TAP'S TIPS

Tap's Tips

Practical Advice
for All Outdoorsmen

by H. G. Tapply

Illustrated by Walter Dower

with an introduction by
William G. Tapply

THE LYONS PRESS
Guilford, Connecticut
An imprint of The Globe Pequot Press

The Lyons Press is an imprint of The Globe Pequot Press.

10 9 8 7 6 5 4 3 2 1

Printed in the United States of America

Library of Congress Cataloging-in-Publication Data

Tapply, H. G. (Horace G.), 1910-
        [Sportsman's notebook and Tap's tips]
        Tap's tips : practical advice for all outdoorsmen everywhere / by
H. G. Tapply ;
        Illustrated by Walter Dower.
                p. cm.
        Originally published: The sportsman's notebook and Tap's tips.
New York : Holt,
        Rinehart and Winston. 1950.
        Includes bibliographical references (p.).
        ISBN 1-59228-214-8 (cloth)
1. Fishing. 2. Hunting. I. Title.

SK33.T36 2003
799—dc22

2003070079

INTRODUCTION

It keeps happening to me.

I'm sitting on the bank of a trout stream in Vermont or Montana. Or I'm hunting quail in Georgia or woodcock in New Hampshire or ducks on Cape Cod. Or I'm launching my canoe on a Maine lake or wading a beach on Martha's Vineyard. Or I'm poking around a fly shop or shooting sporting clays. I meet a stranger. He might be a college kid, or a genuine Old Timer, or anywhere in between.

We talk, of course. We know what we have in common.

Sooner or later we exchange names and shake hands. Then, always, the stranger cocks his head and says, "Did you say Tapply?"

I smile and nod. I know what's coming.

"Tap Tapply?" Now he's grinning. "Tap's Tips? I grew up reading your stuff. When I was a kid, it was the first thing I turned to when my new issue of Field & Stream arrived. I used to clip out your columns. Somewhere in my mother's attic there's a big notebook stuffed with them. You were like my favorite uncle. What an honor to meet you."

"Sorry," I have to tell the stranger. "That's not me. Tap was my father."

"Your father? Well, lucky you."

Yes, indeed. Lucky me.

* * *

In 1964, when he started putting this book together, Tap had been writing his monthly column for fourteen years. That's a full career in the magazine business. Six Tips and two Notebook articles per month—it added up to 1008 Tips and 336 Notebooks, give or take a month's worth or two. Anybody who knows the agony of trying to come up with just one good idea for a monthly column will appreciate what those numbers mean. Tap had committed himself to thinking up eight ideas every month, and he'd been doing it since September, 1950. Not just any old eight ideas, either, but six fresh and useful ideas that could be explained fully and clearly in five typed lines adding up to between forty and fifty words (those were the Tips) and two more expansive ideas that required between 400 and 500 words (the Notebook items).

He did it, month after month, and only those of us who lived with him appreciated how challenging the job was for a man with Tap's high standards. He didn't steal ideas. He didn't recycle old ones. He was always grateful when his readers or his sporting companions suggested ideas to him, but he never took them at face value. Every idea had to be thoroughly tested in the out-doors before Tap would pass it along.

This meant that he had to do a lot of fishing and hunting and camping and boating and cooking and dog handling and trapping and ice fishing and snowshoeing. He called it field-testing. Research. The truth was, he loved to spend time in the out-of-doors, and the monthly column was a neat excuse— or rationalization—whenever he felt he needed one.

Most of the time, I got to go along with him.

Lucky me.

* * *

H. G. Tapply became managing editor of Boston-based National Sportsman/Hunting & Fishing magazine in 1935 (at the age of twenty-five) and editor a year later. In 1940 he became editor of Outdoors, which post he held until 1950 when the magazine was purchased by a Chicago group. During those fifteen magazine-editing years he bought stories from just about every fledgling outdoor writer of that generation. Many of them became household names. They also became Tap's lifelong friends and sporting companions.

During the decade of the forties, Tap also wrote Tackle Tinkering and The Fly Tier's Handbook. Both books were packed with practical and instructive information for fishermen and were written in precise, easy-to-understand language. Tap had found his calling.

When he declined the offer to continue as editor of Outdoors (it entailed moving his family to Chicago, and Tap was a New England Yankee to the marrow), he became, for a few years, a free lancer. Hugh Grey, one of the legion of outdoor writers whose career Tap had nourished, had by then become editor of Field & Stream. Hugh immediately hatched the idea of a monthly column packed with practical lore for outdoorsmen. He thought it was right up Tap's alley.

Tap thought it should be called "The Sportsman's Notebook."

Hugh came up with "Tap's Tips."

It ended up being both.

* * *

This book is not merely a collection of fourteen years' worth of Field & Stream columns. Tap intended it to be a book of lasting value for outdoorsmen. He did not compile it; he wrote it. He discarded everything he thought was -- or might soon become—outdated. He combined ideas, refined them, updated them, expanded or contracted them, and organized them in ways that he believed would be most coherent and useful to his readers. He was liberated by having no rigid word-count requirement. Some Tips he condensed into two lines; others he expanded to ten.

You will find remarkably little in this book that even now, forty-odd years after it was published, is out-of-date or impractical or superseded by current wisdom. In fact, I found exactly one Tip that I can no longer use:

Cutting strips from soft metal toothpaste tubes and wrapping them around your leader for sinkers. It's actually a pretty good idea, but I can't find those metal toothpaste tubes anymore.

All the rest will forever be useful and readable stuff—general strategies, specific tactics, practical tips, all leavened with Tap's humor and down-to-earth philosophy.

Every time I thumb through this book—and I still do it often—I never fail to spot something I'd either forgotten or had failed to notice. Just now, for example, I opened randomly to page 193: "Avoid getting stuck in mud or snow by carrying a few strips of asphalt shingles in the back of your car. Placed in front of the wheels, rough side down, they provide excellent traction." Why didn't I think of that?

How many ways can you use aluminum foil in outdoor cooking? See page 309. Oh, and you can also use it to add flash to lures and flies.

* * *

Like Tap's monthly columns, this book was aimed at sporting generalists, the all-round outdoorspeople who took advantage of whatever the season offered, folks who preferred to be proficient in many things rather than expert in one. In his later years, Tap was saddened by the trend towards specialization among sportsmen. He felt they were missing out on a lot if all they wanted to do was fly-fish for trout or bow-hunt for deer.

If your outdoors interests have narrowed, this book will remind you of what you're missing, and it will give you enough information to enable you try something new with a reasonable expectation of success.

I think it's the perfect book for young outdoorsmen and women. It's down-to-earth, clearly and unpretentiously written, and packed with useful lore. It will open their world to possibilities.

* * *

After this book was published in 1965, Tap continued writing his monthly columns. The very last one appeared in the September, 1985 issue of Field & Stream, thirty-five years to the month after the first one—420 straight monthly issues, never a missed deadline, never a carelessly written word, never a tip that Tap could not guarantee. That was a long time, a lot of words, many hours in the outdoors . . . and at the typewriter.

In early 1985 when Tap wrote to Duncan Barnes, then the editor of Field & Stream, of his intention to call it quits, Barnes replied:

". . . my sincere thanks for your dedication and professionalism in writing what is probably the most widely read outdoor column in the world—certainly in the outdoor magazine field."

The magazine continued to publish reprints of the old Tips for another ten years. Tap, typically, agonized over selecting those that would be of interest and use to outdoorsmen.

When my father died on January 24, 2002, he had outlived most of his friends, that wonderful generation of outdoors generalists that included Lee Wulff, Ed Zern, Frank Woolner, John Alden Knight, Harold F. Blaisdell, Corey Ford, Burton L. Spiller, Ted Trueblood, A. J. McClane, Edmund Ware Smith. Most of them credited Tap for "discovering" them back when they were aspiring outdoor writers. Tap, in turn, credited them for sharing their wisdom and expanding his outdoor experiences.

My father would be pleased to know that this book has reappeared. He would hope that it might inspire another generation to explore the outdoors with rod and gun and have as much fun at it as he had in his lifetime as a sportsman.

William G. Tapply
Hancock, New Hampshire
April 2003

A NOTE OF THANKS

THIS BOOK would be only half as thick and considerably less than half as help-ful to the reader if I had drawn only from my own experience for the material to fill it. Although I have fished and hunted and tramped the woods for nearly forty years, I still haven't acquired such a store of knowledge that I could stuff a book with it.

A large portion of this material was contributed, directly or indirectly, by my fishing and hunting companions and, in an extra large measure, by readers of *Field & Stream*. I want to acknowledge here my debt to them all, and to express my sincere gratitude for their help.

I am especially grateful to the publisher of *Field & Stream* for permitting me to use material that appeared originally in that publication. All of this text has now been revised or rewritten, but even so, some long-memoried sub-scribers may recognize bits and pieces they have read earlier in their favorite sporting magazine.

I also wish to express my thanks to the editor and publisher of *Sports Afield* for permitting me to include the story "Duck Blinds I Have Shot From," which that excellent magazine printed some time ago; to my old friend Harold Blaisdell for his invaluable help with subjects about which he knows a great deal more than I do; to another old friend, Hugh Grey, Editor of *Field & Stream*, for encouraging me to tackle the job in the first place; to Walter Dower for illustrating the subjects with such clarity and skill; to my son, Bill, and daughter, Martha, for their lively interest in the project throughout the long months I spent working on it; and, finally, to my patient wife, who made perhaps the biggest contribution of all by typing every last word of it.

Gratefully, H. G. T.

CONTENTS

FISHING

HUNTING

Fishing

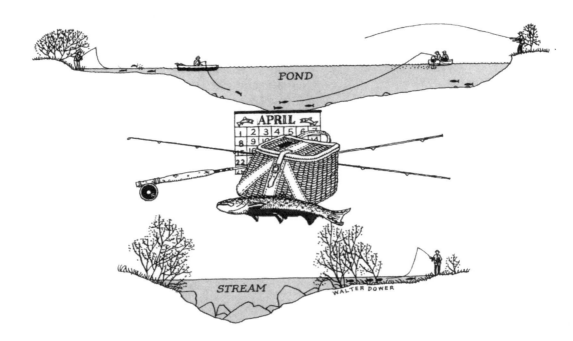

POND

APRIL
1 2 3 4 5 6
8 9 10 11 14
22

STREAM

WALTER DOWER

TROUT

Where to Catch Trout on Opening Day

TELL you first where you may *not* catch many: in your favorite trout stream.

If your last opening day was anything like mine, you found the water much too high, too cold and too dirty for good fishing. The best pools— in this day and age, that means those close to the highway where the hatchery trucks unload—were lined with early-bird fishermen nudging one another for elbow room. The water temperature was probably in the middle or low 40's, and the trout were simply too sluggish to chase flies or spinning lures or even to scoop up a worm.

Their reluctance to feed during early-season conditions is due to their low rate of metabolism. When the water remains uncomfortably cold for a prolonged period their bodily processes slow down to half speed. They don't need much food, any more than an idling motor needs much gas. Therefore, they don't move around much once they find a comfortable resting spot. That's what makes early-season trout fishing so tough. You must put your bait or lure right in front of their noses, and even then the chances are 50-50 that they will ignore it.

So unless you get a spell of balmy weather just before the season

3

opens, your pet river probably won't treat you as kindly on the first day as it will a few weeks later.

But it's unthinkable to stay home—especially if you know of a trout pond within driving distance, preferably one with brook trout in it. Brookies tolerate cold water better than browns and rainbows and normally become active earlier. Many fishermen overlook this factor in making their early-season fishing plans.

You will almost surely find the pond at fishable level, reasonably clear, and perhaps as much as 10 degrees warmer at the surface than your trout stream. You may even find fish dimpling in a shallow, sun-warmed bay and enjoy the rare pleasure of taking trout with dry flies on the very first day of the new season. And because of the nature of pond fishing, the other fishermen will probably be scattered enough to give you room to swing your rod.

Ponds and lakes offer you a wide choice of fishing methods. You can spin-cast from shore, covering all depths from surface to bottom, or you can simply toss out a worm and let it lie in the path of cruising fish. If you have a boat you can troll streamer flies, wobblers, or a spinner with a worm trailing behind it; and you can try different depths until you find the level where the trout are gathered. Or you can hang a baited hook over the side and drift with the breeze, which is an excellent way to catch pond trout.

That should be your best bet for opening day. However, if you still feel that you should pay your respects to the river, here's a tip: look for a shallow cove or a place where the stream has flooded a field edge. Normally the water here will be a few degrees warmer than in the main river. Trout often move into such places, unlikely though they may seem, to escape the chill and push of the heavy currents. You may have to cast in the grass and brush, but it could prove worthwhile. At least, you'll be fishing where you have a better chance to catch trout. And you'll probably have such improbable-looking places all to yourself.

TAP'S TIPS

《 Release undersized trout as quickly as possible. Small fish that have been handled roughly or allowed to struggle till exhausted seldom survive when tossed back into heavy, icy water.

《 The size and weight of the sinkers you use are important in early-season fishing. To get a variety of sizes, from BB and Buck to 4 and 6, open shotgun shells and split the pellets halfway through with a sharp knife blade.

《 When trout refuse to bite, give the suckers a try. They "run" in the early spring, and a worm rolled along bottom will usually take them.

4

Trout in the Trickles

Opening day on most well-known trout streams produces about everything except solitude and fish, so if you want to escape the bargain-counter mob and can't get on a trout pond, seek out the small pasture brook. You may not have it all to yourself, but you'll probably find room to fish, and those little brooks often give you better early-season fishing than the larger streams, flooded and muddy from the spring runoff.

This doesn't mean that trout in small streams are always easier to catch. Actually, brook fishing offers a pretty severe test of your skill as a trout fisherman. If the trout sees you before he sees your bait, he usually won't bite, so you can't bumble along the bank like a cow moose. Sneak from pool to pool, keeping low to avoid casting a shadow ahead of you. Fish upstream if you can, or from the side, and use all the line you can handle to keep as much distance as possible between you and the fish.

The real trick of fishing the trickles, though, is to pass up the open, inviting stretches and concentrate on the hard-to-get-at places. Trout like such holes, and most trout fishermen don't. If you can't get a baited hook through the tangle of alders, float it down on a chip or leaf and twitch it off when it drifts over the spot you want to reach. This takes patience and a knowledge of the kind of water trout like to lie in, but it pays off.

While trout in small brooks may lack the suspicious nature of fish in the larger streams, they won't fall for coarse tackle or for baits that don't look natural. So pay them the compliment of a light leader and a lively bait rolling free and enticingly with the current. Avoid drag just as you would if you were fishing a dry fly.

Best bait? In the very early season, it's worms; later, you may have better luck with grasshoppers. However, you're not limited to bait. Try a small fly-rod wobbler. Let the current carry it into the deep pools and beneath the undercut banks. Twitch your rod tip to keep the wobbler darting and fluttering. When a 10-incher boils up to take a crack at it, he'll seem like a whale.

These little jump-across brooks will really test your skill as a trout fisherman. You'll find them fun to fish at any time of year, but especially so in the early spring. Fish 'em right and they'll produce a skilletful of trout for you, too.

TAP'S TIPS

◖ Trout love to lie under stream banks that have been undercut by the twisting current. Look ahead for such places and roll a bait into them before you approach close enough to flush out the fish.

◖ If boot tracks in the mud show that another fisherman has beaten you to a fishy-looking pool, try it anyway. He may have given it just a lick and a promise, or perhaps he frightened the fish by stumbling or approaching too closely. By the time you come along the fish may be ready to bite again.

◖ How do you carry your rod through the brush—tip first or butt first? It can become tangled either way. But I like to keep my eye on that fragile tip, so I believe that tip first means safety first.

Bottom Baiting

Come hail or high water, a few fishermen will catch a few fish on opening day this year. Ask the lucky ones how they did it and, if they're truthful, they will probably tell you they simply heaved a gob of lively nightcrawlers out into a big pool, propped their rods in forked sticks, and sat. It really works.

Figure it out for yourself. The water is still very cold, and the trout

6

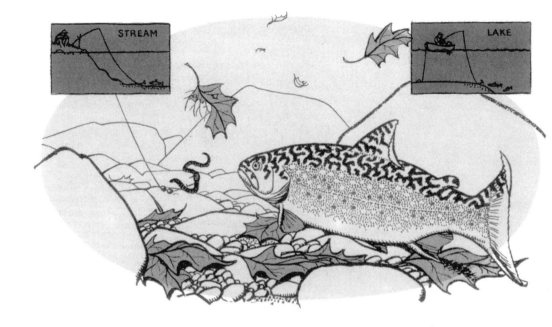

are sluggish. The calm, perhaps slightly warmer, water of the pool is more to their liking than the icy quick-water stretches. The fish aren't ravenous, either, so they won't chase their food if they don't have to. But if they run their noses up against a nightcrawler writhing on the bottom, they are not likely to pass it by. So the rod starts bouncing in its forked stick, and the system pays off again.

Now I don't suggest that you should plant yourself at a pool and sit there all day. Maybe there aren't any fish in this particular pool, although that's not too likely on opening day. Fish it first in your usual manner. If that doesn't pay off, pinch on a couple of split shot, drape on a fresh bait, heave it out, and cut yourself a forked stick. Give the pool as much time as your patience will permit—a half hour, say, or even an hour. If nothing happens, try another pool.

This basic idea often pays off in ponds and lakes, too. You face the same troublesome combination of cold water and sluggish fish, and you may troll or cast for hours without a strike. In that case, try fishing the lake as if it were a giant pool, with a large, lively bait lying on the very bottom. Get it on the edge of a bar if you can, just where the bottom drops out of sight. .

Slow fishing? Maybe. But when you ask the trollers and casters how they fared, you might find you had faster fishing than you realized.

TAP'S TIPS

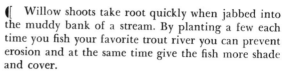

❰ Willow shoots take root quickly when jabbed into the muddy bank of a stream. By planting a few each time you fish your favorite trout river you can prevent erosion and at the same time give the fish more shade and cover.

❰ Try Eagle Claw hooks for worm fishing. The bait stays on this type of hook better, and the curved point prevents shake-offs. Size 6 is my choice, because it is too big for small trout to swallow.

❰ Skittish trout shy away from a baited hook with a sinker close to it. If you use split shot to carry your bait close to bottom, pinch it on about a foot above the hook, where the fish won't notice it.

Winning Ways with Worms

A worm is such a shapeless creature there doesn't seem to be very much a fisherman can do with it except to jab it on a hook and toss it into the water.

And that, as you may have observed, is exactly what a great many fishermen do. This is grossly unfair to the worm, and damaging to its reputation as the world's most popular bait.

The way to hook a worm is just once, in the middle. Not twice or three times, and certainly not skewered on the hook like a shishkabob. The hook should be as small (unless you start catching undersized trout) and the leader as light as you dare use. You'd be surprised what a difference it makes.

The way to get the most out of a worm is to fish it without drag. That means no sinkers, or as little weight as the speed of the current or depth of the water permits. In streams, the worm does its best work when cast upcurrent, or across and up, and allowed to drift down just as a free worm would drift, rolling and writhing and making little inviting gestures. If you are fishing the worm with a fly rod, you will find it helpful to mend your line to avoid drag, just as you would when fishing a dry fly.

But an even better way to fish a worm is with spinning tackle, and the lighter the tackle, the better. The ultralight stuff that handles lures in the 1/16-ounce class is just the ticket for worming. I have never put a worm on a scale, but I imagine a prime 4-incher, well-fed and in fighting trim, would weigh pretty near as much as a tiny UL spinner. With hairline monofilament and a soft spinning rod you can lob a worm 40

8

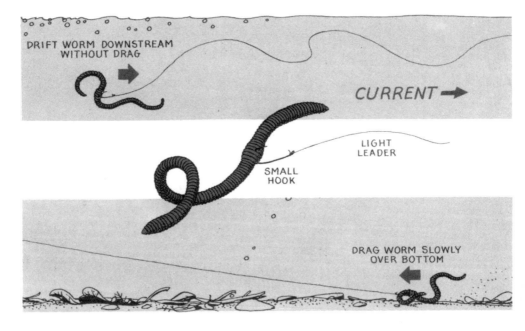

DRIFT WORM DOWNSTREAM WITHOUT DRAG

CURRENT →

LIGHT LEADER

SMALL HOOK

DRAG WORM SLOWLY OVER BOTTOM

or 50 feet. That's farther than most of us could "fly cast" a worm without snapping it off the hook.

In still pools and ponds, you can let the worm settle naturally to the bottom and just leave it there, hoping that fish will find it—which in time they will. However, a better way is to crawl it over the bottom by turning the reel crank in slow motion. If the line tightens, wait a bit; you may have hung bottom, but on the other hand, you may have hung a fish.

Worms or nightcrawlers? I really can't say that one is any better than the other. As a matter of purely personal choice, I use spade-dug garden worms for trout, nightcrawlers for bass, and when a bait looks as if it has stopped trying, I hang on a fresh one.

TAP'S TIPS

(Cover the lens of your flashlight with red or yellow cellophane when you hunt nightcrawlers in the dark. If you can't find colored cellophane, paint the lens with fingernail polish. To clean off the glass, borrow your wife's polish remover.

(When you keep a supply of worms for several days, give them a bite to eat occasionally. They thrive on crumbled yolk of hard-boiled egg, corn meal, powdered milk, bread crumbs.

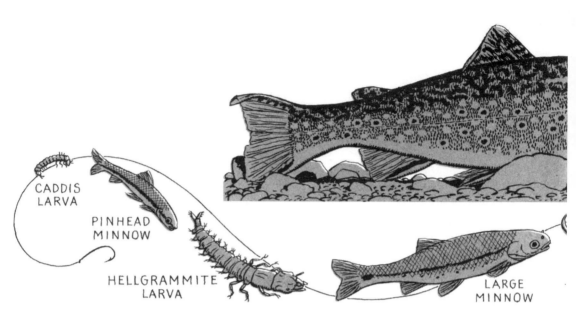

CADDIS LARVA

PINHEAD MINNOW

HELLGRAMMITE LARVA

LARGE MINNOW

Trout Baits Worth Trying

Most trout fishermen do not hesitate to use bait, especially early in the season when trout tend to be somewhat sluggish. And the favorite bait, without question, is the old reliable garden worm.

But there are other baits that trout like, too. For instance, have you ever fished a typical "worming" brook with pinhead minnows—the little fellows about 1½ inches long? Just run a No. 12 hook through both lips of the pinhead and drift it ahead of you, giving it a twitch now and then to attract attention. Pan-sized brookies murder these little minnows, but a lunker won't pass them up, either.

And how about hellgrammites? These evil-looking creatures make especially good bait in the very early season when trout stay close to bottom. Choose the small ones, and hang them by their collars on a No. 6 Eagle Claw hook with a light leader. Hellgrammites have tough skins, so trout can't steal them as easily as worms. With these larvae, nearly every honest strike means a hooked fish.

Caddis larvae, on the other hand, are too soft to stay on a hook well.

10

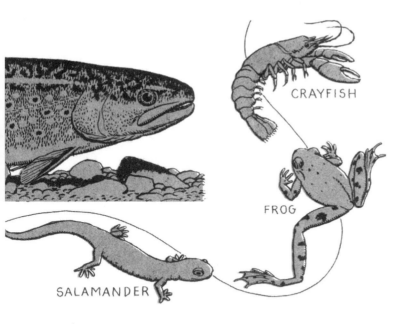

CRAYFISH

FROG

SALAMANDER

But how trout love them! The bigger the larvae the better, but you can't always find the big ones, so tie on a No. 14 or 16 fine wire hook for this fishing. Toss the larvae upstream as gently as possible and let it drift back to you on a slack line. When you get the hang of it you'll be able to coax trout from places where a dangled worm would draw a complete blank.

If you're gunning for really big trout, a 4-inch minnow will out-fish a gob of worms every time (well, almost every time). And don't neglect such rare goodies as salamanders, baby crawfish and live salt-water shrimp. Small frogs, too, have ended the career of more than one old buster. And a friend of mine tells me he once saw a huge brown trout lift himself out of water to make a pass at a low-flying bat.

So worms aren't always the best trout bait you can use, even if they are easiest to come by. Take some with you, by all means, but try some of the other baits, too. They may score for you when worms practically go begging.

TAP'S TIPS

Sewn Minnow: Deadly!

George used to sneer at my "fancy-Dan" tackle when we loaded the canoe for our spring trip into Fifth Lake Stream, up in the Machias River country of northern Maine.

"Here's all you need to catch trout with," he would tell me, holding aloft his fly rod and squinting happily down its twisted length. "This, and a mess of chub, like I got right here in this lard pail."

As you might guess, George was not a fisherman in the sense that you and I are fishermen. He was a registered Maine guide, and his rod seldom came off the nails driven into the side of his spruce log cabin. But when I came up in the early spring, before his sports arrived, he always took a few days off to go trout fishing on the Stream. What he enjoyed most about it, I think, was catching more trout than I did, for all of my fancy tackle.

As far as George was concerned, there is only one sensible and proper way to fish for trout—or to troll for bass, landlocked salmon, togue, or pickerel either, for that matter—and that is with sewn bait. A chub or smelt laced on a well-soaked gut hook was all he ever used at Fifth Lake Stream, and it was a rare day indeed when I could top him with bucktails, streamers, wet flies, or nymphs. Or even worms.

There are several good ways and one best way to lace a minnow to a hook. The best way (George's, naturally) is to run the hook down through the minnow's lower lip, then through the head from top to bottom, and finally in and out of the side down near the tail. Tightening the snell bends the bait into a curve that will make it revolve at whatever speed conditions demand. The slower the better, according to George.

As I say, George used only a fly rod. He fished the bait by plopping

12

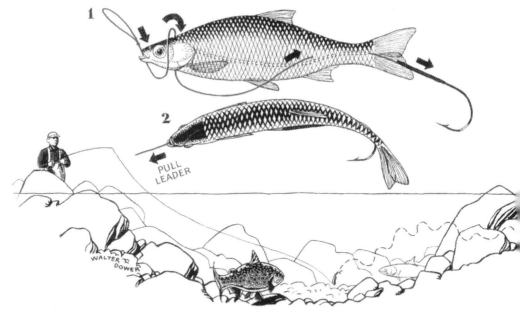

it out as far as he could reach and nursing it back in slow twitches so that it just barely rolled and flip-flopped along. Ever and anon he would let it sink to the bottom of the deeper holes where the larger trout were supposed to lie, and often did.

This method was sure death on Fifth Lake Stream, which was—and, I imagine, still is—inhabited only by wild native brook trout. Later I discovered that it is equally deadly where sophisticated browns and rainbows are found. I also discovered, after spinning came in vogue, that a sewn bait casts beautifully on a light spinning rod, with a couple of swivels to keep line-twist to a minimum.

It has been some time now since I've seen anyone fishing a trout river with sewn bait. The last time was on the Esopus Creek in New York State. A night of rain had killed the dry-fly fishing, and I was standing on the bridge below Phoenicia brooding down on the flood. A fisherman waded into view, and I noted that he was lobbing a sewn minnow around. I also noted, as he passed below me, that he was towing a good-sized rainbow from a rope around his waist, and the sight of it made me feel a lot better, somehow.

TAP'S TIPS

《 To make sure you can always find a swivel when you need one, string a dozen or so on a large safety pin and fasten the pin to the underside of your shirt-pocket flap.

13

❪ Check your sewn bait after each strike, or when it hits bottom. The curvature of the minnow may be changed so it spins too fast or not fast enough. The correct shape can be restored simply by adjusting the snell.

❪ To preserve bait fish, wrap them individually in waxed paper or foil and store them in the freezing compartment of your refrigerator. Don't try to re-freeze leftover baits, as they become soft after they thaw.

Hardware for Trout

In the early part of the season, when streams run high, cold and murky, trout that won't come up for a fly will often fall all over themselves chasing a hunk of hardware. Spinning pays off but it's difficult to spin cast in a narrow winding meadow stream or a small mountain brook where your good water is a series of small pockets. You can hit the pools and pockets all right, but then you have to retrieve your lure all the way back to the rod tip, over boulders, logs, and sometimes even bankings, before you can cast again. It isn't easy, and you waste a lot of precious fishing time.

You'll find you can fish such spots much better with a fly rod and a small, light wobbler or spinner. You can cast the lure into the hotspots on a short line, lob it in underhanded, or let the current carry it there for you. You can even roll cast it easier than you probably think, if you have never tried it. After you've got it where you want it, you can keep it fluttering and darting as long as you want simply by working the tip of your fly rod and letting the current and eddies play with it.

These small mosquito-weight metal lures handle best on a line with a short front taper and a fairly heavy leader. Three feet of 6-pound-test nylon is plenty for this kind of work; trout don't seem to be fussy about what a wobbler is tied to. The flash of the lure probably holds their attention more than a fly does, and of course trout aren't likely to be gut-shy in the first week or two of the season, or when the water is high and discolored.

In this kind of fishing you don't have to retrieve your lure at all. The idea is to put it into a promising spot and keep it there until a fish belts it or you're convinced there's nobody home. You can even let it hang in one spot, allowing the current to keep it flopping. Often trout will look it over for a minute or more, and rush at it as if it were the most tempting thing they'd ever seen in their lives. But usually a darting, fluttering lure that wanders all around the pool brings the most strikes.

What's the best color? Probably the color of the lure isn't important

14

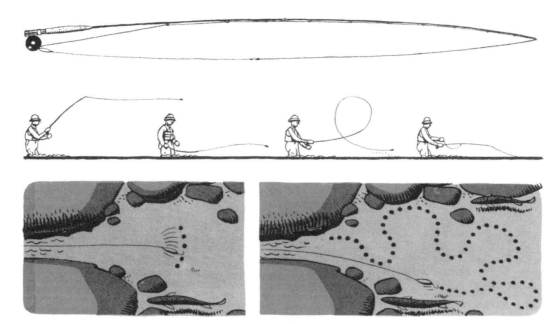

in this kind of fishing, but personally I favor the red-and-white wobbler with a silver underside. The "fly-rod size" with thin blade and small treble hooks is ideal for this kind of fishing. You will use the same lure for trolling with a fly rod, too, as you will discover in the next couple of pages.

TAP'S TIPS

⟨ Some wobbling lures have better action when the treble hooks are removed and replaced with single hooks. You may miss a few strikes, but you won't hang bottom so often, and you will find it easier to unhook small fish without tearing their mouths.

⟨ The great proliferation of fixed-spool reels has resulted in some confusion as to what they should be called. The open-face, under-the-rod reel is a spinning reel. The closed-face reel with nose cone and push button is a spin-casting reel. You spin with one, spin-cast with the other.

Trolling with a Twist

Wherever in a stream you find a long, deep channel of slow-moving water, look for big trout. These stillwater lunkers are cagy customers, but you can fool some of them some of the time by trolling.

You'd think stream trolling would scare the spots off the fish, but it doesn't. Trout will smack a trolled lure in a channel scarcely wider than your boat, so forget your fears on that score. Troll with a motor if you have one—if anything, the flash of the prop seems to stir up more strikes.

For a lure, make your first, second, and third choice a red-and-white wobbler, fly-rod size. After that, pick through your box of spinning lures or try a midget plug. If hardware fails, try spinner-and-night-crawler or spinner-and-sewn bait—then tie on the red-and-white wobbler again and leave it on.

Big trout lie deep, so it's important to get your lure down to 'em. Troll slowly, barely faster than the current. Hang on a sinker if necessary in deep water, or use a lead-core line. Let out line in the straight stretches, shorten up to negotiate the bends, guiding the line around obstructions and through gouged-out holes where big fish live. Twitch the line every once in a while to make the lure flutter. Cover promising stretches of water two or three times before passing on. Stay in the channel and you'll take fish even when the stream is over its banks.

If you haven't tried stream trolling, you've got a treat coming—and maybe some really big fish.

TAP'S TIPS

❴ To keep your hands free for pipe filling and story-telling with gestures while trolling with a fly rod, lean the rod against an oarlock and hook the line over (not around) the reel handle. This prevents the reel from turning and helps to hook striking fish.

([Fish don't feel pain the way humans do, but they certainly deserve a quick, merciful death. Small-to-average trout can be killed instantly by putting the thumb in the gills and bending the head back to break the backbone. Use a priest or knife handle on larger fish, and conk them hard on the noggin.

([When cleaning fish be sure to remove the dark blood along the backbone. I use my thumbnail or a knife point when dressing fish at streamside, but prefer a discarded dessert spoon while working at the kitchen sink.

Try It Upstream

You can't judge a fisherman just by the flies in his hatband or the patches on his waders. If you really want to know how much rod work he has done, notice whether he is fishing upstream or down. The man who works against the current—not all the time, but more than most fishermen do—is generally a man who knows how to catch trout.

This isn't because he can sneak closer to the fish by approaching them from behind. That's part of the reason he fishes upstream, of course, but only a small part, because a good fisherman can get close to fish, or reach them with long casts if necessary, from any direction.

The real reason upstream fishing pays off is that the lure or bait comes to the fish in a more natural manner. This is quite obvious when the lure is a dry fly. The fisherman can see plainly how the currents

17

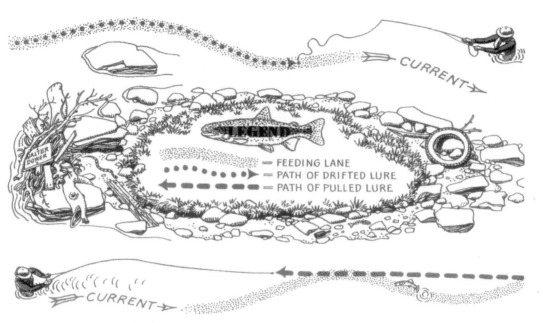

LEGEND

∙∙∙∙∙∙∙∙▶ = FEEDING LANE
∙∙∙∙∙∙∙∙▶ = PATH OF DRIFTED LURE
◀━ ━ ━ ━ = PATH OF PULLED LURE

CURRENT →

CURRENT →

carry it along at the same pace as the naturals; he can watch it bounce down the rips and twirl in and out of eddies just as the hatching flies are doing.

Worms and most sunken artificials behave pretty much the same way when they are cast upstream and allowed to drift back with the currents. Free of leader-pull, they sink naturally and wash through the feeding lanes with the other food carried by the stream. When the fisherman lifts his lure it rises at the same angle as a live nymph or bait fish struggling up from the river bottom. The fisherman can't see this, but the trout can, and that's what counts.

There are even times when streamers and bucktails lend themselves to upstreaming. Drifting back haphazardly with the current, they twist and turn like confused or injured minnows, offering the softest kind of pickin's for a trout. So when fish don't look kindly on streamers that are jerking about on the end of a taut leader, or hanging motionless in the current, it may pay to turn around and chuck them upriver for a while.

You don't see many fishermen casting spinning lures upstream, but when you do see one you can be sure he has served out his apprenticeship. It's tricky, because of the difficulty of keeping the lure working deep, where it belongs, without constantly hanging up on bottom. The trick is to cast upriver from an angle, hold the rod high, and retrieve the hardware just a bit faster than the speed of the current. Upstream spinning is a cinch with ultralight lures, by the way, as they require very little water resistance to keep them fluttering.

Learning how to fish a lure upstream isn't nearly as difficult as learn-

18

ing how to tell a strike from a hang-up on bottom. The line twitches slightly or hesitates briefly; the fisherman sees, or imagines he sees, a faint flicker of movement under the water. Perhaps he doesn't see anything at all; some sixth sense triggers a reflex, he strikes, and he is not greatly surprised to feel the thrust of a fish as the hook digs in.

True, the upstreamer misses more strikes than the downstreamer. But he gets more strikes—usually a great many more, counting those he doesn't know about. If he keeps his hooks sharp, gathers in slack as fast as it builds up behind the drifting lure, and doesn't mind hooking bottom occasionally, he also catches more trout.

TAP'S TIPS

([Facing upstream allows you to scratch bottom with your lure on the retrieve, which is effective when fish are lying deep. The same method works when trout are coming to the surface to feed, too, as the fish often rush the lure just as it reaches the top.

([Trout almost always start feeding when the water temperature begins to rise after a long spell of cold weather. When the weather man predicts a warming trend, you can look for improved surface fishing and the beginning of the fly hatches.

([Avoid handling small fish that you intend to release. Slide your hand down the leader, grasp the fly and twist it back and forth a few times. Unless the fish is hooked deep he usually comes free.

The Brainy Brown

You can always start an argument in a gathering of fishermen by comparing the brook, brown, and rainbow trout for fighting ability, beauty or the flavor of their flesh. But there's seldom much argument on one point: Most experienced trout fishermen agree that the brown is the smartest of the three.

Probably very few rainbows or squaretails die of old age, except in remote places, but many a brown lives out his full life span, even in hard-fished water. Smart as he is, though, the brown becomes vulnerable at certain times, and those are the times to go gunning for the big ones.

The best time of all comes when a heavy shower raises the water and turns it cloudy. Trout then start to move and feed, and even the lunker browns seem to catch the spirit of things. The worm fisherman can clean up if he hits the stream while it's still rising and rolls a fat nightcrawler into the muddied pools. So can the spin fisherman and the man

with a fly rod and weighted bucktail.

The trick in this kind of fishing is to get the bait or lure down deep. If you're casting a spoon or spinner, aim it straight upstream or at an upstream angle and let it swing slowly into the pool, turning the crank handle just enough to keep the lure fluttering. Bucktailing isn't quite as easy, but a split shot or two will help if you cast above the pool and let the current wash the fly into the deep places.

Hitting a stream during a rise of water is mainly a matter of luck. However, there's another time when browns turn bold and hungry. That's at night, after most fishermen have creeled their quota of 10-inchers and gone home.

From dusk until as late as the fishing laws of your state allow is the time to flog the flats and pools with your biggest flies—wets, streamers, bucktails. If you hear trout chugging at the surface, tie on a big, bushy dry, such as one of the Wulffs, or even a medium-sized deerhair bass bug. Forget finesse and aim for the spot where most of the noise is coming from. You may not hang many fish under such conditions, but if you do get a hook into one of those lusty night-feeders, you may have to carry him home with your finger hooked in his gills.

Admittedly, fishing high, dirty water or stumbling over unseen rocks in the black of night isn't nearly as pleasant as casting over a sun-dappled stream when the water runs clear and low. But, if you want to take big browns, that's the price you've got to pay. And when you do drive a barb into one of them—say, a 5-pounder or better—the price seems reasonable enough.

20

TAP'S TIPS

❡ When fishing in discolored water or at night, cut your leader back to a heavier diameter. Trout are not too fussy during these conditions, and the short, heavy leader is easier to cast. It's also strong enough so you can yank it free when you hang up on snags—or apply pressure on a big fish if you hook one.

❡ Rising trout can be very particular during an evening hatch, but after dark they usually come to any floating fly they can see. My favorite floater for dark-of-night fishing is a White Wulff, size 10 or 12.

❡ When you release a completely exhausted fish, hold it upright in the water long enough to let it regain its strength. Otherwise it may not survive the mauling of the heavy current.

How to "Read" Trout Water

Charley Wallant stood on the high embankment overlooking the river and said: "So this is the Lamoille."

As I tugged at my wading shoe I wondered where I would start him off. The water directly below us was shallow and sandy; it usually held a few small trout, but it was not worth fishing in daylight. At the tail of the long flat there was a pyramid-shaped rock, its point barely breaking the surface, where I had taken a 17-inch brown just a year ago this very weekend. That should be a good place, I thought, for Charley to make his maiden cast in Vermont water.

Hurrying, I gave the lacing a yank and it snapped.

"Take your time," Charley said. "I'll go along down and take a look at this fabulous river of yours."

By the time I was ready he had passed out of sight. I sloshed through the edge of the shallow flat and caught up with him at the pyramid-shaped rock. He had a trout on.

I should have known he would find the place. Anyone who can "read" the surface of a trout stream would recognize it as a perfect lie for trout and would know at a glance that the broad, shallow flat above it would be barren except perhaps in the evening, when trout might move into it to cruise for hatching flies.

In a sense, a trout river is like a book; some parts are dull and some are lively. Experienced fishermen recognize the sections that promise action and save valuable time by skipping or skimming over the places that look uninteresting.

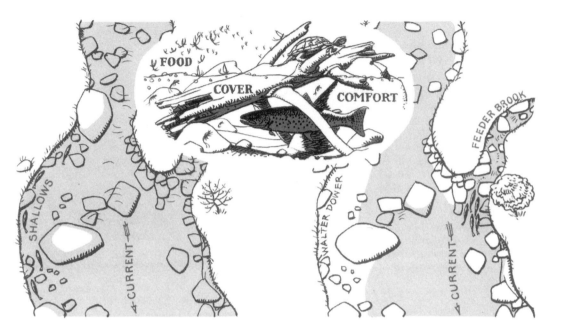

No doubt when Charley first began fishing he had worked many flats like the one on the Lamoille before he concluded that such places seldom yield keepable fish. So he had waded along until he came to the pyramid rock. Having caught a great many trout among the boulders of the Beaverkill and Willowemoc, he probably wasn't greatly surprised when he hung a fish there on his very first cast.

While all trout rivers have different characteristics, the trout in them are pretty much the same. They all have three basic needs: food, cover, and a comfortable place to rest. A fisherman who knows the conditions that create these essentials should be able to catch trout from any river in the world.

Mainly, he will look for current. It is the heavier flow of water that sucks drifting food into feeding lanes, gouges deep holes where trout can hide, creates eddies and cushions where they can rest. Wherever a rock or a log or an upturned tree stump breaks the flow of the water there are currents, and where there are currents there should be trout.

But finding fish isn't quite that simple. Sometimes fish lie out of the current for one reason or another. In the early spring when the water is uncomfortably cold, trout will move into the still, shallow edges where the sun has raised the water temperature a few degrees. In these circumstances, comfort is more important to the trout than cover, or finding a plentiful supply of food.

Late in the season, when the water temperature climbs into the 70's, the same fish will seek the mouth of a cool feeder brook and lie in its

22

flow, often dangerously exposed, possibly hungry, but grateful for the comfort of the cooler water.

So at any time of day or year one of a trout's three basic needs may be more urgent than the others. This is something a fisherman must consider too. Is the stream running high and heavy? Then comfort may be the greatest need. I would look for trout in backwaters and eddies, outside the direct thrust of the main currents, or close to bottom where the rubble breaks the force of the water.

Is it low and clear? The fish must find cover during the day and wait until evening to feed. I would look for them now under a protective ceiling of broken water, beneath undercut bankings, or in the dark holes under logs and boulders.

Some of these holding spots are so obvious that a beginner would have no trouble finding them. Others show only faintly at the surface as gentle boils and creases that form when the current comes to a hidden obstacle and rolls around and over it. These are harder to read, but when a fisherman learns to recognize them he will almost surely find trout there.

TAP'S TIPS

⁅ When wading in swift, heavy water, keep your hip to the current as much as possible; you present a narrower surface for the water to push against. And when your toe meets a rock, sidle around it. Going over might mean going in.

⁅ A new beaver dam often produces fantastic trout fishing for the first few years. If you come upon signs of beaver working, mark it down as a spot to try first thing next year.

⁅ One of the big advantages of spin fishing is that you can get your lure down deep where the big fish

lie. So never leave a "black hole" without scraping its bottom up, down, and across. Remember that big fish aren't eager fish, so give them plenty of chance to strike before moving on to the next pool.

The Merry Month of the Mayfly

It takes 12 long months, but it always gets here right after April. Flies are dancing over the riffs, trout are slurping them off the smooth-water, and it's gangway for the river, boys, and don't forget the fly dope.

Now, theoretically, you should be able to get a rise from every feeding fish you see. And possibly you would, if you made a perfect, drag-free cast every time, with a fly that exactly matched those that were hatching—or one that looked enough like a perfect match to deceive the fish.

However, even during a "duffer's hatch" when trout behave like would-be suicides, you won't raise every fish you cast to. And you won't hook every fish you raise, either.

So how do you improve your chances?

You can start by tying on a fly that matches as closely as possible the size and color of the hatching naturals. You won't need a hundred patterns, either. If the naturals look gray, try a Quill Gordon or Hendrickson; if brown, a Light Cahill or Ginger Quill; if you're not sure, a mixed-hackle pattern like the March Brown or Adams. That's six. Add

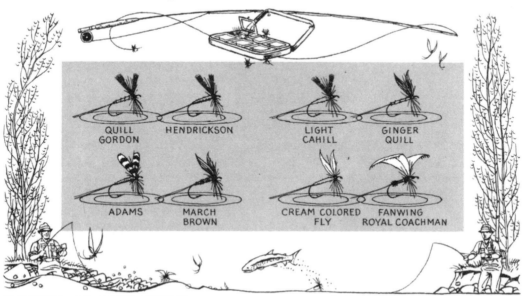

FAST WATER: 9 ft. LEADER - 3X POINT   SLOW WATER: 12 ft. LEADER - 5X POINT

24

a light-yellow fly to take care of the evening "creams" you're likely to see later in the season, plus a nonimitative pattern like a Wulff or Fanwing Royal Coachman for times when fish aren't rising at all. Those eight patterns should see you through nicely.

Next, what sizes? Since I've already oversimplified this subject, I'll oversimplify some more and suggest stocking each pattern in two sizes, 12 and 16. Or, simpler yet, just in size 14.

Having the matching pattern and size of the hatching flies will help, but not much if the fish can see the leader you've tied it to. Make it as long and fine as you dare. For a rule of thumb, let's say 9 feet tapered to 3X for broken water, 12 feet to 5X for flat water.

Now you're set. All you've got to do is drop the fly as soft as a lover's whisper just upstream of where the fish lies, and let it float naturally and cockily down over him without a hint of drag. And right there's where the men get separated from the boys. I could tell you how to do it, perhaps, in several thousand tortured words, but I won't try it here—because I can't catch every feeding fish I cast to, either.

TAP'S TIPS

❲ Here's a trick that sometimes brings fish up to a dry fly: Make your cast high and check it abruptly while it is still above the water. Trout seem to see it fluttering down and rise to it the instant it lands. Try it with a fanwing on smooth water, just for kicks.

❲ When buying dry flies, look for the quality of the material rather than its quantity. Trout like sparsely dressed floaters. Check the hackle for stiffness by pressing it lightly against the lip; good hackle feels prickly.

❲ The swallows often tell you when it's time to tie on a dry fly. They start skimming the surface when flies first begin to hatch, and usually they can see them before the fishermen can. Occasionally one of them will make a pass at an artificial fly, but for the most part swallows tend to be gut-shy and selective.

First Casts with Dry Flies

Most fishermen who use dry flies agree that no other fishing method provides the interest or excitement you can get from taking trout with floaters. For one thing you can see your trout when he darts up to gulp your fly. For another, there's tremendous suspense in watching your fly drift toward a feeding fish, hope and fear mounting steadily together as the moment approaches when he must either take it or refuse it. And

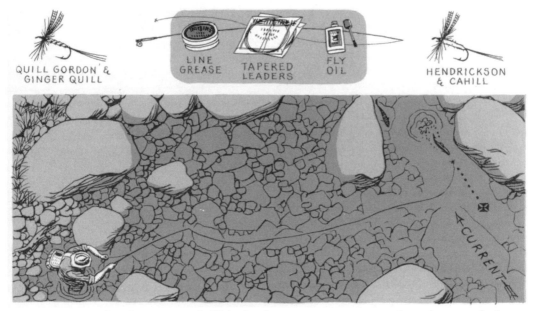

QUILL GORDON &
GINGER QUILL

LINE GREASE TAPERED LEADERS FLY OIL

HENDRICKSON
& CAHILL

there's an extra thrill in having a trout come out of nowhere to slash at your fly when you least expect it.

Unfortunately, many fishermen hesitate to try dry-fly fishing because they think it's too difficult for their limited ability. Some fishing writers like to make it sound difficult, but it really isn't. Anyone who can cast 30 feet of fly line can take trout with dry flies. Shucks, make it 20.

It doesn't even matter if you can't tell one kind of mayfly from another. When gray-colored flies are hatching, just tie on a gray-colored artificial of about the same size and start casting it. Basically, dry-fly fishing is just about as simple as that.

It helps, of course, to have a few of the most common dry fly patterns in your fly box—some Quill Gordons and Hendricksons, for example—in sizes 12 and 14. Add some Light Cahills and Ginger Quills if you insist, and you can be pretty sure of putting up an acceptable imitation of almost any common mayfly that hatches. Grease the line to make it float, tie on a leader tapered to 3X, dip the fly in oil and you're ready for the Great Experiment.

Most fly hatches develop in the late afternoon and evening. That's the time to look for rising trout. The idea is to locate one that seems to be feeding steadily in one spot. Make the cast well above him, so the fly drifts down to his position in a natural manner. Strip in slack line as the fly comes toward you, and be ready to strike at a splash or dimple, because that's him, and that's the fun of fishing with a dry fly.

Sure, there's more to dry-fly fishing than that. It really helps to recognize the various mayflies, to be able to call them by name, and to

26

know about when they will hatch. It helps a lot if you know how to cast curves into the end of your leader so it follows the fly over the fish. But all that can come later. To start, all anyone needs is a rising trout and a fly that will float long enough to ride over his nose.

TAP'S TIPS

❲ Ideally, the line and fly should float and the leader should sink when fishing with dry flies. So be careful not to handle the leader while dressing the fly line with floatant. Rubbing the leader with fish slime sometimes encourages it to sink.
❲ The best dry-fly fishing usually comes at dusk, just when you can't see to change flies. A small pencil-type flashlight clipped to your shirt pocket and aimed downward solves that problem nicely.

How to Avoid Drag

Anyone who has taken trout with a dry fly learns sooner or later—and usually, pretty darned soon—that trout will not come to a floating fly that moves at odds with the current. In fact, after a dragging fly passes overhead they sulkily refuse to rise to anything for a while, even juicy naturals.

How much drag will kill a float? The merest bit, generally. Just as in cooking there's no such thing as a little garlic, in fishing there's no such thing as a little drag. Sometimes it takes only a quiver to kill your chance. A fish may stop rising for a few minutes or he might show his concern by staying down for half an hour or longer. Either way, you've hurt your chance of taking him.

A fly drags when the leader and line pull it from a natural, free float. It skids, in other words. Living insects do not skid, and trout know it. They become so upset upon seeing a fly behave unnaturally that they simply stop eating.

On perfectly smooth water, the extended line, leader and fly all float along at exactly the same speed, and the fly does not drag. But in broken currents, the fly may move faster or slower that the leader and line, and thus get pulled off course. That is drag. And most trout live among broken currents.

One way to avoid drag is to stop the forward cast abruptly. Line and leader spring back, dropping on the water in loose curves. During the time it takes the currents to pull out the curves, the fly floats without drag.

27

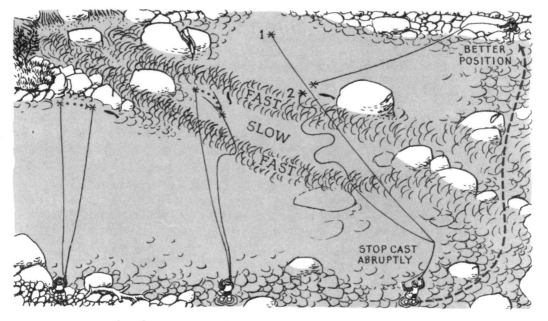

Another way is to look for "draggy" places and avoid them. You may have to move about to put smooth water between you and your fish, or even aim at him from directly above or below his lie. But somewhere in the pool there's usually a spot that offers you a good chance for a drag-free float. The experienced dry-fly fisherman looks for it as a matter of habit, noting the direction and speed of the currents without really thinking much about it, and holds his first cast until he has waded into the best spot.

The first cast over a rising trout is always the important one. If the fly drags and puts the fish down, the second will probably be only a waste of time. But if the fly floats over him naturally and freely the first time, you probably won't have to cast again.

TAP'S TIPS

⟨[When you see a trout rising in moving water, don't cast to the ring he makes, because the current immediately carries it below where he lies. Mark the spot by lining it up with an object on the opposite side of the stream. Then aim your cast a couple of feet above it.

⟨[Check the bite of your fly if you have trouble hooking rising trout. Some heavy-bodied patterns have so little space between the point and the body that the hook slides by without catching in the trout's jaw.

28

⟨ "Rising" trout that refuse dry flies actually may be feeding on nymphs just under the surface, or nosing bottom with their tails breaking water. Under these conditions dry-fly fishing is almost useless, but a sunken nymph or wet fly should be just what the trout are looking for.

Sometimes It Pays to Have Some Drag

Having just established the fact that a little drag is bad, I am now going to state that a lot of drag may be good. This sounds contradictory, but it really isn't.

In this case, drag is a matter of degree. A floating fly that drags just a tiny bit looks like a living mayfly, but it doesn't act like one; that is why timid fish shy away from it. However, a floating fly that drags so much it neither looks nor acts like a real fly is another matter. It moves, and hence it appears alive, and therefore to a fish it must look edible. I'm sure trout don't actually think it out that way, but I'm just as sure that this is what triggers them when a fly skitters wildly over their heads.

Here's how it works. Tie on any dry fly that will float well—a large bivisible, a hairwing Wulff, or any standard pattern with an abundance of hackle. In this case, the color and dressing, even the size of the fly, are less important than its buoyancy.

Now cast it crosscurrent and retrieve it over the top of the water just as if it were a streamer. Bounce it over the rips, twitch it over the flats, always working the rod tip to give it as much motion as possible. When the fly completes its swing, strip it back in short jumps and hitches. Then extend line and cast again, reaching beyond the water you have just covered.

This won't work when trout are rising to naturals, but it is worth trying when they are not taking sunken lures or showing themselves at the surface. The commotion of the dragging fly often brings up fish that are preoccupied with nymphs and other stuff down in the basement. Since the trout are not, at that particular time, in the habit pattern induced by free-floating surface food, the exaggerated drag seems to attract them rather than alarm them. Trout often boil at the dragging fly two or three times before catching it. Frequently fish that miss the fly appear to remain in the same spot, seemingly watching the surface hoping it will return, and smother the fly when it skids over them again.

Controlled drag can also be used, with sometimes riotous results, with wet flies. Most sea-salmon fishermen know this, but I know of very few trout fishermen who have tried it. I learned how to do it while fishing several years ago on Portland Creek, Newfoundland, with Lee Wulff, and often since then I have used the trick successfully on the trout rivers of New England.

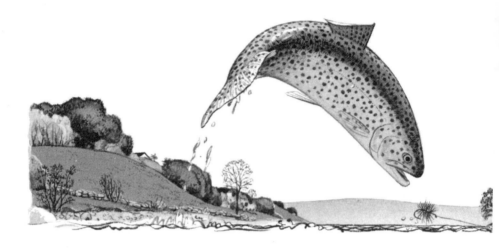

In this kind of fishing, the fly must ride over the water in an arc, cutting a V-wake on the surface. This can be done only if the fly is attached to the leader so that it sets off at an angle with its head up and tail down. To obtain this angle, tie the fly to the leader in the usual way, with a Turle knot. Then pass a half-hitch over the head of the fly and tighten it so the leader comes off the bottom or side. This is the "Portland hitch." When a fish strikes, the hitch slides off the head of the fly without knotting or kinking.

With the fly hanging from the leader at an angle of about 45 degrees, cast directly crosscurrent. Keep the line as straight as possible and hold the rod tip high as the fly swings around. The angle of fly to leader, plus the straight line and high rod, will make the fly plane like a single water ski, creating a distinct wake. I believe it is the wake, more than the fly or its pattern, that brings up the fish. Whatever it is about the hitched fly that attracts them, there are times when this seems to be the only way to make salmon and trout sit up and take notice.

There are some bugs in controlled-drag fishing. Rough water may drown the fly. Its commotion may frighten nervous trout lying under a clear, glassy surface. When the dragged fly does bring up fish, they often miss it in their nose-over-teakettle rush for it, or if they connect, they may break the tippet as they turn back against the straight leader. However, it sometimes stirs up fish better than any other way, and for that reason it is worth knowing about.

30

TAP'S TIPS

⟨ It isn't necessary to use an ultralight leader when fishing a fly with controlled drag. A 1X tippet creates no more commotion on the surface than a strand of 3X or 5X, and the heavier diameter will hold fish that might break a fine tippet by striking hard against a taut line.

⟨ When you feel or turn over a striking fish without hooking him, take a moment to check the point of your fly. You may find that it has been dulled or broken by ticking a rock on your back cast.

⟨ To keep trout cool and fresh in your creel, line the bottom with damp moss, a wet sponge, or a baby's diaper soaked in river water. The gradual evaporation refrigerates the creel and helps to preserve the flavor and freshness of the fish.

"Cast and Carry" Fishing

Every time I wade into a trout river with one rod in my hand and another fastened to my fishing vest I seem to invite jocular comment. "Hey," my witty companion will say, "you left your antenna up," or: "What's the matter, afraid of lightning?"

I suppose the rod shaft spearing up over my head does suggest the

31

radio antenna on a Volkswagen or a lightning rod on a barn roof. Anyway, I don't mind. The extra rod doesn't get in the way much, and often I am glad I have it with me. As a matter of fact, some of the humorists I fish with have begun to carry a spare rod too, so the idea does seem to have a little merit.

When you leave the car to fish a stretch of trout river you seldom know for certain-sure whether you will fare better with a spinning rod or a fly rod. If you decide to take the tin-tosser, sooner or later you are sure to come upon some trout rising busily at the tail of a pool, and wish you had brought the feather-duster instead. If, on the other hand, you start off with the fly rod you may flog away for an hour or more without raising a fish, and then meet a spin fisherman who has been cleaning up with a wobbler. By the time you decide that you brought the wrong rod you are so far from the car it doesn't seem worthwhile to trundle your waders all the way back to get the other one.

But if you take both rods with you there is no problem at all. You can fish downstream with hardware, change rods and fish back up again with feathers, or switch back and forth as you wish. In my case, I like to start fishing about midafternoon and work downriver with spinning lures until the sun gets off the water. Then I change over to the long rod and fish back up with flies, timing it so I will arrive at the car about dusk. On the way back I often pick up fish that I had located on the way down—trout that nudged the spinner or started for it and then backed off, or fish I flushed by wading carelessly. By the time I get back to these fish they are usually ready to come again, and if flies have started to hatch in the meantime they may be pushovers for a floater.

The extra rod doesn't get in the way nearly as much as you might think. Carried in two pieces, my light 5½-foot spinning rod sticks up over my head only a couple of inches, and my 7-foot fly rod only a little more than that. The loops in my fishing vest hold the spare rod tight against the front of my left shoulder so it doesn't interfere with casting. I carry both rods in my hand when walking through the brush, and when I stop to spend some time working one of my favorite pools I often leave the spare rod on shore until I am ready to move on. Frequently I keep both rods set up with their warheads on so I can fish a promising pool both ways, first giving it a once-over with a streamer or brace of wet flies, and then dredging it with a deep-going spinner or wobbler. Many times a quick switch from the spinning rod to the fly rod enables me to get a floater over a rising fish while he is still in the mood to take. And quite often a trout that shows interest in a fly, but can't quite convince himself that he should take it, will belt a spinner without an instant's hesitation.

Some days I never use the extra rod at all, especially when the trout show even a little bit of interest in flies. Even then, however, I find it comforting to have the spinning rod along, just in case they change their minds.

TAP'S TIPS

◖ Easiest trout to catch with a dry fly are those that lie in shallow, fast water; hardest are fish that hover in a still, glassy patch where they can examine the fly at their leisure before deciding to take it. So if you would like to practice with a dry fly, stick to the ripply runs.

◖ Big fish like to lie in or close to deep water. Therefore, fish deep for lunkers. This is probably the most important single factor in the search for a mounting-size fish.

◖ When you have a long walk from the car to the trout stream, wear light shoes or low-cut sneakers and carry your waders. When you arrive, stuff the sneakers in the back of your shirt and put them on again when you walk back to the car. It makes walking much easier, saves wear and tear on waders, especially those with felt soles.

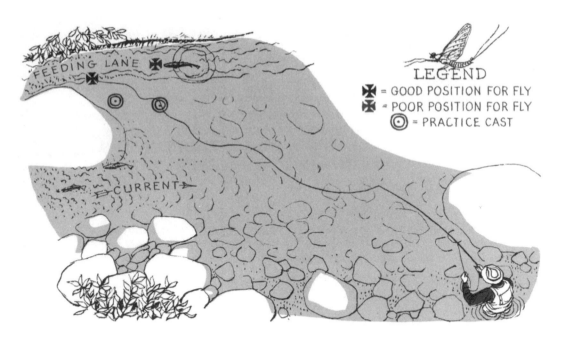

FEEDING LANE

CURRENT

Big Trout on Little Floaters

Late spring—mid-May to mid-June, in most areas—brings you your best chance of taking a big trout with a dry fly. Earlier than this, they're not interested in surface food. Later than this, they become shy, and nocturnal in habit. But the biggest and juiciest flies hatch in late May and early June, and lunkers that ordinarily stay away from the surface will move up now and gorge themselves on fat drakes. With luck, plus a little know-how, you might get a hook into a couple of them.

Whenever you find big trout sloshing around in a hatch of flies, certain factors begin working for you. Once a lunker trout starts surface feeding in earnest, he generally isn't too fussy, especially around dusk, which is when most of this sort of thing goes on. In many cases fly pattern won't be important if the size is about right. Also, the trout are feeling bold and hungry, and they're watching the surface. That's all in your favor.

Even so, a trout that's lived long enough to put on two or three pounds of meat isn't going to be a pushover. You've got to go at him right and he won't give you a chance to correct any mistakes you make.

Since you will almost surely get only one float over him, take a little time to size up the situation before you start pitching line. Fly fluffed and ready? Leader long enough, strong enough? Line floating nicely? Okay. Now where's the best spot to try from?

Personally, I like to cast from a position across stream and a bit

34

below the fish, when I can. Casting straight upstream is the storybook way, but that may require throwing a wide curve to prevent the leader from passing over the fish before the fly reaches him, and curves sometimes don't develop the way you plan. Casting from cross-stream on the other hand, permits you first to make one or two short casts to measure the distance without danger of putting the fish down. Your business cast, if you judge it right, will float your fly right into the leading edge of his feeding zone—and that's where you'll hang your fish if he comes.

In other words, the trick is to avoid making a forcing cast, one that either raises the fish or puts him down for good. By coming at him from the side, you edge your fly in toward the spot on the surface that he's watching, and if your fly hits his feeding lane without drag, he'll take if he's ever going to.

TAP'S TIPS

❲ When a rising trout refuses a well-placed dry fly, he may object to its size more than its pattern. Before you start experimenting with some different patterns, try the same one in a smaller size. Many times trout that ignore a size 12 will come readily to a 14 or 16.
❲ As dusk settles over the river, trout like to move into the shallow tails of the big pools where they can pick flies off the smooth water. Once a big trout settles in such a spot you have an excellent chance of getting him to come to a dry fly.
❲ Don't gauge the size of a rising trout by the size of the ring he makes. Big trout often make only a tiny dimple when they rise. If you see such a dimple in a place that looks as if it could hold a good fish, cast to it with extra care.

Fishing without Flies

As you may have noticed, there appears to be a definite correlation between fishing success and the activity of biting insects. When fish feed, so do the carnivorous bugs, the one on a hatch of flies, the other on a hatch of fishermen. This supports a treasured theory of mine, that for every reward there must always be an offsetting penalty. In the case of fishing, it works out almost every time. Whenever you enjoy good fishing you pay for it with an equivalent amount of suffering, whether from cold, rain, hunger, headache, loss of sleep, or the torment of biting insects. The better the fishing, the more it costs you, either in money or misery.

The relationship between fishing and insect activity has nothing to do with cause and effect, although it would appear to. The fish certainly don't bring out the bugs, and the man-eating varieties of bugs don't bring out the fish. There is, however, a significant relationship in time and place. Fishing always reaches its peak at the time when the bugs are thickest. And bugs are thickest at the places where fishing is best, as anyone who travels to Florida, Alaska, or Labrador will agree.

So whenever or wherever you enjoy good fishing you can expect to find mosquitoes, black flies, midges, or deer flies, all lusting for your life's blood.

As it happens, these pests share certain characteristics that make them vulnerable to protective measures. They can't maneuver well in the wind. They prefer to work in the shade, but are attracted to light, and to light-colored skin and clothing. They don't like smoke. And certain odors are repugnant to them. By exploiting these factors a fisherman can get along with bugs, at least as long as the fish keep biting, by wearing dark clothing with sleeves and pant cuffs tightly closed, staying in the sun and wind as much as possible, and keeping his pipe lit. If necessary he can also wear a head net, preferably one with dark netting.

Most important of all, he can plaster himself with bug juice. There are three basic types of insect dopes: repellents, insecticides, and protective coatings. Most prepared dopes have a little of each in them. In my opinion, commercial preparations are far more effective than home-brewed mixtures, and well worth their higher cost (one manufacturer frankly admits that his repellent is "outlandishly expensive"). Pressure

36

cans and spray guns are the most convenient to use, but they don't fit easily into the pocket of a fishing jacket. Most commercial dopes have an agreeable odor. Many, however, do not leave a durable residue, and must be applied frequently.

Some fishermen enjoy making up their own dope. The ingredients most commonly used in kitchen-sink concoctions include oils of pennyroyal, citronella, lavender, and cedar, usually mixed with pulverized or gum camphor, creosote, kerosene, or pine tar. Then the mixture is blended into a base of castor oil, lanolin, or warmed petroleum jelly to delay evaporation. Castor oil is excellent, except that it evokes such unhappy memories.

Or perhaps you would like to try the Indian method. When the bugs first appeared in the spring, they smeared themselves with pork rind from moccasins to scalp lock and then scrupulously avoided contact with water until the first September frost brought the fly season to a merciful end.

TAP'S TIPS

◖ The itching of insect bites can be relieved by covering the welts with a watery paste made by mixing bicarbonate of soda with water. If that isn't available, try a gob of mud.

◖ To prevent ticks and chiggers from climbing aboard when you fish in areas where they are common, rub kerosene into ankles, wrists, and neck, or dust these parts with powdered sulphur.

◖ A small jar of petroleum jelly belongs in every outdoorsman's kit. It can be used as a lubricant, rust preventive, medication for insect bites, water repellent, even as a floatant for flies and fly lines. The man who invented Vaseline even ate the stuff.

◖ Skunks shouldn't object to odors, but they do— to that of camphor, anyway. If woods pussies insist on coming to visit when you are camping out, a handful of mothballs will keep them away.

Sight-Savers

The next time you see a fisherman hold a fly as far away as the length of his arms will let him and try to poke the end of his leader through its eye, don't laugh. You may be doing the same thing yourself, one of these days.

No matter how falcon-eyed you are as a stripling, when you enter middle age your eyes will begin to lose some of their ability to focus

sharply for close-up work like tying on a fly or adding a 5X tippet to
your leader. Your distant vision will remain about as keen as it ever
was, but things right in front of your face turn fuzzy. Of necessity, you
will hang a pair of glasses on the bridge of your nose, and discover, as
I have, what a nuisance they can make of themselves when you're
fishing.

If you must continually put your glasses on and take them off while
you're fishing, invest a dollar in one of those cords with loops on each
end. All optical stores carry them. Force the loops over the earpieces
and drape the cord around your neck. The glasses hang conveniently
on your chest, easy to slip on and off, and you can't lose them overboard.

Another suggestion is to have your oculist make a monocle for you.
I know of a fisherman who did it. 'Ung the bloody thing from a string,
screwed it into his eye while changing flies, and let it dangle safely inside
his fishing weskit the rest of the time. It sounds like a practical idea,
but I think I'd feel a little self-conscious about using it.

Dimming vision brings other problems, not the least of which is
following a dry fly as it dances down a current. If you have trouble seeing such misty patterns as the Quill Gordon, remember that highly
visible flies like the Fanwing Royal Coachman, White Wulff, or a
bivisible all take fish, too.

When it becomes necessary to match a hatch with a dun-colored
floater, forget the fly and watch only its estimated position. By judging
the length of your cast and the speed of the current, you can follow the

38

water where the fly should be, and strike at any disturbance in that area. You may do that now, when fishing in the evening dusk. With a little practice you can learn to watch your fly without actually seeing it at all.

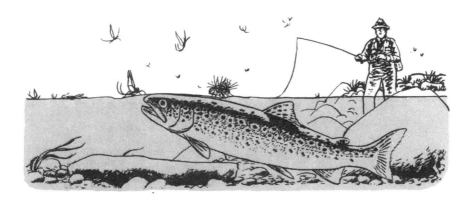

TAP'S TIPS

(Watch out for "wind knots" in your leader when you fish after dusk. They greatly reduce the strength of the leader and may break—in fact, probably will break—if you hook a heavy trout. Stop every so often to run the last two or three tippets through your fingers. If you find a knot, tie in a new tippet.

(Trout grow bolder as darkness settles over the water. They cruise more, rise to floating flies with greater confidence. When you can't locate a rising fish exactly, cast in his general direction, but above him if possible. If the fly doesn't pass over him, he will probably leave his feeding position to take it. Strike at the sound of any surface disturbance in that area.

(Wings are the least essential part of a dry fly. They look pretty to the fisherman, but trout will come to a wingless pattern if it matches the size and color of the hatching "natural."

How to Beat the Heat

Although trout fishing slumps off badly in hot weather, it never becomes completely hopeless. You can still take trout at certain times and places.

For example, last August I fished a stream in western Massachusetts where the water temperature registered 81 degrees at sundown. My

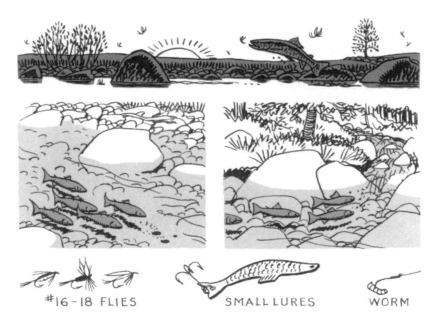

#16-18 FLIES   SMALL LURES   WORM

partner and I hadn't seen a trout move all afternoon, although we had fished hard with an assortment of lures and baits. But just at dusk the water began dimpling, and soon trout were rising steadily. We had to stalk our fish and cast to them delicately from a respectful distance, but we managed to hook enough of them to make the day worth remembering.

During the dog days of summer it pays to fish early and late, and usually only then. The water is cooler in the evening and early morning, and streamlife—flies, nymphs, bait fish and trout—will be moving then, for they must eat some time to stay alive.

It pays to watch for sources of cool water, too. Trout often gather in spring holes and near small brooks that bring colder water into the main stream. A stream thermometer will help you find such places; a drop of as little as a couple of degrees indicates that cooler water is coming in somewhere above.

For hot weather fishing, stick to small lures. The smaller insects are hatching now, and you'll do most of your business on sparsely dressed dries, wets, and nymphs in sizes 16, 18, even 20. Leaders should be both long and light, tapered down to at least 5X. Ultralight spinning lures, miniatures of the wobblers and spinners that produced so well in the early season, come into their own now, too. And while worms are far from your best bet in hot weather (except in rising water after a rain), a pinch of worm on a No. 14 hook will sometimes turn the trick. Fish it with upstream casts, just as you would a nymph.

So you don't have to stop trout fishing because the weather's hot.

40

You may not take as many fish as you did in the spring, but you're more likely to take bigger ones.

TAP'S TIPS

⟨ When you don't find trout lying below the mouth of a cold feeder stream in hot weather, explore the stream itself. The fish may have left the river in the morning to lie in the brook during the heat of the day. Even if it is only a trickle, the first pool may be full of trout.

⟨ Many fishermen prefer to wade wet in the summer. Body heat inside boots and waders causes evaporation, so it is almost impossible to keep your feet and legs dry anyway. Wading in sneakers give you better mobility, too.

⟨ It is often difficult to detect the gentle strike of a trout when dead-drifting a nymph or wet fly. You can make a "strike indicator" by scraping the leader about two feet above the fly. This forms a coil, which serves as a bobber. When the coil straightens a little, strike.

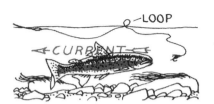

Trout Fishing in September

It's easy for a fisherman to get into a groove. For example, years ago I used to fish for trout and salmon in May and June, for warm-water fish during July and August, and in September I worked my bird dog and hung storm windows.

Back in the spring, though, the sporting camp people kept telling me about the perfectly fantastic fishing I'd have if only I'd come back to their place in September. So one year I went up to try it. Sure enough, I had to agree the fishing was fantastic, because it rained all during the weekend and I caught one 7-inch brook trout.

But that's not the point of the story. The point is that just before I got there a party of fishermen had caught trout and salmon until it was embarrassing, and a couple of days after I left someone brought in a 7-pound squaretail along with a mess of 3- and 4-pound speckled trash hardly worth the bother of cleaning.

Since then I've enjoyed some September fishing that really *was* fantastic, and not only for trout and salmon, either. I mention it here because it seems to me a lot of fishermen are passing up a good thing when they quit fishing in August, as I used to.

Think of all the things you have working for you in the cool of the year. For one, fishing pressure is light. You can go almost anywhere and

41

MAY   SEPTEMBER

have the place pretty much to yourself. For another, the fish are becoming active again after sulking through the heat of August. The fall spawners, stirring with the urge to perpetuate themselves, start gathering around the mouths of the tributaries, and they are mature fish that average bigger than the fish you catch in May and June. If you like dry-fly fishing you can have it in September. You probably won't have to fuss around trying to match a hatch, either, because flies don't hatch much at this time of year, and a Fanwing or Wulff will do about as well as anything.

September fishing is fly fishing for those who like to cast feathers. But it's light tackle fishing with plug and spinning rod, too, because all fish are nearer the surface now and feeling frisky again. So between putting up storm windows and working the bird dog, try to steal some time during the month for fishing. Like the camp owner said, it could be fantastic.

TAP'S TIPS

(The first heavy rain of late summer often brings trout out of their summer quarters for good. Unless the rain is followed by a long spell of hot weather, they will probably settle down in the same holes that produced such good fishing for you in the spring.
(In general, the chance of taking large fish improves as the season advances. For one thing, spring-

42

stocked fish have added length and weight. For another, the larger (and therefore wiser) fish remain in the stream after most of the small fish have been caught. And, of course, mature fish start moving around as the spawning season approaches.

⟨ When pond trout that seem to be feeding at the surface ignore a dry fly, try a nymph. The "rises may be caused by trout swirling at emerging nymphs just an inch or two from the top. Retrieve the nymph very slowly just under the surface, sink your leader if you can, and strike every time you think you see a flash or bulge near your lure.

How Much Does It Weigh?

If you know the length and girth of a fish, and carry pocket scales, you can always find out exactly what it weighs. If, on the other hand, you know the length and girth but do not have scales, you can guess at the weight. Personally, that's the method I prefer.

Some people, however, feel it is terribly important to know exactly how much a fish weighs. So for the benefit of those who cannot be happy until they have evaluated a defunct aquatic vertebrate in terms of pounds and ounces, here is a formula by which its weight can be calculated almost to the gram: $G^2 \times L \div 800 = W$

Suppose, now, you have just caught a trout 15 inches long and 9 inches around. Nine (G) squared is 81. Multiply that by 15 (L) and you get 1,215. Divide that figure by 800 and it comes out 1.50. So the weight (W) of the fish is $1\frac{1}{2}$ pounds.

The formula is surprisingly accurate when applied to medium-sized fish, but it should not be used on fish in the record class, even as a quick estimate. I tested the formula on some large fish of known length and girth, and found that a record muskie that weighed $62\frac{1}{2}$ pounds on accurate scales weighed $81\frac{1}{2}$ pounds by the formula. That record was subsequently broken by a $64\frac{1}{2}$-pounder which, according to the formula, really weighed only $41\frac{3}{4}$. Then along came a third giant muskie whose $G^2 \times L \div 800$ totalled $84\frac{1}{2}$, but whose weight on official scales was but $67\frac{1}{2}$ pounds, still a very large fish.

The margin of error narrows when the formula is applied to smaller fish, however, so it is worth remembering. Readers who don't like to mix figuring with fishing can make a tracing of the accompanying chart and carry it in their tackle box. As the index line shows, that 9-by-15 trout is going to weigh only $1\frac{1}{2}$ pounds if you happen to have the chart with you at the time. If you haven't, just call it a 2-pounder and dress it out fast before someone produces his pocket scale.

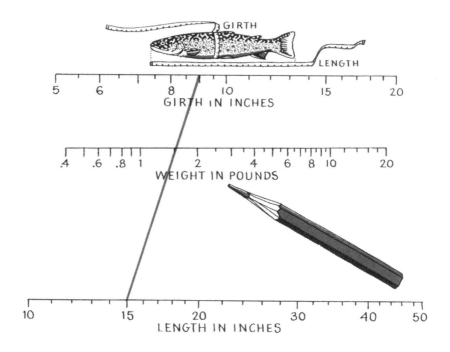

GIRTH

LENGTH

5   6   8   10   15   20
GIRTH IN INCHES

.4   .6 .8 1   2   4   6 8 10   20
WEIGHT IN POUNDS

10   15   20   30   40   50
LENGTH IN INCHES

TAP'S TIPS

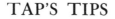

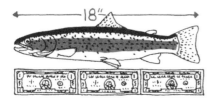

⟨ Fish begin losing weight, mostly through dehydration, immediately after they are killed. However, the loss is not as great as many fishermen think. It averages about one ounce per pound of fish the first few hours; after that shrinkage is negligible.

⟨ To measure a fish when you have no ruler, look in your wallet. Paper currency is 6 inches long (6⅛, to be exact) and 2½ (actually, 2⅝) inches wide. For measurements between 6 and 12 inches, fold the bill carefully once, twice, or three times.

⟨ Check your state fishing laws to see if trout fishing is legal in October and November. Cooling surface waters stimulate fish into a flurry of feeding, and sometimes the late fall fishing is better than it was in the spring.

Trout Are Trout

Whether we like it or not, trout fishing is fast becoming a put-and-take proposition. Many of our trout rivers have become so warm and polluted that fish cannot survive in them from one season to the next. The streams that have so far escaped the curse of what we call civiliza-

44

tion often can't produce nearly enough native fish to meet the ever-increasing pressure, and they must have help from the hatchery truck.

Yet many fishermen still hold man-reared trout in contempt. Stocked fish are too easy to catch. They can't fight. They taste like liver. They are but pale copies of the real thing.

Easy to catch? Sometimes, yes. But many fishermen still fail to take their legal limit on opening day, when the stream is full of freshly stocked trout. And often, when fishing remote waters, I have caught wild fish cast after cast till I tired of it.

No fight? Give them time to get used to their new environment. Modern hatchery production methods produce a remarkably strong, healthy fish, compared with pool-reared trout of only a few years ago. Given time to develop their muscle in the river currents, they can run and jump with the zing of a native.

They taste like liver? That's odd, because hatcheries don't feed with liver any more. In fact, hatchery trout have a more balanced diet than wild trout, which is one reason for their faster rate of growth. The diet even includes elements that give the fish better color, inside and out.

Trout are trout. And since today it's pretty much a choice of fishing for hatchery-produced trout or not fishing for trout at all, the tolerant fisherman will be grateful for what he has and not care whether the trout he catches was born in the rubble of the stream bottom or in an egg tray under electric lights.

And trout are trout whether they be brookies, browns, or rainbows. Some fishermen admire one kind extravagantly and despise the others. In much of the Northeast, for example, oldtime trout fishermen insist that the native squaretail is the only trout worth catching, and scorn the alien brown and the rainbow of the West. But Westerners love their rainbows, and dry-fly fishermen of the Middle Atlantic States esteem the brown.

I always thought the brook trout was the sweetest-meated of them all—until I ate a fresh-caught rainbow from an icy river in Colorado. The rainbow was considered the jumper—but one of the jumpingest fish I ever hooked was a spring-tailed brown from the Squannacook River in Massachusetts. And the brown trout was always the dry-fly fisherman's delight—although remembering how the brook trout slurped mayflies off the pool below Night Dam on Fifth Lake Stream in Maine one evening, I sometimes wonder.

So let's just say that trout are trout, and feel grateful for having them, whether they were born in a hatchery or go by the name of *fontinalis, irideus,* or *fario.*

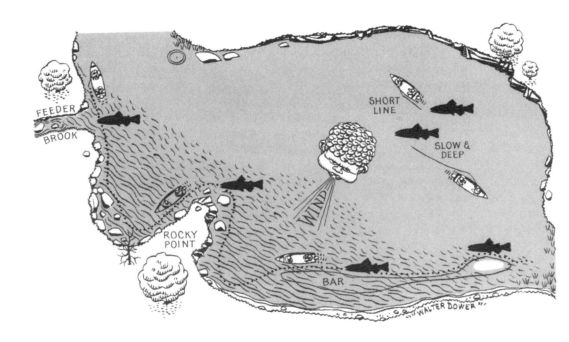

FEEDER BROOK

ROCKY POINT

WIND

BAR

SHORT LINE

SLOW & DEEP

WALTER DOWER

SALMON AND LAKERS

Trolling in the Spring

SOME fly casters tend to curl their lips when they speak of trolling. This is unfortunate, because trolling is an interesting, ethical, and, at times, exciting way to take fish. It can also be a productive one, if only because trolled lures spend more time in the water where fish can get at them.

In the spring of the year, before warming surface waters drive the fish down, towing a lure behind a boat is without question the most practical known way to take any lake-dwelling game fish, from trout and landlocked salmon and even lakers, to bass and walleyes. It is light-tackle fishing, too, as the troller can use the same gear the fly-swisher uses, except that he will want a sinking line, and he can choose from a wider variety of lures—streamers, small spinners, wobblers and, of course, live bait.

Trolling speed is important. Trout and landlocked salmon seem to enjoy chasing a fast-moving lure, while bass and walleyes usually prefer one that is just loafing along. However, fish are capricious, so the troller will have to experiment a little by opening and closing the throttle until he hits upon the rate of speed the fish seem to like.

While fiddling with the throttle, the man at the motor should also saw the tiller back and forth. Steering an erratic, zigzagging course swings the lure over a wider area of water and at the same time makes it rise and sink to different levels. As in stream fishing, fish often strike just as the lure darts upward after a slow drift.

Surface trolling is mainly shoreline fishing, and the best shoreline is always the one on which the wind is blowing. The heavier the wind, the closer the fish lie to the shore, doubtless feasting on small stuff caught up in the wash and roll of the waves. Salmon and trout often cruise into the very surf, so close to the rocks it is impossible to reach them with a trolled lure. The only way to get at these fish is by casting a fly or spinning lure up against the shore. If the fish don't smash it instantly, they may follow it out and take one of the trolled lures as it goes by.

Other hot spots are rocky points and bars and the mouths of feeder streams. It will often pay to linger at such places, circling and cutting figure-eights over them several times before leaving. Often a sufficient number of fish will have congregated in these areas to keep a pair of fishermen happily occupied for hours.

Surface fishing usually slumps off badly when the wind dies and the lake flattens out. When this happens, it may help to move away from the shallow waters near shore, reduce speed, and perhaps nip on a piece of lead to take the lure down into deeper water. If this fails, fishing the lure close to the boat on a very short line sometimes stirs up some action. Often fish will charge into a miniature rooster tail to nail a fast-moving lure.

One thing about trolling: the fish usually hooks himself. Members of the Annual Sebago Lake Landlocked Salmon, Beef Stew and Draw Poker Expedition, in which I was active for several seasons, classified trolling strikes as tip-dippers, rod-bouncers, and reel-screechers. A tip-dipper resulted when a fish merely bunted the lure with no serious intention of taking it; a rod-bouncer was when the fish actually belted the lure but failed to hook himself. In either case, the fish could some-times be teased into striking again by circling over the area a few times.

But a reel-screecher signalled a smashing strike, almost always a solidly hooked fish, and action of the kind we had come to Maine for. Since it was the concensus of the ASLLSBS & DPE membership that fast trolling increased the incidence of reel-screechers, you can be sure we lingered not nor dawdled long as we made our rounds of the Sebago Lake shoreline.

TAP'S TIPS

(When trolling with oars, vary the speed to put more kick into the lure. Take several quick strokes, let the boat glide almost to a dead stop, then dig in with a few more short, hard strokes. This causes the lure to dart up, sink slowly, and dart again, simulating the actions of a live bait fish.

(Towing a string of flasher spoons from the stern of the boat often brings in fish that might not see the trolled lures. Shorten one trolling line so the lure follows 10 or 15 feet behind the flashers.

(To row in a perfectly straight line without continually turning to point the boat, drag a floating fly line directly off the stern. Either aim the line at a spot on shore or just concentrate on keeping it straight. If the line bends you know you have wandered off course.

FLY LINE

Fishing with a Mandolin String

Most fishermen like to hang on a pair of streamer flies when they troll the northern lakes for landlocked salmon, trout, and, for a short while after the ice goes out, even lakers. This gives the fish a choice of two different patterns in two sizes—for example, a No. 8 Dark Edson Tiger, which resembles a chub, and a No. 4 Green Ghost, which looks more than faintly like a smelt. The two-fly setup also gives the fisherman a chance to score an occasional double, an event that can lend quite a bit of spice to a day's fishing.

Now here is a way to troll three flies at a time. And if two flies catch more fish than one, certainly it stands to reason that three should catch more than two.

You'll need a mandolin E string, although a banjo A string, which is slightly heavier, will do. Cut off a 12-inch length, measure in about 5 inches from one end, and bend it there, forming a small loop closed with two or three twists. Before you twist it, slide a small barrel swivel into the loop. Next make small loops at both ends and form the wire into the shape of a wishbone.

You now have a light, strong, virtually invisible spreader with two flexible arms of unequal length. Attach short leaders of equal length to the end of each arm. Then tie a fly to each leader, making sure the short arm of the spreader has the larger of the two flies. This balances the weight so that both flies will swim properly in the water.

The third fly is fished as a dropper from the main leader, a foot or two above the spreader. Tie a barrel knot into the leader at this point

49

and leave one end from 4 to 6 inches long to serve as the dropper strand. The dropper fly should be the largest of the three—a No. 4 or 6. The fly on the short arm of the spreader can then be an 8 and the other a 10.

As you can see, the spreader prevents the flies from tangling with themselves or the leader. More important, the springy wire gives the flies unusually lifelike action. Each time you pump your rod the spreader arms open and close, which makes the tail flies dart and weave like a brace of scurrying bait fish.

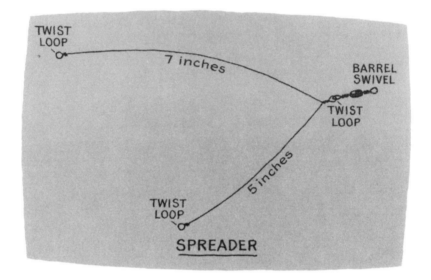

As with streamer flies trolled in the orthodox manner, the spreader rig should be fished fast—not just moderately fast, but quite fast. Land-locked salmon seem to enjoy chasing after their food, particularly in windy weather when the water is choppy. How fast? Well, faster than you can row a boat or paddle a canoe; up to half-throttle with, say, a 5 h.p. motor. So if you try the spreader, adjust your trolling speed to the weather and fish fast on a windy day, slower when the water is barely ruffled or flat calm.

I learned this trolling trick from Lewis Brown, one of the top fishing guides at Grand Lake Stream, Maine. Lew told me that his father, who was a Maine guide before him, developed the idea more than thirty years ago. Lew's dad claimed that it worked mainly because the three-fly tandem looked like a couple of small fish following a larger one. This may be so, but the idea appeals to me mostly because I've never scored a triple on landlocked salmon, and the mandolin string may give me a chance to do it.

50

TAP'S TIPS

❰ To make a set of tandem hooks for trolling night-crawlers and large minnows, use two hooks with ringed eyes and force the barb of one through the eye of the other. Fasten the bait to the forward hook. The trailing hook often hangs short-striking fish.

❰ When surface trolling for salmon and lakers, carry a spare reel filled with wire or lead-core line. If the wind dies and fish move into deeper water, use the wire line to get your lure down to them.

❰ Try using an extra-long leader when trolling streamer flies. Many lake fishermen like to have 25 or 30 feet of monofilament in front of their flies, especially when the surface is calm or barely rippled. Fasten leader to line with interlocking loops so the connection will pass easily through the rod guides.

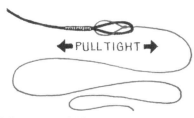

PULL TIGHT

Bar Tender's Guide

Some people would think it a very funny joke if a fisherman said he spent the evening hanging around a bar and came home loaded. They wouldn't find it quite so funny, though, if he showed them what he came home loaded with. There's nothing comical about a mess of eatin' fish dangling from a stringer.

No question about it, a bar is a fruitful place to fish in a lake. You can't name a fish that doesn't come in from deep water every so often to enjoy the good living around the shoals, and this includes everything from the lordly landlocked salmon to the humble perch, the trout, lakers, walleyes, and both kinds of bass. At one time or another you're sure to find them up on the bar chasing bait or, oh happy hour, even rising like crazy to a hatch of mayflies.

The big trouble with fishing a bar is that you can't always find one unless the water is very clear or the shoals have been marked with buoys. Most of the larger bodies of water have been charted for pleasure boating by now, however, so if you can get a navigation map of your favorite lake you can easily pinpoint the shallow spots by means of the depth-in-feet numbers sprinkled over it. A tight cluster of 8's and 10's surrounded by a scattering of 30's and 40's marks an area well worth investigating. So does a string of low numbers running out from a point of land.

Without such a chart, you may have to hunt blind by letting your lure hang bottom or by feeling for it with a sounding bob. A simple way to find a bar is to tie a 4-ounce sinker on a 20-foot length of mono-filament and hold it over the side as you troll at slow speed. When you

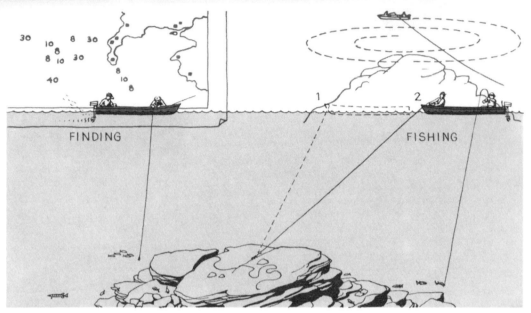

feel the sinker hit something, you have probably come upon the edge of a bar. You can then probe with the sinker to get an idea of its size and shape, and fix its location by lining it up with objects on shore.

How you should fish the bar depends on what you're fishing for, the method you prefer, the time of day, and season of year. Generally, cold-water species lie in the deep water during the day and move onto the bar as evening approaches. Their behavior is determined by such factors as water temperature and the kind of food they're looking for.

A good way to find where the fish are lying is to drop your anchor on the very top of the bar and let the wind carry your boat over the downwind side. By letting out anchor line a few feet at a time you can fish a bait or a deep-running lure along the dropoff all the way down to black water.

If you prefer to troll, follow the general contour of the bar in widening circles and let out more trolling line each time you complete a circuit. As evening approaches and the wind starts to die, reverse the process. By the time dusk has blotted out your shore markers the fish will probably be up on the shallowest part of the bar. That's the time to let your anchor down real easy and break out the fly rod. If salmon or trout are present you could have a circus with a streamer fly or nymph, or even a floater. If it's a bass lake, by all means tie on a loudmouthed popping bug.

I can't guarantee you'll leave the bar loaded, but if you're lucky you'll know you've been to a party.

TAP'S TIPS

⟨ When trolling two lines, start by running one of them long and deep, the other short and shallow.

Game fish move up and down as the water temperature and other conditions change. As soon as one line begins to produce strikes, raise or lower the other one to that level.

⟨ Two men can fly-cast from a boat without getting in each other's way if the man in the bow faces one direction and the man in the stern faces the other. When both cast off the same side of the boat their lines often become tangled on the back cast.

⟨ To make a line-holder for dropline fishing or for sounding bottom with a sinker, rivet two metal pie plates back to back and cover the seam with waterproof tape. By adding handles or passing a rod through a hole drilled in the middle it can be used to let out and bring in line quickly, without snarling or twisting.

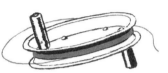

"Pulling Copper"

My friend Lenox Putnam came back from upper New York State last summer looking a little wild-eyed and smelling strongly of fish. It seems he had been deep-water fishing with some friendly natives up in the Finger Lakes country, and had learned their fabulously successful method of snatching lake trout off the bottom of the deepest lakes.

The locals call it "pulling copper," and according to Len, here's how it's done: Copper-pulling is simply handline trolling with enough metal line to drag the lure along the bottom of the lake. Jerking, or "pulling" the line by hand causes the lure to lift off the bottom and flutter slowly back. The trick is to keep the lure in contact with bottom entirely by feel, while giving it an erratic, zigzag motion. Light, thin treble-hook spoons of chrome or stainless steel are the favorite lures.

Some fishermen who dislike handlining use a bait casting rod with a star-drag trolling reel and 600 feet or so of fine-diameter wire, often Monel. The rod makes it somewhat more difficult to feel bottom, but it can be done with practice.

Most deep-lake floors are surprisingly smooth and free of debris, so copper-pullers don't hang up as often as you would expect. However, it helps to know the shoals and ledges, and to avoid shallow areas where weed growth becomes a problem.

As a rough rule of thumb, five feet of line will sink about one foot at normal trolling speed. In other words, 250 feet of wire line will put the lure on bottom in 50 feet of water. Then the trick is to keep it there by taking in or letting out line as the depth varies. Since wire has no elasticity, it carries the feel of bottom directly to the hand. And that is the real secret of pulling copper—recognizing when the lure is scraping bottom, and keeping it down there.

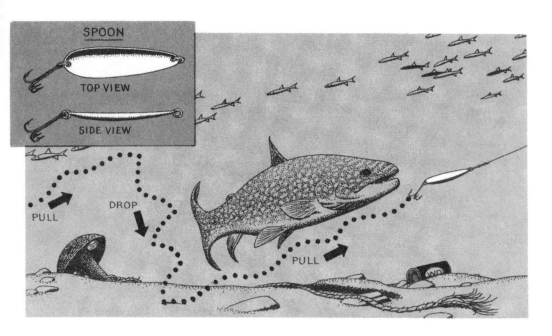

During most of the fishing season the big lakers and brown trout keep their fat bellies right on the lake bed, in deep, cold water. Pulling copper makes it possible to put a lure where they can't help seeing it, and where the laziest of them can take it without putting themselves to any great amount of trouble.

TAP'S TIPS

⟨[Wire line breaks easily when it becomes kinked. To make sure a line is free of twists, let it pass between your fingers as it runs out. When you feel a bump, either straighten the wire or break it off and splice it with interlocking loops.

⟨[Because wire has no elasticity it is especially important to keep the rod tip high while playing a fish hooked with wire line. The rod's flexibility prevents the fish from tearing the lure free on sudden twists and turns.

⟨[When leaving trolling gear set up in the boat between fishing trips, cover the reel by slipping a plastic bag over the butt of the rod and fastening it with wire, a pipe cleaner, or rubber band. The bag keeps sand out of the reel and, if the lure is left hooked to a crossbar of the reel, it may prevent someone from getting caught on it.

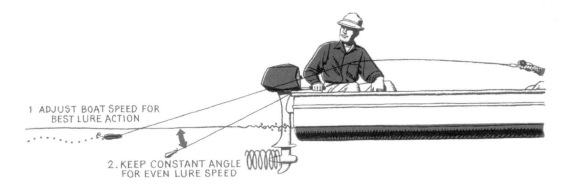

1 ADJUST BOAT SPEED FOR
BEST LURE ACTION

2. KEEP CONSTANT ANGLE
FOR EVEN LURE SPEED

Trolling with a Speedometer

A genial French-Canadian who had come down from Quebec to seek his fortune in the pulp mills of northern Maine once described for me the tackle he used for lake trout and landlocked salmon fishing. "She's want dam' beeg rod for pull those dam' beeg spin*nairs*," he told me, "an' two-t'ree dam' swi*vell* so she's don' kinkle t' dam' line, wit' long lea*deur* an' be sure he's don' forget some nice frash smaaalt."

Jean was referring, of course, to deep trolling with sewn smelt and the famous old Dave Davis rig, a string of flashing blades nearly the size of saucers. A Dave Davis bucks as hard as a 4-pound togue, but it is a lethal thing to fish with.

In this enlightened age (that, as you will shortly see, is intended to be a pun), you don't see so much of that kind of tackle being used on the northern lakes. The trend today is toward much lighter trolling gear—glass fly rod, fly reel, and wire line, generally Monel or copper, sometimes lead core. With this gear it is possible to probe quite considerable depths with plugs, spoons, or sewn bait, and playing a fish on such relatively light tackle is a great deal more enjoyable than winching it in with a star-drag reel.

The trick to this fishing is to find the level where the fish are lying and then to put your lure through it at the speed that gives it the best action.

Len Putnam, who has made a specialty of wire line trolling, tells me he takes by far the great majority of his fish over sunken bars and along shelving shorelines where the thermocline rests on bottom.

That's nice to know. But once a lure sinks out of sight, how do you know when it has reached the depth you want? If you have marked your line at, say, 25-foot intervals, you may know that paying out 150 feet of line at 3 mph should take the lure down to around 30 feet. However,

55

it's easy to knock that calculation cockeyed. A Mooselook wobbler, for example, should be trolled at about twice, maybe three times, the speed of a Flatfish. Monel trolls deeper than lead core. And varying speed as little as 1 mph can lift the lure out of the strike zone or hang it on bottom.

Running the motor at a predetermined setting isn't the answer, either, because the boat will travel faster downwind and slower upwind. You may not notice the change in speed, but it will affect not only the trajectory of the line but may also kill the action of the lure.

Obviously, the important thing is first to find the correct speed for whatever lure you've tied on. That's simple. Let out 6 or 8 feet of line and drag the lure beside the boat where you can see it. Fiddle with the motor throttle until you hit the speed that gives the lure its best action. Now let out line and try to hold that rate of speed.

There's a quite ingenious trolling speedometer on the market, called the Trolex, which makes it easy to maintain uniform speed. I wouldn't go deep-trolling without one, and I recommend it without reservation for anyone who fishes with wire line. However, if your sporting goods store doesn't carry it, you can make a crude version. Just tow a 2-ounce sinker from a length of monofilament long enough to hold the sinker 6 or 8 inches under water, and note carefully the angle of the tow line when the boat is moving at the desired speed. If you keep the line at exactly that angle you can be sure of maintaining proper speed on upwind, downwind, or crosswind legs, with your lure working hard for you every foot of the way.

TAP'S TIPS

([Watch the rod tip when trolling with a Flatfish— an excellent lure, incidentally, for landlocked salmon and lake trout. Its violent action makes the tip throb, and a change of speed varies the beat of the tip noticeably.

([When deep-trolling with two lines, keep them separated by using different types of wire. This prevents them from running side by side at the same level and tangling on sharp turns.

([Sometimes it pays to keep a fly rod rigged and ready when trolling deep with wire. Occasionally fish will chase bait to the surface, and take a streamer fly if it is cast over them quickly.

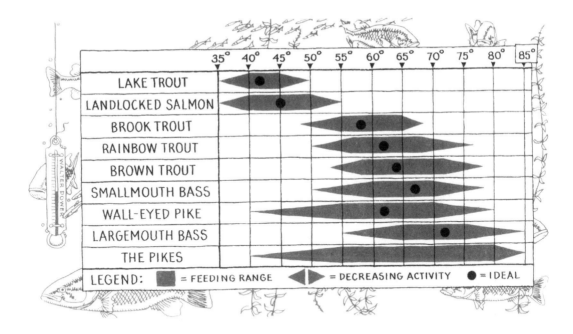

	35°	40°	45°	50°	55°	60°	65°	70°	75°	80°	85°
LAKE TROUT											
LANDLOCKED SALMON											
BROOK TROUT											
RAINBOW TROUT											
BROWN TROUT											
SMALLMOUTH BASS											
WALL-EYED PIKE											
LARGEMOUTH BASS											
THE PIKES											

LEGEND: ▮ = FEEDING RANGE ◀▶ = DECREASING ACTIVITY ● = IDEAL

How to Find Fish with a Thermometer

Water temperatures affect fish just as much as changing weather affects humans, although of course in a different way. When the water becomes too cold or hot, fish seek more comfortable surroundings, or else they just mope around and pick listlessly at their food until the temperature becomes comfortable again.

Serious fishermen know how important the temperature of the water can be to their success, and they know how to put this knowledge to good use. That's why some people can catch fish when other people can't. It's not the only reason, of course, but certainly it is an important one.

Anyone who owns a water thermometer can use it to find fish. First, however, he must know what temperatures the different species of fish like best. To simplify this, I made up the above chart showing the temperature most of the common game fish prefer. The pointed bars cover the temperature range in which these fish are most likely to feed. The tapered ends indicate their increasing or decreasing activity as the water temperature changes from just warm enough to a bit too warm. The wide part of the bar shows the optimum, or ideal range. The dot is the exact water temperature each species seems to prefer.

The chart does not show the coldest and hottest temperatures fish can stand, remember. We are not interested here in survival, but only in the conditions that affect fishing, so we will know where to look for fish and how to fish for them.

You will notice that the chart shows no ideal temperature for members of the pike family—northerns, muskies, pickerel. Actually, the musky is somewhat more selective in this respect than the northern, and the northern more than the pickerel. But all three have great tolerance for temperature extremes, and it would be necessary to use a long bar, rather than a round dot, to show the temperature range in which they are active.

At the other extreme, lake trout are very persnickety about the temperature of their water. Ice fishermen can catch lakers off the bottom in 39-degree water; summer trollers may take them at mid-depth in water up to 50 degrees. But if a lake holds a layer of water that is exactly 42 degrees, it's almost a sure bet you will find lakers there.

Naturally, your choice of lures, as well as the way you fish them, has a great deal to do with your fishing success, even when you find water the fish should like. In general, you should be able to take fish on topwater or shallow-running lures when the surface water is in the optimum range. However, if the temperature is in the tapered end of the bar—for example, if the water is 75 to 80 degrees and you're fishing for smallmouths—you would improve your prospects by fishing a deep-going lure or dropping a bait down into 65- to 70-degree water.

Knowing how water temperatures affect fish can also help you to choose the best method of fishing. If you can't locate comfortable water, then the fish may be forced to stay a while in water they don't like. In that case, fish your lure very slowly, because the fish probably won't feel much like chasing after it. On the other hand, fish lying in comfortable water are likely to be hungry and active, and a fast-moving lure would look good to them.

So a thermometer can pay off double for you, first by helping you find fish, and second by tipping you off to the best way to catch them. Used with the chart, it can prove to be a valuable item of fishing equipment.

TAP'S TIPS

(In the very early spring, usually just after the ice goes out, lake trout often come near the surface and mingle with the landlocked salmon and trout to feed on smelt. They take streamer flies readily, and put up a stubborn, if not spectacular, fight.

(To find spring holes and patches of cool water when wading a stream, let a fish-finder thermometer hang in the water from a thong attached to your belt. Checking it occasionally may lead to pools where fish are concentrated.

(Fish often start feeding just as a cold front moves in. When the weather bureau predicts a drastic change in the weather, plan to be on the water before it arrives.

(A red flag with a white diagonal stripe serves as a warning to boaters that a skindiver is under water somewhere close by. If you see this flag, either attached to a float or flying from a boat, steer clear of the area—especially if you are deep-trolling with wire line.

Fishing the "Comfort Zone"

During the months of hot weather the water in all large, deep lakes settles into three layers. This is a matter of more than casual interest to trout and salmon fishermen because one of those layers now holds practically all the cold-water fish in the lake.

Reading from top to bottom, these layers are called the epilimnion, thermocline ("comfort zone"), and hypolimnion. They form because the dense cold water settles to the bottom and the lighter warm water remains on top. Sandwiched between them is a relatively thin sheet of cool water with a high oxygen content. That's where the fish are. They are concentrated in a very small part of the lake's total water volume and they are healthy, happy, and hungry. All you've got to do is find the layer and put a bait or trolling lure into it.

The drawing shows what a lake looks like in cross section after it has stratified in summer. The depth and temperature figures were taken from an actual survey of a 1,500-acre lake in Maine on a day in mid-August. As you can see, the temperature dropped very slowly through the warm top layer. At the 25-foot level it began dropping fast—about 8 degrees in 15 feet—and then dropped slowly again between 40 feet and bottom. So in that lake, on that day, the comfort zone was about 15 feet thick and started 25 feet down.

During the summer stagnation period the surface water is too warm for salmon and trout, although they will move into it occasionally to chase food. However, the warm-water species—bass, the pikes, panfish —prefer the surface layer and stay in some part of it throughout the summer.

Below the comfort zone the water is colder than salmon like and often lacks sufficient oxygen to sustain them for long. Lake trout, which

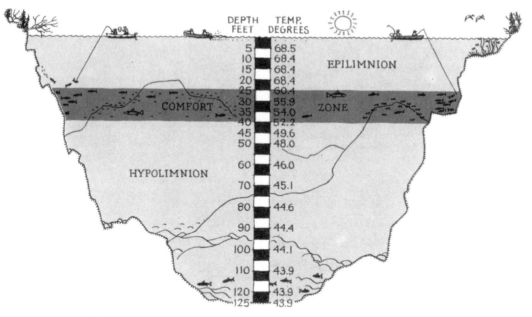

DEPTH FEET	TEMP. DEGREES
5	68.5
10	68.4
15	68.4
20	68.4
25	60.4
30	55.9
35	54.0
40	52.2
45	49.6
50	48.0
60	46.0
70	45.1
80	44.6
90	44.4
100	44.1
110	43.9
120	43.9
125	43.9

EPILIMNION

COMFORT ZONE

HYPOLIMNION

insist on very cold water, have the bottom layer pretty much to themselves during the summer months.

So now nearly all the fish in the lake have taken summer lodging
in the layer of water they like best. And happily for us, the landlocked
salmon and trout are concentrated in the thinnest of the three layers.

This poses the problem of finding the comfort zone. Because its
depth and thickness are determined by the depth of the lake, the clarity
of the water, and other factors, the only accurate way to find it is to
probe with a water thermometer until you come to rapidly dropping
temperatures. This takes some time and patience—but then, so does fishing aimlessly in barren water.

It is possible to find the comfort zone with an educated guess plus
trial and error. If the lake is large and deep, start fishing at about the
35-foot level and then try it 10 or 15 feet above and below. If the lake is
known to be very deep, start at about 50 feet. In smaller bodies of water
try the 20-foot depth for a starter. Remember that wind action drives
the thermocline down, and that it will be deeper in clear lakes because
the sun's rays penetrate farther.

After you find the right depth, look for shorelines that drop off into
deep water, and if you have a survey map of the lake, check it for the
location of underwater bars and ledges. While you can expect to find
trout and landlocks in almost any part of the comfort zone (more likely,
however, near the top of it), the hottest spots of all are those places
where it rests on bottom. When you start scratching rocks at thermocline depth you're really zeroed in.

BASS

Different Fish, Different Methods

BASS may come a lot easier if you treat them as separate species and cater to their respective habits in your choice of tackle, lures, and fishing methods.

Locate largemouths by reading the shorelines. Old stumps standing at the waterline often mark the location of submerged trees and underwater brushpiles—always hotspots for bigmouths. Look for brushy, overhung banks and shoot your plug or bug far under the foliage, as close to shore as you can put it. Investigate coves and pockets; surface debris accumulates in these places and affords excellent largemouth cover. Beds of lily pads may shelter bass, so give them a thorough combing, paying special attention to the edges and open pockets.

Largemouths tend to move out into deeper water during the heat and brightness of midday. Go down for them then with deep-running plugs and bait—frogs and large minnows held just above the bottom growth with a bobber, weighted plastic worms dragged slowly across the floor of the pond, a weedless spoon with pork rind, or just a big gob of nightcrawlers. Toward evening the fish move back toward shore again. Follow them in and pepper the shoreline with surface lures—floating plugs, pork chunks, bass bugs, and fly-rod poppers.

Smallmouths prefer a different kind of environment. Look for them in deep water over a rocky bottom. Probe with a sounding weight to locate reefs. When you locate one, fish just over the dropoff. Explore water off stony points and rubbly shores if the bottom drops away sharply.

You can frequently locate a glory hole by this method: Fish ten minutes or so in one spot, raise the anchor and drift or row a few yards, fish again, drift, and so on. If the anchor suddenly plummets toward Hong Kong, locate the brink of the chasm and fish over the edge of it.

Use deep-running lures for smallmouths and stick to the smaller sizes; in general, largemouths like bigger baits than smallmouths do. Fan your casts out like the spokes of a wheel to cover all surrounding water. On calm evenings try bass bugs along the shores and off the weed beds and rockpiles.

Lay in a variety of natural baits to match the everchanging tastes of smallmouths. They may like hellgrammites one day, minnows or crickets the next, or nightcrawlers, live shrimp or crawfish. Offer smallmouths a tasty snack; treat largemouths to a hearty meal. They really don't have much in common, except for the family name and quarrelsome nature.

62

TAP'S TIPS

⟨ When casting for bass from an anchored boat, toss out a live bait on a bobber, and then cast around and beyond it. Fish that follow the lure without striking will often take the bait instead.

⟨ Try this sometime when fishing for bass in very clear water, on a bright day, or wherever or whenever the fish are playing hard to get. Cast your lure as far as you can, let it sink to bottom, and leave it there as long as your patience lets you. Ten minutes is none too long. By the time you start to retrieve it the bass will have forgotten the disturbance it made, and may pounce on it the instant it moves.

⟨ As insurance against running out of live bait, carry a few No. 14 or 16 hooks. Baited with a tiny morsel of worm or rolled pellet of sandwich bread, these small hooks are just right for catching minnows, shiners, or baby bluegills.

Bass at Their Best

Any way you fish for him, the bass is a fighter. But on a fly rod he always seems to feel a little heavier, a little scrappier, a little more inclined to strut his stuff above the water.

Although most bass are caught with plugs and live bait, both the largemouth and smallmouth take fly-rod lures readily. In fact, just about anything that can be cast with a fly rod can be considered a bass lure, and probably a good one.

Dry flies, for example. River smallmouths will rise to just about any of the conventional trout patterns. Largemouths like them bigger and buggier, something along the lines of a bushy bivisible or hairwing Wulff, in size 10, 8, or even 6. Lesser fish will come up to them, too—bluegills, crappies, sometimes big yellow perch.

Bass bugging is almost a sport apart from all others. We used to think you needed a heavy rod for heaving bass bugs around, and you do need some power to drive a cork-bodied popper into the wind. But if you enjoy light-tackle fishing, tie on a deerhair bug, not too big but as big as the rod can handle comfortably, and see how easily it casts—and how the bass go for it.

Bug fishing still wears a black eye administered by the die-hards who insist that you can't get big bass on bugs, and that bugs won't take

smallmouths. Don't let those two fairy tales keep you from discovering how deadly a bass bug can be, and how much sport it is to fish one with a light rod. But give the bug a chance to show what it can do by fishing it on calm, fairly shallow water, where the bass can see it.

In rippled water, and during the bright part of the day, try a large, brightly-colored bucktail or streamer fished at moderate depth. Or hang a small spinner ahead of the fly and troll it slowly just off shore, close to the pads and weed beds in largemouth water, over gravel bars and around rocky points if you're looking for smallmouths.

Will bass take nymphs? Sure! Nymphs are a bit too small for a gluttonous largemouth, perhaps, but river smallmouths are heavy nymph-feeders, and at times the lake fish feast on them too. Fish the nymph just about as you would for trout, remembering that the larger sizes seem more appealing to bass.

Bass may not be as pretty as trout, but on almost every other count they rate just as high for fly-rod fishing in size, abundance, willingness to bite, and ability to fight. If you stop to think of it, trout wouldn't be held in such high regard if most of them were caught on plug casting tackle.

TAP'S TIPS

❰ Largemouth bass like to lie under overhanging bushes close to shore. To get a bass bug into such places, make a hard side-arm cast aimed at the edge of the overhang. If the bug hits hard enough, it will bounce into the hidden pocket.

❰ In general, trout prefer small, sparsely dressed flies, whereas bass like them big and bulky. Most fishermen carry a few trout flies that should be transferred to the box of bass lures. You will recognize them by their thick hackle and fat bodies.

❰ Every time a tree falls into the water it creates a home for bass. When nature fails to provide such spots, they can be created by chopping down dead trees near shore and letting them fall into the water. Be sure to get the landowner's permission first, though.

Light-tackle Bass Bugging

Present company excepted, most fishing writers will tell you that you can't catch as many large bass on bugs as you can on plugs, spoons, plastic worms or bait. They also say that you need a heavy, powerful fly rod to heave a bug any distance at all, and that you must fish the bug very, very slowly.

Anyone who accepts this as gospel will miss a lot of the fun of catching bass with bugs. Take it from me, an addict.

It is true, of course, that large bass spend more time in deep water, where you can't get at them with bugs, than small bass do. They come into the shallows later in the afternoon, leave them earlier in the morning. Therefore, anyone who throws bugs about in broad daylight is certain to catch more small bass than big ones. However, from the time the evening shadows creep over the water until the wind and sun strike it again the next day, the chance of catching a buster on a bug is tempting enough to make sleeping seem a waste of time.

This fishing, exciting though it can be at times, loses some of its zing when your arm aches from flogging about with a 6- or 7-ounce fly rod. Such a weapon is needed to drive a heavy bass bug through a spanking breeze. But bass are seldom much interested in bugs when wind is whipping the water.

In my case, I found that by trimming the arms and legs off an ordinary deerhair bass bug I could cast it easily with a light trout rod and a forward-taper line. This is a pleasant outfit to handle in calm weather, and the light tackle greatly magnifies the joy of playing fish. In addi-

66

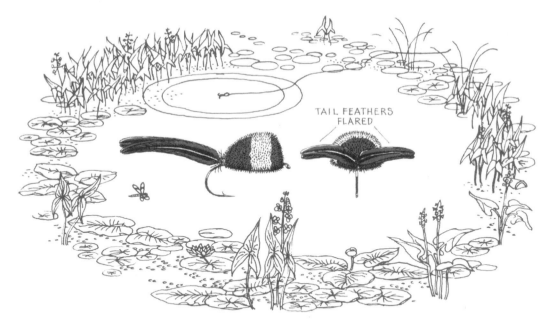

TAIL FEATHERS
FLARED

tion, the streamlined bug seems to raise as many large bass for me as the big featherdusters ever did, and offers the extra advantage of casting more accurately into the bassy holes deep in the pads and brush.

First, let's be sure we understand what I mean by "light" bug-fishing gear. To be arbitrary about it, call any fly rod light that weighs around 3 ounces. That's strictly rule-of-thumb, of course. Everyone knows that the action of the stick has more to do with its performance than either its weight or length.

Such a rod—and in this Age of Glass the sporting good stores are full of them—can throw a line quite a goodly distance. If you insist on figures, 60 or 70 feet. That's plenty far enough for most bass waters, whether you're operating from a boat or sloshing along the shore in waders.

Two things make it possible to bug-fish with light fly tackle. One is the forward-taper line and the other is a streamlined bug.

Because the light rod is shorter and consequently less gutty than the 6-ounce wrist-breaker that has always been considered standard bug-fishing equipment, it is necessary to shoot line rather than to work it out by false casting. The weight-forward line gives you an easier, longer shoot than either a level or double-tapered line.

A fairly stiff 7½-foot rod that weighs around 3 ounces will probably want a GBF line to perform properly. If the stick comes closer to the ultralight category, like those beautiful little 6½-foot, 2-ounce, impregnated bamboo rods that Orvis makes, then HCF should be just right.

But the bug must be streamlined, because casting most surface poppers is something like trying to throw a silk stocking against the wind. The sketch shows you the deerhair bug my friends and I developed for light-tackle bass fishing. It casts as easily as a fanwing or Wulff dry fly, and the bass seem to like it as well as any dish-faced balsa bug with arms and legs sticking out all over it. This bug—we've never given it a name —floats nicely on its clipped deerhair body, and the back-to-back hackle feather tail has just enough kick to arouse the predatory instincts of any fish that sees it.

This brings us to the matter of how the bug should be fished. Nearly everyone who writes about bug fishing (again, present company excepted) recommends a very slow retrieve, with long periods of complete rest between twitches.

True, bass sometimes like to give a bug a long and leisurely inspection before they make up their minds to take it. Often a deliberate retrieve with long pauses takes fish when a fast retrieve doesn't. It's always worth trying. However, the fast retrieve with its greater surface commotion frequently stirs up fish that might lose interest in a motionless bug. So the fast retrieve is worth trying too. If you insist on a rule to govern this situation, try the slow retrieve in pockets where you feel certain a good bass should be hiding, the fast retrieve when you are fishing blind in open water.

The streamlined hair bugs needed for light-tackle bugging do not "pop" like the explosive floaters made of cork, balsa, or plastic. But they burble, and that's just as good. The trick is to lower the rod until it is nearly parallel with the water and bring the bug in with a series of good hard yanks. This makes it plow across the water with a bubbly uproar that shatters the dusky silence and leaves a trail of foam in its wake. If there's a bass anywhere around, it would be a lethargic specimen indeed if it didn't come charging out to see what all the fuss was about.

TAP'S TIPS

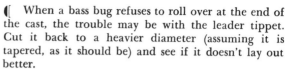

([When a bass bug refuses to roll over at the end of the cast, the trouble may be with the leader tippet. Cut it back to a heavier diameter (assuming it is tapered, as it should be) and see if it doesn't lay out better.

([Bass love to lie in the shade. When you cast to a rock or stump, aim your first cast for the shaded side. If a bass is at home, that's probably where you'll find him.

([Color seems to be of little importance in bass bug fishing. I tie my bass bugs mostly with natural gray deerhair, and add a white band only so I can follow

it on the water easier. However, most bass fishermen agree that color is important on underwater lures.

❨ Don't change a deerhair bass bug because it has absorbed some water. The loss of buoyancy causes it to ride a little deeper, and in this position it creates more surface commotion when retrieved.

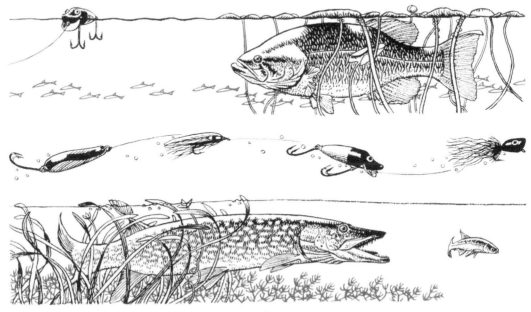

Try Fishingfaster

If you believe everything you read about bass fishing (including, I suppose, what you read here), you should be able to catch a boatload every time you go out. The big secret, which fishing writers have been revealing in hushed tones ever since I started reading outdoor magazines, is to fish slow, very slow, usually spelled *slooooooooow*.

According to this sacred scripture, you should cast out your plug or bug, and let it lie perfectly motionless for a long, long time. Then you should twitch it very gently, just once, and resume dozing over your rod. Sooner or later a large fish—and this is practically a money-back guarantee—will lift himself up and inhale your plug, bug, or whatever it was that died out there. That's absolutely all there is to it.

On days when fishing slooooooooow is the best way to catch fish (and you can always find out by trying it a while), you can take a lot of fish that way. But on days when the fish feel restive, you can't. And such days seem to come along pretty often on the waters I visit, even those containing the classic example of fish that should be fished for slow, the largemouth bass.

69

I generally haul a popper in pretty fast—fast enough to leave a wake of bubbles behind it. I make my go-deepers dart and dive and my streamers twitch along at a pretty good clip, the way a scared bait fish moves when he realizes with a start that he has wandered into enemy territory. At the moment I can't think of a fish, except possibly a carp or a bullhead, that doesn't like a fast-moving bait occasionally.

People who study such things say that the iris of a fish's eye cannot expand and contract the way a human's can, and as a result all fish are desperately nearsighted. Therefore, a fish groping myopically through the water isn't very likely to see your artificial lure if it doesn't move. And of course he can't hear it or smell it either. So a moving lure is bound to attract more attention from the customers.

I don't suggest that you should always fish fast. Sometimes fish just don't seem to feel like chasing after their food, and then you have to tease them a little. But fishing at a fast clip is a welcome relief from fishing in slow motion, and that way you'll get to see what's around the next bend in the river.

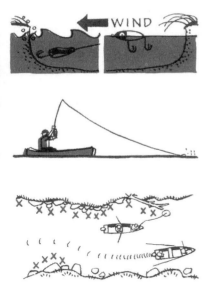

TAP'S TIPS

(When fishing a shoreline for bass, let the wind conditions dictate your choice of lure or fishing method. Use a top-water lure on calm water, a sunken lure in areas rippled by the wind. Change from one to the other as the water changes.

(To retrieve a sinking lure just beneath the surface, hold the rod tip as high as you can and reel fast. Sometimes the fish come best to a lure that stays within the top 12 inches of water.

(There are two ways to prospect for bass when fishing along shore from a boat. One, comb all of the water thoroughly. Two, fish only the most likely spots, passing by all the water between them. I have tried both ways, and find the second one most productive on the waters I fish.

Lunkers or Nothing

Big bait, big fish? Not necessarily. Small lures have accounted for many a prize winner over the years. But you wouldn't set a mouse trap to catch a mountain lion, and by the same token, you won't catch many lunkers with No. 18 dry flies or tiny dabs of bait. If you want to catch big fish, you've got to fish big for them.

More fishermen would concentrate on gunning for trophies if it

meant nothing more than using king-size baits and lures. However, trophy fishing means passing up the fun of taking smaller fish. It's all or nothing, and mostly it's nothing. Since most fishermen want quantity as well as quality, the field is wide open to the lunker-hunter. You, too, may catch a big one, if you fish big enough long enough.

No matter what rod you use, you've got a chance. If the fly rod's your weapon, use nothing but big bucktails or streamers tied on heavy-wire No. 2 or No. 4 hooks, flog away day and night—but mostly night—and some sweet moment you may tie into something you can take to the taxidermist in a wheelbarrow.

Spin fishermen who gun for trophy trout simply hang on a wobbling spoon or spinner big enough to choke a musky and keep flogging it out till it lands in front of a trout capable of coping with it. Ditto the bait casters who use musky plugs for bass, and striped bass plugs for muskies.

Just imagine how big a bass would have to be to tackle a 1/4-pound pond shiner. I know a fisherman who brings home bass that big, using shiners that big. He also considers 12-inch suckers the ideal bait for northern pike. He probably doesn't average more than one strike per day's fishing, but think of the strikes he does get!

You can fish big for just about anything that swims in fresh water or salt. I don't recommend it as the way to get the most fun out of fishing. But if you're looking for a trophy to hang on the wall of your den, that's the surest way to get it.

TAP'S TIPS

[When bass turn up their noses at minnows, frogs, and other common baits, try something different. Garden slugs, for example. You'll find them under boards and flat rocks in moist places. Hook the slug lightly through the back, fish it as you would a night-crawler.

Weed 'Em Out

Never give up on any bass water until you've given the weeds a thorough raking. Largemouths love to lurk beneath the shelter of the matted growths, especially during the bright of the day. And that, of course, means casting right into the spinach. The problem is, how do you keep from getting fouled in weeds every cast?

Bait manufacturers offer a variety of lures suitable for weed-bed fishing. The best are the casting spoons with a single rigid hook and wire weed guard. When retrieved properly, these lures plane on their back right over the top of the weeds, or through them, with the hook riding upright so it seldom collects much green stuff.

The pork chunk is another excellent weed-bed lure. Hang your chunk on a weedless hook and you can make it scamper across the matted vegetation to suggest a frog going places in a hurry. And don't forget that old favorite of the cane-pole fisherman, a sinuous strip of fish belly. Old-fashioned, maybe, but deadly on bass when chucked far back into the weeds and slithered along the surface.

No bait or lure is completely weedless by itself, however. Fully as much depends on how you retrieve it as on its design. The trick is to

72

start it back quickly. Begin reeling the instant it strikes the surface, or a half-second before. Then if you keep it coming at a merry pace it will skip and skim over the weeds instead of plowing through them.

To do this properly, you must keep the tip of your rod high, which means actually reeling with your hands right up at face level or higher. This holds most of your line off the water, and the upward pull causes the lure to plane along the top. If your boat is stable enough, stand up and gain that much extra advantage.

Hold your rod as high as you can reach and reel like the dickens. This sounds as if you were sacrificing the natural action of the lure for the sake of keeping it free of the weeds. It ain't necessarily so. Bass lurking beneath thickly matted weed growth can't see surface objects clearly. When something kicks up a fuss overhead, they're pretty apt to sock it first and ask questions later. The fast retrieve doesn't give them much time to study the situation. They've got to grab whatever it is that is causing all that commotion while the grabbing's good. And as often as not, that's just what they do.

TAP'S TIPS

❪ When floating duckweed completely blankets the water, pretend it isn't there and fish just as you would in open water. Duckweed doesn't foul a lure the way lily pads and water chestnuts do, and most lures pass through or over it without collecting much weed.

❪ Bass taken from weedy water often have a "muddy" flavor. They taste better if they are skinned, rather than merely scaled. Adding condiments helps to disguise the muddy taste, too.

❪ Sometimes you can stir up bass by attaching a plastic worm to the hook of a weedless casting spoon. Let the spoon settle on bottom, then retrieve it very slowly. As the hook rides upright, it seldom becomes snagged. The same lure can be used for jigging in deep water, too.

❪ If you have trouble catching crawfish, try this: Cut both ends off a large tin can. When you spot a crawfish, plunk the can down over him. You can then fish him out at your leisure.

Bass after Bedtime

Want to know how to lick a hot-weather slump in bass fishing? Go after 'em at night. Daytime fishing often goes to pot simply because the bass have knocked off to cool their fins in some deep hole where you can't reach them. But at night it's a different story. With darkness and cooling water they move back in to shore where they cruise about looking for such tempting tidbits as minnows, frogs, bass bugs, and Hula Poppers.

Blackout casting poses problems, but you'll leave fewer lures hanging in trees if you use your flashlight sparingly so your eyes can adjust themselves to the gloom. You can cut down still further on overshooting and backlashes by making shorter casts. From a fish-taking point of view, a short line works as well at night as a long one does, probably because bass grow bolder under cover of darkness and let you get closer to them.

Being bolder at night, bass come into open water they normally avoid in daylight. So don't be surprised if you draw blanks in your favorite daytime hotspots and raise bass where you never find them after breakfast. Take your water as it comes instead of concentrating on just the coves, pockets, and weed beds—although you'll find them there, too.

The blacker the night, the better your chances. A full moon and a big spangle of stars make a romantic setting, but bass like darkness better. They move about more, feed more. So fish when it's dark—and fish when it's late. Each hour of darkness means still cooler water and more active fish. The best fishing usually starts after midnight.

Most fishing writers advise using an all-black lure at night, on the theory that a fish can spot it easier against the silvered surface of the water. That may be so. But a white or yellow plug is easier for *you* to see, and you should think of your own convenience, too. In my experience, color isn't that important; it's the noise and action that attract fish to an artificial lure, and to many baits as well. Just be sure to make them kick up as much fuss and sputter as you can, for at night bass are likely to slam at the cause of the disturbance without studying the situation first. Set the hook when you hear the slosh, and don't be surprised if it feels like a big one.

TAP'S TIPS

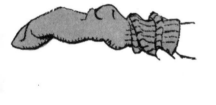

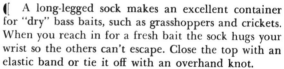

⟨ A long-legged sock makes an excellent container for "dry" bass baits, such as grasshoppers and crickets. When you reach in for a fresh bait the sock hugs your wrist so the others can't escape. Close the top with an elastic band or tie it off with an overhand knot.

⟨ If you hook an eel while bass fishing at night, don't try to land it with a net, or you will have a slimy mess you won't be able to clean up till morning. Sprinkle sand on your hands or hold the eel with a cloth while you remove the hook.

⟨ Hook live minnows lightly through the back between the head and dorsal fin. Game fish always swallow bait fish headfirst, so placing the hook near the head gives you a better chance to hook a striking fish.

—And Bass Close to Bottom

Shoreline bass fishing starts to taper off soon after the first frosty days of fall. As the temperature at the surface drops out of the 70's and sinks through the 60's, bass drift back into deeper water and display little interest in what happens overhead or in their shallow haunts of summer. From that time on, the secret of catching bass is to get down where they are with something they want.

That's why one of the surest ways to take October bass, either large-mouths or smallmouths, is to hang on a live bait with just enough sinker to carry it close to bottom. Minnows, crawfish, hellgrammites, frogs, crickets, and grass shrimp too, if you can get them, usually produce most consistently in the fall. To improve your chances still further, use the smallest hooks and lightest leaders you dare. The light end gear will fool bass too cagy to be taken in by coarse tackle, especially after they've spent the summer watching the lures go by.

If you make your bid with a casting rod, switch to sinking plugs. Let them settle close to bottom before starting your retrieve. Reel slowly, to keep the lure down where it belongs. Make the plug dart, just as you would when fishing close to the surface, but remember to let it settle back again before resuming your retrieve. Bass will hit a plug that is moving, standing still, or sinking slowly, so long as you keep it down where they can see it.

When you fish for smallmouths, be sure to take your spinning rod along. Metal wobblers and spinners are deadly on smallmouths, and it's easy to keep spinning hardware down deep where the fish can see what's on sale. Midget-sized plugs, the $\frac{1}{8}$-ounce size, are perfect for the spinning rod, and especially for smallmouths.

Another way to fill a stringer with autumn bass is to troll a plug or spoon on a wire or lead-core line. Just chug along slow and easy and let the line keep your lure down where it should be. Because getting down there, remember, is the secret of taking bass in the fall.

TAP'S TIPS

《 Use light terminal gear when fishing with crickets —fine leader, small hook, only a single split shot. If you can't find large crickets, two or three small ones clustered on the hook will do just as well.

《 As an alternative to deep-trolling for bass, try

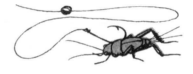

jigging for them from a drifting boat with a metal spoon or spinner. All deep-water fish are attracted by these shiny lures as they dart up from bottom and flutter back.

 Here's a quick way to put a baited hook on bottom when you don't want to use a sinker: Roll the line in a stone. When you feel it hit bottom, lift the line until it unwinds from the stone.

 When bass retreat into deep water during the dog days of summer, go down after them with bottom crawlers. Killing lures for this kind of fishing include weighted plastic worms, jigs, single-hook spoons (the Johnson Silver Spoon is a longtime favorite) tipped with pork rind. Let the lure settle on bottom, then "walk" it back with a slow-motion retrieve.

A Good Man at the Oars

Casting from the bow of a boat or canoe can be a pleasant and highly productive way to fish. But it can also be frustrating and unproductive, too. It all depends on the man who's wielding the paddle or oars.

If your skipper steers a course that keeps you constantly in position to hit the best spots from the most favorable angle, you're in business. But if he zigs this way and zags that way, plowing through the good water and dawdling over the barren stretches, you're not going to take many fish. Actually, the man with the paddle or oars should be "fishing" just as hard as the man with the rod.

The secret of skillful boat handling lies in putting yourself in the place of the man who's fishing. Look ahead for spots you'd want to cast to if you had the rod, maneuver into position, and hold the boat there till the spot yields a fish or it's time to move on. Turn the bow at an angle if necessary, to give the caster room for a back cast. Avoid splashy strokes and banging of paddles and oars.

In cramped quarters the man at the oars has a more difficult job. Winding through a brush-choked stream or maneuvering among stumps and weed beds calls for a certain amount of navigating skill. The point is to put the caster in position to fish, even if the oarsman has to horse-collar himself in bushes to give his partner a clean shot.

The man who turns in a competent guiding job with oars, paddle, or the tiller of an outboard motor is fishing just as much as his partner —and often he's the one who deserves most of the credit for the fish that get caught.

78

TAP'S TIPS

(You can prevent loose hooks from scattering all over your tackle box by putting a small magnet in the compartment with them.

(If you have trouble setting the hook in fish that strike on trolled flies when you are fishing alone, try this technique. After letting out line, take a couple of turns around a smooth, flat stone and lay the stone in the bottom of the boat. When a fish strikes, the weight of the stone helps to set the hook, and you have time to grab the rod while the line unwinds.

(When a blustery wind makes it difficult to cast a bass bug, shorten your leader or tie on a heavier, stiffer tippet. Work your rod parallel to the water to get line and lure "under the wind."

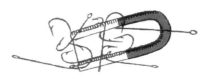

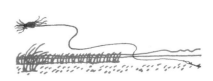

The Look-Alikes

Knowing how to tell the difference between a largemouth and a smallmouth bass, a white and black crappie, and some of the other confusing species is one thing, but remembering how to do it is something else again. Here's a system that may help you.

The largemouth's mouth is so large that the end of the upper jaw-plate extends beyond an imaginary line dropped from the back of the eye, while the smallmouth's smaller mouth does not. The largemouth also has larger scales, with room for only about ten rows on the cheek, as compared with the smallmouth's seventeen rows of smaller scales. The largemouth also has a larger, and hence deeper, notch in its dorsal fin. And being larger and perhaps a little lazier than its cousin, you'll generally find the largemouth yawning in warmer, more sluggish water.

Crappies look pretty much alike, but look closely and you'll find a

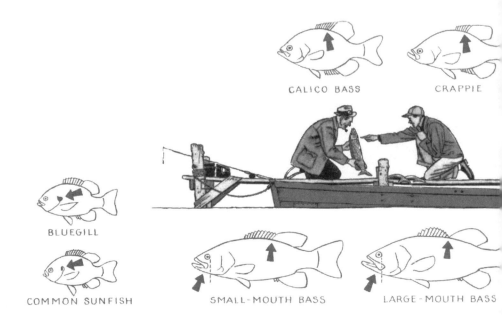

CALICO BASS

CRAPPIE

BLUEGILL

COMMON SUNFISH

SMALL-MOUTH BASS

LARGE-MOUTH BASS

difference in the spines of the dorsal fin. When in doubt, count 'em. The white crappie has five or six; the calico bass, or black crappie, is back-happy, and shows off seven or eight spines in its dorsal.

Among the common sunfishes you will discover noticeable differences that distinguish one from the other. The bluegill has an all-blue gill flap, and a large one. The common sunfish flashes a bright red sun-spot on its smaller flap, with usually a touch of sky color mottling its cheek. The long-ear sunfish has a flap that looks like a long ear, just as the name suggests.

The three members of the pike family may give you a little more trouble. When in doubt, look closely at the scales on the cheeks and gill covers. The pickerel's are completely covered with scales. The pike's cheeks are scaled, too, but the lower half of the gill cover is bare. The hulking musky grew so fast his scales couldn't keep up with him, so the lower half of both cheek and gill cover remain naked.

The color and marking of the pikes also help to identify them. The pickerel is mostly yellow overlaid with a dark-green chainlike design. The pike is dark with oval yellow spots. The color of the musky varies,

80

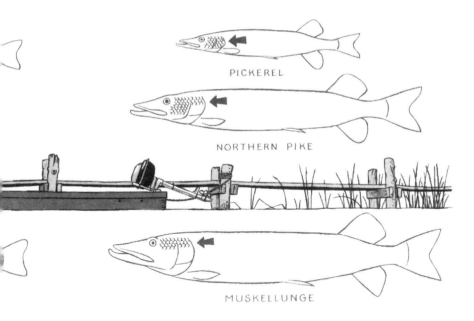

PICKEREL

NORTHERN PIKE

MUSKELLUNGE

generally in shades of gray, but the markings never resemble either a chain or long oval dots. As for size, it's easy to remember that the pickerel is the littlest and the musky the huskiest.

TAP'S TIPS

❪ When hanging fish on a stringer, be sure to hook them through both lips. Then if they are dragged behind the boat they won't drown, as they would if they were hooked through one lip so they couldn't close their mouths.

❪ An excellent fish stringer can be made from a length of chain and some shower curtain hooks. The chain links should be just large enough to allow the hook to pass through up to the clasp.

❪ When bass turn up their noses at plugs, tease them by adding a thin rubber pennant to one of the tail hooks. Brightly colored balloon rubber is ideal, as it does not interefere with the action of the lure.

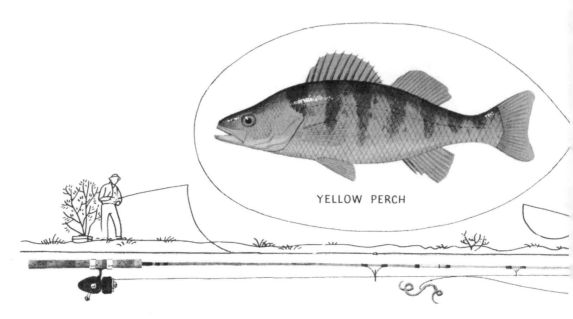

YELLOW PERCH

PIKE, PERCH AND PANFISH

The Early Biters

IN SPRING a young (and even a not-so-young) man's fancy lightly turns to thoughts of perch and bullheads . . . if he's a fisherman and if he knows a little about the habits of these two species.

As soon as the water has warmed up to about 50 degrees, the yellow perch come in close to shore to spawn. Always hungry in the spring, and never finicky about diet, they are seldom difficult to catch. But proper tackle and suitable bait make a good catch doubly certain.

The neatest tool you can use for spring perch fishing is a light spinning rod rigged with a No. 8 hook and a plastic spinning bubble, or bobber. Half-fill the bubble with water so you can make long casts without using a sinker. This counts in your favor, for perch will grab your bait more eagerly if it settles slowly and naturally through the water.

Generally, you'll need no other bait than the traditional can of worms, but once in a while perch turn fins-down on worms, even in early spring. When this happens, a lively two-inch minnow will almost always turn the trick, so it's wise to bring along a well-stocked minnow bucket, too. Whatever the bait, set the hook at the first gentle twitch, for perch seldom hang to a hook very long.

82

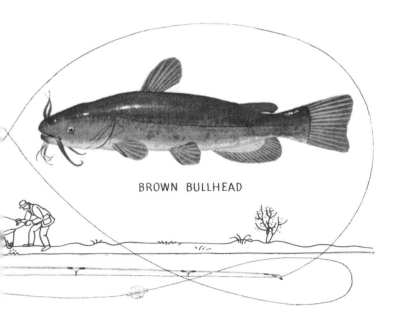

BROWN BULLHEAD

The white perch is basically an anadromous fish that migrates from salt water into tidal inlets and brackish water. It also thrives in ponds and lakes without ever tasting sea water. The white perch is both a blessing and a curse—a blessing because it is a hearty feeder, enormously abundant, and one of the tastiest fish on the North American continent; a curse because it proliferates so fast in many waters it almost literally drives out the other species.

Like the yellow perch (to which, incidentally, it is not related), the white perch spawns in the spring—quite early in salt or brackish water, but in fresh water not until the temperature gets up near 60 degrees. The same tackle and baits serve equally well for both species during the spawning season.

Many fishermen relish perch roe, and even compare it with roe of shad. If you have never eaten fried perch eggs, by all means try them. They lack the delicate flavor of fresh shad roe, in my opinion, but a true roe-lover would almost certainly enjoy it.

Shortly after the perch finish spawning the night-prowling bullheads begin adding a new multitude to the old one. Whether they are spawning or not, bullheads eat practically anything they find lying on the bottom. They don't even mind if it happens to be dead, although they prefer live bait when they can get it. They feed on crawfish and minnows (this surprises some fishermen), but the best bait beyond any question is a juicy nightcrawler gobbed on a large hook. The worm can be fished on bottom, which actually means buried in the mud, but it is better to suspend it about an inch above bottom if possible. The bullheads can find it easier that way—or at least that is what many bullheaders believe.

When you remove the hook from a bullhead, watch out for the long, sharp spines in the leading edges of the pectoral and dorsal fins. A stab wound from these spines can be very painful and slow to heal. The best treatment is a slab of bullhead meat rolled in flour, fried nut-brown in sizzling pork chunks, and applied promptly to the taste buds.

TAP'S TIPS

([Chumming with chopped bait attracts fish to an area and holds them there long enough to provide fast fishing. When chumming for bottom fish such as bullheads, put the chum in a paper bag with a small stone, tie a line to the neck of the bag, and lower it to bottom. When the line sags, yank. The stone will break out of the bag, dumping out the chum.

([Many catfishermen make their own doughball baits from secret recipes. The following aren't secret, but you can catch catfish with them: Flour flavored with limburger cheese; any strong cheese kneaded into a small piece of sponge; limburger, hamburger, and flour; blood and flour; bran, oatmeal, and flour moistened with honey; flour and cornmeal flavored with licorice and sugar.

([Yellow perch and bullheads are both fond of fresh-water clams. Use only the head and muscle for perch; everything but the shell for 'pout.

"Bumping" for Walleyes

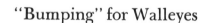

Walleye fishing hits its peak early in the spring, usually when the water temperature gets up to around 50 degrees. As the spawning urge draws them out of the deep water, the walleyes congregate along the shorelines in great numbers. They are active and hungry and, even more important, they are available. Later, when they finish spawning and scatter back into their summer haunts, they won't be nearly so easy to find or to catch.

84

Trolling is by far the most dependable method of taking walleyes. A light trolling outfit is fine; an ordinary bait-casting rod and reel will serve just about as well. The terminal tackle is designed strictly for bottom-scratching, with a sinker hanging from a three-way swivel, and the lure or bait following at the end of about four feet of monofilament. The size of the sinker will depend on the depth of the water, but it should be big enough, for sure, to stay in contact with bottom. Old hands call this "bumping" for walleyes, and if there is any secret to catching walleyes, that is it. If there is another secret, it is to fish at night, for walleyes are nocturnal in habit and feed most actively after the sun goes down. However, daytime fishing is not a waste of time, by any means, especially during the spring spawning season.

For a lure, the first choice, and also the second and third, is a June Bug spinner ahead of a nightcrawler hung on a single hook. Word has leaked out, however, that walleyes can also be taken with a small live minnow hooked through both lips and dragged behind a slow-moving boat, and even with small deep-running, jointed bass plugs. Walleyes also eat frogs and crawfish. Even so, the spinner and worm is the old reliable, and definitely the thing to try first.

A hooked walleye should be handled gently, for these fish have tender mouths. Tender meat, too—some say the tenderest, sweetest meat of them all. The way to find out is to fillet a 2-pounder, broil the slabs and slather them with butter.

Although walleyes are generally called walleyed pike, they are not even distantly related to pike. Actually they belong to the perch family, and it would be more accurate to call them walleyed perch. However, "walleye" is a simpler, better name, and descriptive of the large, milky eye which always identifies the walleye and its smaller cousin, the sauger.

TAP'S TIPS

(To hook more biters when still-fishing with bait,

use a light, slender float. Large bobbers offer so much resistance that biting fish often become suspicious and drop the bait.

¶ Small walleyes and large saugers look very much alike. To tell them apart, examine the front dorsal fins. The walleye's has a single dark blotch at the rear; the sauger's has a sprinkling of small black spots, but no blotch. The sauger's eyes are smaller than the walleye's, too.

¶ Walleyes return to deep water after spawning, but often come up to feed near the surface at night. After dark, try trolling with unweighted spinners and worms, small plugs or minnows. Even if the water is 50-feet deep, walleyes may be found within a few feet of the top.

Drifting and Dredging

"Troll to find fish, anchor to catch them," I once read somewhere. It's true, too. Trolling is the best way to locate fish in a broad expanse of water, particularly the restless, schooling varieties like perch, walleyes, and crappies. When you find them, dropping an anchor and a baited hook is the recommended way to fill a basket.

Mark Burlingame, the genuine original Old Fisherman, showed me his method of finding fish and catching them both at the same time. Mark simply drifted with the breeze, letting the boat carry his baited hook along till it blundered into a bunch of fish. Then he gentled the anchor down and hauled them in till the school broke up, moved on, or dwindled away.

There was a little more to Mark's method than that, though. If the wind pushed the boat too fast, he rigged a sea anchor to hold it back. He weighted his line with split shot on a whisker of gut, and stripped them off or added more to keep his bait down exactly where he wanted it. And he kept a condiment tray at hand, with small shiners for crappies, worms or goldenrod grubs for perch, crickets for smallmouths, usually a few leopard frogs for the big stuff. He used very long leaders and very small hooks, and he always caught fish.

Sometimes Mark and I drifted cross-pond, sometimes we let the wind carry us parallel with shore, depending on the season, the hour, the weather, or how badly his corns ached. Nearly every drift took us into fish; when it didn't, we rowed back upwind to try again. An essential part of Mark's system was that the other guy should do the rowing.

If you try this, you will find that you snag bottom frequently, so you might as well have the rest of the Old Fisherman's system: Use a very light leader tippet. When you hang up, just yank and tie on a new hook.

86

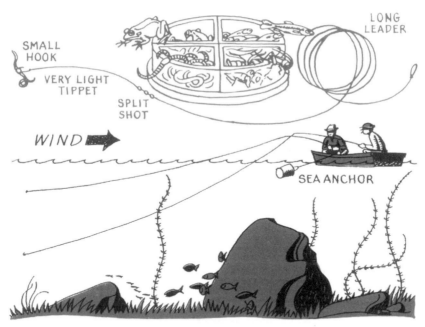

LONG LEADER

SMALL HOOK

VERY LIGHT TIPPET

SPLIT SHOT

WIND ➡

SEA ANCHOR

TAP'S TIPS

❨ If you run short of minnows while fishing for bass, try tadpoles. Hook them through the nose for drift-trolling, through the top of the tail for still-fishing. You will find lots of them in the muddy shallows close to shore.

❨ When a fish takes a bait, make sure the line is straight before setting the hook. Often the fish will carry the bait to one side, leaving a belly in the line. Strip in the slack gently until you can feel the fish, then strike him.

❨ Drag a bottom-scratching bass lure behind the boat when drifting for panfish. A weedless spoon is perfect, as it rides with the hook up and rarely hangs on bottom. Dress the hook with a plastic worm or strip of pork rind, and if necessary weight the lure so it "walks" right on bottom.

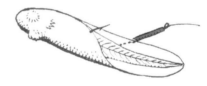

Floaters for Flatties

If you believe, as so many trout fishermen do, that dry-fly fishing ends with the trout season, it's a sure bet you have never dropped a bivisible among hungry bluegills. One session would convince you that dry-fly fishing is where you find it, whether on a famous trout stream or along the shaded shore of a nearby pond.

Fight? A saucer-sized bluegill will put a bend in a fly rod that would do credit to any fish his size or bigger. Ounce for ounce, this little scrapper can slug as hard as a trout, bass, or almost any other game fish you care to mention.

Your lightest fly rod and a few heavily-hackled dry flies put you in the bluegill business. Pick a cove or shoreline sheltered from the wind and drop your floater along the edges of the pads and in the pockets that look "fishy" to you. Let your fly rest a moment, then twitch it, rest it and twitch it again. A high-floating fly like a bushy bivisible or hairwing Wulff on a No. 10 hook is the thing to use. Bluegills aren't very bright, and they rise trustingly to almost anything that floats and moves. After a season of catering to the finicky appetites of trout, it is a joy to be able to tie on the first fly you find in your box knowing that you can take fish with it.

If you like to eat fish, you can bring home a generous mess of bluegills with a perfectly clear conscience. In the case of bluegills and other warm-water panfish, keeping fish is good conservation. It works like this: Every time we take a game fish we make room for more panfish. The panfish begin multiplying faster than the remaining game fish can eat them. Before long, hordes of hungry, stunted sunfish and perch have taken over the water, and bass fishermen report mournfully that the pond has been "fished out."

Nature normally strikes a balance of so many small fish to every large fish in a given area of water. By taking only the large fish we upset that balance. The answer to that is simple. Every time you keep a game fish, balance it off by taking some panfish too.

When you get home, cook the commoners right along with the more aristocratic species and serve them on the same platter. If you detect any difference in taste, you may decide it's in favor of the panfish.

TAP'S TIPS

◖ Although bluegills and crappies often live together, they have completely different eating habits. Bluegills like bugs, crappies prefer minnows. To interest crappies, tie on a streamer fly or small spinning lure. To take both, use worms.

◖ Because bluegills have small mouths, they are hard to hook, especially when they are rising to surface lures. The trick is to delay the strike just long enough to let them get their mouths around the hook.

◖ When worm-fishing for bluegills and other panfish on a sunny day, try dropping the bait close to the boat every once in a while. Fish often gather in the shade of the boat and refuse to budge until the bait comes closer.

◖ Here's a trick worth trying when you are still-fishing with bait for panfish: Use a floating bass plug as a bobber. It not only tells you when a fish nibbles at the bait, but its dancing may attract bass. Attach the bait leader to the eye of the plug.

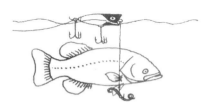

Worms When You Want Them

Repairing to the back of the barn to dig a can of worms has long been the time-honored prelude to a day's fishing. But alas, worms are not always easy to find.

To make sure of having an ample supply of garden hackle on hand at all times, many fishermen keep a well-stocked worm box in a cool part of the cellar or buried in a shaded corner of the back yard. Given tender loving care, worms grow fat and sassy in confinement, and even reproduce more of their kind.

The worm box should be roomy, rot-resistant, and well drained. A butter tub, large flower pot or earthenware crock makes an excellent container for a modest supply. A sturdy wooden box is even better, because it holds more. One or two holes bored in the bottom and covered with copper screening provide the necessary drainage.

Fill the container up to within a couple of inches of the top with clean, damp—but not wet—moss. Scatter in some well-rotted leaf mold if you can find some, but omit dirt. Pack the moss firmly and dump the worms on top. As they burrow down into the bed they create ventilation holes and scour themselves at the same time. About once a week cull out the dead and flabby-looking worms and repack the container with fresh moss.

The moss has no food value, so the worms must be fed. They thrive

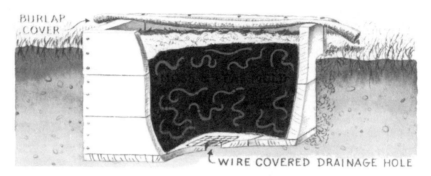

BURLAP COVER

WIRE COVERED DRAINAGE HOLE

on powdered milk, crumbled yolk of hard-boiled egg, molasses, coffee grounds, bread crumbs, corn meal, and, for rich fare, rotten manure. Sprinkle the food on top of the moss and serve it sparingly. Keep the bed moist at all times, but never wet. To delay evaporation, provide shade, and to discourage flies, cover the box with a dampened burlap bag. Whenever you need a canful of worms in a hurry, you'll know where to find them.

TAP'S TIPS

(Traditionally, worms are carried in a tomato can, but a small plastic bag is much more convenient. Put a handful of damp moss in the bag, leave the top open for ventilation, and carry it in a jacket pocket.
(Fresh, lively worms are more attractive to fish than bait that hangs motionless on a hook. You will get more bites if you change baits frequently, and leave plenty of loose end to wriggle and squirm.
(Fish like a moving bait, even if it moves in an unnatural manner. You can attract fish and make them more eager to bite by lifting the bait every once in a while, or lobbing it out and drawing it back slowly, or just by jigging it. Try it when the fish aren't biting as fast as you would like.

Minnows, Dead or Alive

Of all the baits used for catching fish, the one most fishermen would vote Most Likely to Succeed is the minnow. There are several reasons why this is so. For one, practically all fish eat minnows. For another, you can fish a minnow in a dozen different ways, all of them wonderfully effective. And for still another, minnows offer you a variety of

90

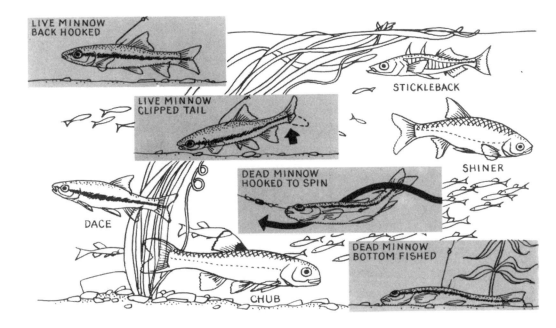

LIVE MINNOW
BACK HOOKED

LIVE MINNOW
CLIPPED TAIL

STICKLEBACK

DEAD MINNOW
HOOKED TO SPIN

SHINER

DACE

DEAD MINNOW
BOTTOM FISHED

CHUB

sizes, shapes, and even colors, if by "minnow" you mean shiners, dace, sticklebacks, chubs, smelt, and all the other small forage species.

The simplest and perhaps most popular way to fish a live minnow is simply to hook it lightly through the back, between its dorsal fin and head, and let it dangle a few inches from bottom. To make sure the bait keeps moving, cut off about half of its tail. This makes it difficult for the minnow to stay upright in the water, and the harder it struggles, the easier it is for fish to find it.

If you're just fishin' and not fussy about what you catch, try still-fishing a dead (but fresh) minnow on bottom. Eels, catfish and other bottom feeders will give you some fun. Don't be surprised if you tie into a bass, pike, or pickerel, too. In fact, the same merchandise will attract a very high class type of customer in cold-water lakes and streams, because big trout won't turn up their noses at a dead minnow, either, especially during the nighttime hours. Some dead-minnow-on-the-bottom fishermen partially skin their bait to make it even easier for cruising fish to locate.

Another virtue of minnows is the choice of sizes they offer. For muskies and pike, you can't buy minnows too big. For pickerel and largemouths, the 4- to 6-inch size is generally your best bet, while small-mouths and walleyes like them just a bit smaller. Pick out the 2- to 3-inchers for trout, depending on the size fish you hope to catch. The 2-inch babies are just about right for crappie and perch.

91

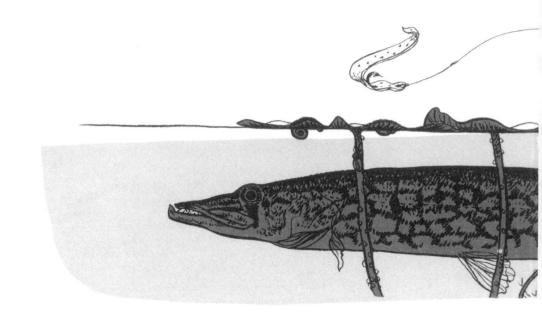

TAP'S TIPS

❨ Minnows can be lured into a trap with cracker or bread crumbs, loose oatmeal, or crumbled dog biscuit. One of the best minnow baits is an oatmeal "bomb." Moisten dry oatmeal with a little water and form a lump the size of a golf ball. The "bomb" lasts longer than crumbs.

❨ Never, never dump surplus bait fish into the water after a day's fishing. Introducing a new species can upset the balance among the native populations and eventually ruin the fishing. This is especially true of goldfish, yellow perch and white perch.

❨ Save dead minnows and use them for bullhead bait after sunset. Cut the bait into chunks and fish it just off bottom. Bullheads are scavengers and don't care if their food is alive or dead.

❨ Big pike like big baits. One of the best is a live sucker 6- to 8-inches long, trolled slowly or still-fished on tandem hooks. Lip-hook the sucker to the small hook, tied in about 3 inches above the big one, and hold the larger hook to the body of the sucker with a rubber band. When a pike takes the bait, give him plenty of time to get it in his mouth before setting the hook.

Pickerel Pointers

If you've never tasted the delights of pickerel fishing the old-fashioned way, try skittering with a cane pole. Twelve to 15 feet is about the right length, and pick one with a springy tip. To this tie a stout line a little longer than the pole; to the line, a short, heavy leader; to the leader, a long-shanked No. 2 hook; and to the hook, a strip of pork rind, a pork chunk, a frog, a strip of perch belly or, better yet, a belly strip from the first pickerel you catch.

Flip the skitter bait to the edge of the weeds or pads and twitch it along the surface, giving it as much seductive wiggle as you can. When a pickerel surges out to take the bait in a boiling swirl, lower the pole and let him chew a while. Then derrick him in.

If you can't bring yourself to cane-pole fishing, you can handle skittering bait just about as well with a heavy fly rod. And of course the spinning rod will cast a belly strip almost as far as you want to throw it. However you do it, you'll still get a thrill when a pickerel nails your bait and starts to fight you for it.

When pickerel are feeding you will find them easy pickin's for the spinning rod and a Dardevle or a bait-casting rod and ditto. Pickerel show a distinct preference for red-and-white lures, and so do most pickerel fishermen.

To get the most sport out of pickerel fishing, be sure to tackle them with a fly rod. The pickerel is a minnow-feeder and a cannibal, and takes large streamer flies and marabous—the longer and brighter the better. Give your streamers plenty of action, and set the hook hard on the strike. Remember to use a heavy leader out of respect to the pickerel's sharp teeth.

Maybe you like to troll. The pickerel is still your meat. A lazily wobbling spoon or almost anything and a spinner will take pickerel if you troll slow enough. So will a live minnow still-fished under a bobber. Whatever method you decide to use, just be sure to use it near a weed bed. And don't be surprised if the same methods work just as well when you are fishing for pike.

TAP'S TIPS

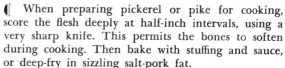

《 When preparing pickerel or pike for cooking, score the flesh deeply at half-inch intervals, using a very sharp knife. This permits the bones to soften during cooking. Then bake with stuffing and sauce, or deep-fry in sizzling salt-pork fat.

《 All the pikes have sharp teeth. To avoid painful cuts when unhooking these fish, keep a pair of needle-nose pliers handy. Grasp the hook at the bend and twist it free.

《 To give a trolled lure more action, hold the line in your hand while you paddle or row. This is a trick the Indians used when they caught pickerel commercially.

《 Pickerel take bass bugs readily, even eagerly. Be sure to use a heavy leader and expect to change bugs often, because they won't survive the chewing. Bugs with long tails (I tie in a half-dozen white saddle hackles) seem to look most appetizing to pike and pickerel.

Floatin' for Fishin'

First, take two guys who love to fish. Next, put in a light boat or canoe they can carry on a car. Then add a lazy stream. Mix well and let

simmer before an open fire. When one of the guys yells "Float trip!" remove and serve. Recipe feeds two—all the fishing they can handle in one day.

Float fishing makes an appetizing dish for several good reasons. First of all, most winding, deep-running streams are seldom fished except in spots which can be reached easily from shore. For every such place there are dozens of deep, protected retreats that almost never see a lure or baited hook. On a float trip you can dip into these virginal pools one after the other as you drift slowly along, just flicking a paddle now and then to hold the course. You'll have very few dull moments, I promise, for always around the next bend lie new pockets to explore and bigger fish to catch.

Take a variety of baits and lures on your float trip. One hole may be the private domain of a big old pike who will go for a wobbling spoon or a large live minnow. The next may hold a school of jumbo-sized perch or bullheads who can't resist a juicy nightcrawler. Bass, pickerel, walleyes, catfish may be in store for you if you can offer them what they like best.

When you're constantly changing baits and artificials, nothing will serve you quite as well as a spinning outfit. With a plastic "bubble" and live bait you can drift your hook through all the likely spots. A quick change lets you toss a wobbling spoon or a small plug where you think it will do the most good. All the time you're drifting downriver with the least possible fuss and bother.

Whatever tackle you use, a float trip will pay off in fun and probably more fish than you'll care to keep. First chance you get, grab yourself a stretch of river and try it.

TAP'S TIPS

《 If you catch a perch or walleye while drifting through a pool, lower the anchor quickly (but quietly).

95

Both species generally hang out with the crowd, so wherever you find one you will probably find more. ⟨ To keep warm and dry while fishing in the rain, wear waders under your raincoat or parka. It's like being in a snug tent, except that your arms and shoulders are free for casting, rowing and playing fish. ⟨ You can always patch torn boat canvas quickly and easily if you carry a roll of waterproof adhesive tape and a tube of Ambroid cement. Just slap a piece of tape over the rip or tear (be sure the canvas is perfectly dry first) and cover the patch with cement. It will probably last through the rest of the season. ⟨ Rope used to tie down a car-top boat may become frayed where it chafes against bumpers or other sharp edges. You can protect the rope by slipping short lengths of rubber tubing over it and placing them over points of friction.

How to Clean a Perch

Some people profess to relish the flavor of yellow perch, especially when taken out of icy water in the winter. I am not one of these, but my friend Harold Blaisdell is, so I asked him just what he did to make a small bony fish like a yellow perch worth cooking.

First, he said, reacquaint your knife with the whetstone. That is very important. Then cut down through the backbone just behind the head, but leave the head attached to the body. Next, hold the perch belly-down in the palm of your left hand with head toward you, and rip along either side of the dorsal fin. Grasp the tail end of the fin and lift it out. Turn the fish over and slice back toward you under the anal fin. Instead of completing the cut, press the base of the fin against the

96

knife blade with your thumb and pull it out. This takes care of a few long bones which would be troublesome otherwise.

Turn the perch over once more, with head pointed away from you, and with your knife work a corner flap of skin loose on each side and draw each flap down until the rib sections are exposed. Grasp the flesh in your left hand, the partly severed head in your right, and pull the head down toward the tail. Head, skin, entrails and remaining fins will come away with the single operation.

Complete the job by slicing the ribs from the backbone exactly as you would whittle kindling from a pine stick. Cut them tight to the backbone and you'll have a perch that can be eaten with relish and confidence.

Waste meat? According to Harold, all you throw away is a mouthful of bones.

TAP'S TIPS

(To remove the slime from fish before cleaning them, dip them in a kettle of water in which a cupful of salt has been dissolved. This makes them easier to handle, reduces the risk of cutting yourself while holding a slippery fish.

(Here's another fish-cleaning trick: Scrape off the scales while holding the fish under water in a dishpan. The scales come off easier, and don't fly all over the kitchen.

(Keep a pair of pliers nearby when dressing out a mess of fish. They're handy for ripping out dorsal fins and gripping the skin to peel it off.

(When perch aren't biting fast enough to suit you, try this: Drop your bait to bottom and leave it there. Perch that refuse a bait suspended in the water will often scoop it off the bottom.

Finding Fish in Winter

Anyone with guts enough to go ice fishing on a sub-zero day in the dead of winter should never feel guilty about taking advantage of any little loophole he can find in the fishing laws. And I have found a loophole in every one of the winter fishing regulations I have ever read. In all cases the law limits the number of lines you may set out but, and mark this well, never the number of holes you may cut. So without violating either the letter or spirit of the law you can fish, say, five legal tip-ups in ten holes or twenty, or as many as you have the energy to cut, just by shifting them from one hole to another. And it stands to reason

that the more different holes you try, the more chance you have of locating some fish.

It seldom pays, I've found, to stay with a hole that doesn't produce some action after a reasonable length of time. "Reasonable" might be only ten or fifteen minutes if you are fishing for bluegills or perch, as long as a couple of hours or more if you are trying for lake trout. All fresh water fish become somewhat sluggish during the winter when their colder environment lowers their metabolism and hence reduces their need for food, so they move around less than they do in the summer. In addition, they tend to scatter after the ice forms, due to uniform water temperatures and lack of weed cover. So for these reasons, plus a few others, it is usually more difficult to find fish in the winter, and thus more important to try different spots.

On the other hand, most wintering fish remain in pretty much the same general areas they occupied in the summer. You can expect to find pickerel, pike, and sunfish still cruising the shallows; walleyes, perch, and trout in deeper water; lakers, whitefish, and smelt down in the deep holes. That simplifies the fish-finding problem a little, because often the best winter grounds are the very same places where you found fish in the summer, particularly over bars, ledges, and channels and off the mouths of tributaries. And of course holes left by other ice fishermen are often worth reopening, especially if you find scales or flecks of fish blood around them.

When you have set out the legal number of lines there isn't much you can do but wait for some action. If the first flag flies up in one of the holes close to shore, then it might be smart to spud out another hole close by. Many times, in fact, peppering a small area with a tight cluster of holes will produce rattle-bang fishing for a while. And sometimes the one last hole chopped in desperation just as the sun goes down is the one that yields the biggest fish of the day.

True, hacking holes through a foot and a half of diamond-hard ice, even with an auger, one of the greatest laborsaving inventions since the outboard motor, is no one's idea of happy holiday fun. But not catching fish isn't the gayest kind of sport, either, especially with the mercury standing a half inch high in the glass. Even if the extra holes don't produce any fish, cutting them isn't entirely a waste of time. At least, it will keep you warm till it's time to go home.

TAP'S TIPS

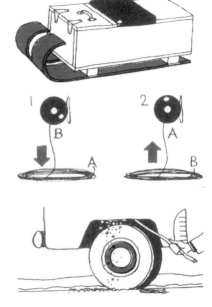

❨ An excellent sled for hauling ice-fishing gear can be made out of broken toboggan runners, available for the asking at most winter sports areas. A large wooden box mounted on a pair of matched boards from the front of a toboggan will carry a surprising amount of equipment. The wide slats will support the load even in deep, soft snow.

❨ Winter is the time to reverse bait-casting lines and both level and double-tapered fly lines. Swapping ends between seasons will lengthen the life of the lines. Forward-taper lines cannot be reversed, of course, but should be checked for signs of wear.

❨ Here's a tip for ice-fishermen who drive over back roads in winter: When tires spin in ice or packed snow, tap loose or scrape off the dirt that has collected under the fenders. Unless the car is new, enough dirt will shower down to provide digging-out traction.

How to Prime an Ice Hole

Quite possibly you don't care for cold hard-boiled eggs any more than I do. Nevertheless, I suggest that you put a couple of them in your lunch box the next time you go ice fishing. Whether you eat the eggs or not, be sure to save the shells. If the fish don't bite as briskly as you would like (and do they ever?), grind the shells between your palms and sprinkle the pieces into one of the unproductive holes. As the bits of shell sink, twisting and flashing in the light filtering down from above, they may catch the eye of any fish that happens to be lurking nearby, or perhaps toll in some hungry minnows which may in turn attract larger fish.

I don't mean to suggest by this that there is anything original about the idea of chumming an ice hole to advertise that it is open for business. Ice fishermen have done it for years. The original thinking is exercised in the choice of materials used for chumming. Mashed eggshell happens to be an old favorite. Another is oatmeal, which is almost certain to bring in some bait fish, often followed by a pickerel or a school of roving perch.

Any well-stocked kitchen shelf will provide an infinite variety of good chum baits. Offhand, I can think of canned corn, split peas, white baking beans, cornmeal, cracker crumbs, rice, and almost any breakfast food, especially Cream of Wheat. Some ice fishermen claim that ground clamshell is better than any of them, while others report sensational results with confetti. However, if you want to try chumming and have forgotten to bring anything, just hold the first fish you catch over a hole and scrape some scales into it. Then gut the fish and bait the bottom with its innards.

But there are still other ways to draw fish to an ice-fishing hole. For example, you can scrape the sinker with a knife blade to make it shiny. Or in place of a sinker, weight the line with a highly polished wobbler body. Another trick worth trying is to remove the hooks from a small, free-turning spinner and tie the shaft into the leader. Each time you raise the line to stir up the bait the twirling blade will flash an invitation to any fish near enough to see it. When fishing in deep water with a heavy sinker, reverse the blade so it spins on the way down.

No spinner handy? Then remove the aluminum foil from a cigarette pack and wrap it around the line or leader, shiny side out. Crimp the foil tightly between your teeth. This creates a multitude of reflecting surfaces that will give off sparks of light when the line moves. To prevent the foil from sliding on the line, string brightly colored beads above and below it.

And finally, try using a gold-colored hook. It's dark down there under the ice, remember, and sometimes just a little flash of color, plus a pinch of chum, can make a world of difference.

TAP'S TIPS

(You will never need a ruler for measuring fish if you know the span of your outstretched hand. Measuring from the tip of the thumb to the tip of the little finger, a small hand covers about 8 inches, a medium-sized hand 8½, a large hand 9.

(Save old chamois skin that can be no longer used

for washing the car. It can be used to catch fish. Wash the skin thoroughly and cut it into strips. It's almost as good as pork rind—supple when wet, convenient to carry in a pocket when dry.

〔 Bait hooks can be carried in the pocket if they are stuck between strips of cellophane tape. When a new hook is needed, select the desired size or shape and slice it from the strip with a knife.

What To Do While Wishing You Had a Net

I saw the trout clearly when it swirled at my fly. I got a good look at its speckled flank as it turned in a boil of lake water, noted the width of its tail as it burrowed down with the streamer stuck in its jaw, and I'd have bet my whole fly book against one moth-eaten bucktail that it would go 3 pounds, maybe 4.

But assuming that I could hang onto it and drag it up on top, there remained the problem of getting it into the canoe. One doesn't just grab the leader and derrick a fish that size aboard. One dips it out with a net. Only my net was hanging on a nail in my closet, some three hundred miles due south.

Our departure from home the day before had been marked with unseemly haste. Bob Elliot had wired from the State House in Augusta, Maine, that Moosehead Lake had "busted wide open" after two weeks of desultory fishing. So Tom and I swapped phone calls, gathered some fishing gear together, and set sail. In the confusion I neglected to take the net off its peg.

"Now what are you gonna do?" Tom asked morosely. He laid his paddle across the canoe gunwales and rested his elbows on it. "You're the guy who forgot the net."

Cranking in a few turns of fly line, I looked around for a boat from which we could borrow a scoop. I then surveyed the shore, now nearly a half-mile distant, for a sand beach where we might land, providing we could tow the fish that far, and drag it out. But there were no beaches, either; only steep banks and jagged rocks tumbling down into the lake.

The fish bored sluggishly under the canoe. Tom picked up the paddle and levered the blade against the gunwale to slide the canoe away. At that instant a light flickered in my mind.

"Look," I said, "I think I know how we can save this fish. I'll lead him down to your end of the canoe, and when he's in the right position I'll slack off on the leader. Then you take that paddle in both hands and chop him over the head with it. That ought to stun him and we can scoop him in as easy as pie."

"You think so?" Tom shrugged and picked up the paddle. "Well, it's your fish. Lead him down here."

Carefully I guided the trout down toward the stern of the canoe. It lay on the water with its back awash and its broad tail waving feebly in the ripple. I lowered the rod tip until the leader hung slack. "Bash him!" I said.

The wet paddle blade flashed down. Its edge cracked the fish's head with a resounding whock. The blow drove the fish down into the water, but it bobbed up again a second later and lay stunned and inert on the surface. Reaching out, I hooked a forefinger through its gills and hoisted the critter aboard.

"Nothing to it," I said. I hung the fish on my De-Liar. The needle sagged down to the 2-pound mark. I jiggled the De-Liar and picked up an ounce. "Three pounds on the nose," I told Tom, putting the scales away. "Nice fish."

"All the same," Tom growled, "we're going ashore and borrow a net from someone. I'd die a thousand deaths if we had to try that stunt on a fish of mine."

He turned the canoe, pointed its bow for the boat landing, and started paddling. If he had elected to pass Cranberry Island on the windward side he might have paddled us out of this narrative without further incident. But he swung around under the lee shore just as a swirling rise bulged the flat water. Tom drove the canoe over to it. As we glided within casting range we each heaved a streamer fly at the widening circles. Mine fell short, but Tom's hit the X-ring. The fish bulged again, clamped its jaws on the fly, and swaggered off with it. I started looking again for a sand beach.

Beaching a fish is as simple as ladling it from the water with a net. You just step ashore and back up about a rod's length from the edge of the water. Play the fish until it's pretty well tuckered out. Then snake it up on the sloping shingle and hold it on a taut line while you or your partner grab the creature or scoop it out high and dry. Once you've hauled the fish out so far it can't get a purchase on the water with its tail, it's practically in the creel.

But you won't always be fortunate enough to find a suitable beach nearby when you hang a fish which you are particularly anxious to save, and some idiot has forgotten the net. As a case in point, let me recount an incident that occurred a couple of seasons back on Sysladobsis Lake in Washington County, Maine.

The villain of the piece was a larger than average landlocked salmon which I hooked, fought and, technically, conquered in a fair and sportsmanlike manner. However, I was without a net at the time, having lent it to someone who then lent it to someone else who had gone off fishing on another lake. At this crisis the idea struck me that by tipping the boat far enough I might be able to slide the fish in over the gunwale.

102

Instructing my partner to lean over as far as he dared, I added my weight to his until the starboard oarlock was nearly awash. Then I lifted on the fly rod. The bemused salmon slithered aboard as docilely as a catfish. But with it came half a boatful of icy lake water. Before I could grab the fish it came to its senses, took a running jump, bounced off the oarlock and splashed back into the lake. The leader, caught under a floorboard cleat, hung over the gunwale, making a rubbery sound. Quickly I plunged my hand into the water and closed it around the fish. As I did so the leader parted, the salmon's tail squirted through my fingers, and that was that.

As the cop said when told that the car on which he had hung a parking ticket belonged to the mayor, if I had that to do over again I'd handle it a little differently. I'd play out the fish, coax it close to the surface, and seize it behind the head, clamping my fingers into the gill openings. This method is effective with almost any fish large enough to make a handful and small enough to lift—say, from a pound weight up to the size of an average pike or musky. The trick is to bracket the fish with thumb on one side and closed fingers on the other and clamp the vise firmly. The fish will flop around some as you hoist it from the water, but the gills provide enough of a finger-hold to enable you to hang onto your victim until it is safely aboard.

At least two species of game fish, sea salmon and fresh-run steelhead, can be lifted from the water by grasping them around the thin part of the body next to the tail. The caudal structure of these fish is firm and hard, the tail itself broad, and the body narrow enough to offer a secure grip. This immobilizes the fish almost completely; it hangs from your hand like a wet sock.

Hand-tailing would be the easiest of all methods of capturing fish, short of using a net, gaff or tailer, if all fish were large enough and their tails firm enough. Unfortunately, the good Lord didn't make 'em all that way. Even Atlantic salmon may become soft in the stern after they have lived in fresh water a while. This I learned one August day on the Serpentine River in New Brunswick. Fishing the Big Salmon Hole with Vic Miller, who leased the river, I hooked a bouncing salmon of about 8 pounds weight, wore it down, and made ready to hand-tail it.

"You better wait till I run up to the cabin for a net," Vic said in my ear.

"Don't bother," I told him. "I'll snake him out by the tail. Done it lots of times,"

The salmon rolled wearily. I reached out with my hand, grasped the fish ahead of its tail and squeezed. As I started to lift the fish from the water its tail folded slowly under my hand. The salmon slid through my fingers and plopped back into the pool.

"Won't take me a minute to get the net," Vic said.

Stubbornly I shook my head and reached for the salmon once more.

But again the tail collapsed. The salmon dropped back into the river and lay sluggish in the eddy, pumping water through its gills.

Without saying a word, Vic ran his hand down the leader, twisted the Black Dose from the salmon's jaw, and with his booted foot pushed the weary fish into the current, where it righted itself and sculled slowly into the deep water of the pool.

"Don't you think you abused that poor fish enough?" Vic said.

I nodded ruefully. "But what was the matter? His tail folded like a fan."

"Well, these salmon have come a long way from the sea. It's two hundred miles or more from this pool to salt water. Maybe being in the river so long their tails grow soft. I dunno. But I've seen other fishermen try to tail fish out of this river, and except for bright fish, fish that come right through on high water with the sea lice still on 'em, they didn't have any better luck than you did."

I know better than to argue with a man who understands his river and his river's fish as well as Vic does, so I let it go at that. But only a few months earlier I had hand-tailed black salmon—slinks—out of the Miramichi, and those fish had been in fresh water nearly half a year. You figure it out.

When you hook a fish you plan to kill for table use, it doesn't matter if you injure it in the process of landing it. Grabbing a fish around the gill openings damages the delicate membranes of the gill rakers, and the fish will almost surely die if returned to the water. The best way to release a fish unharmed is to slide the fingers down the leader, as Vic did, grasp the hook by the shank and twist it free. If the barb is imbedded so deeply you cannot loosen it, cut the leader and let the fish keep the hook as a souvenir.

Pike, pickerel, and muskies are difficult fish to land without a net or gaff. Some musky fishermen use a .22 pistol, but its use is fraught with hazard. The bullet may conceivably ricochet off the water and fetch up in the ribs of a neighboring boat or fellow fisherman. It might even do what an errant .22 slug did to a friend of mine who was fishing muskies up in Ontario.

He had hooked a large musky, between 18 and 20 pounds, he claims, and had licked it on 12-pound line. He brought the fish up close to the side of the boat, drew his pistol, and aimed carefully at the musky's baleful eye. At the split-instant he pulled the trigger the fish thrashed wildly. The slug, lunging out at 1,200 feet per second, pinged off the wobbler that hung from the musky's upper jaw, ripped through the boat at the water line, and exited a scant inch from the guide's foot. In the ensuing excitement the musky shook the wobbler loose and staggered off to brood upon the vicissitudes of life.

The favorite way to lift a spent pike or musky from the water is to

104

grasp it by the eye sockets, much as a bowler holds a bowling ball. These deep holes in the fish's skull offer a convenient grip, but if the fish should nevertheless escape or prove too small to keep, its eyesight must surely suffer some impairment. Lifting a musky or pike by the leader is simple enough. Those who do not use wire leaders when fishing for pike or muskies have no landing problem anyway; their fish seldom stay with them long enough to become candidates for the stringer.

Bass, on the other hand, pose no problem at all. You can catch bass and release them unharmed until the cows come home. When the bass makes its last weary jump, draw it close, clamp its lower lip between your thumb and forefinger, and lift it from the water. Held in this manner a bass comes in with hardly a quiver. Some fishermen hold the mistaken idea that bass are toothless. Reference to any standard book on the anatomy of fishes will disclose that they have teeth "on jaws, vomer and palatines in broad villiform bands" but you could rub your finger on them all day without suffering a scratch.

The lip-hold is effective for landing bass even when the fish has a cluster of gang hooks fastened to its face. You must exercise caution in getting the thumb-and-forefinger grip, but once you clamp down on the lower jaw the fish is rendered virtually helpless. However, the timid soul who shrinks from the flashing eye and frothing mouth of a man-eating bass can always lift it by the leader or grab it by the gills.

The small, run-of-the-hatchery trout with which most of our streams are stocked these days offer little enough sport as it is, and swinging a net at a 7-inch fish always struck me as analogous to batting a no-see-um with a sculling oar. Besides, most trout streams are boobytrapped with brush, brambles, and barbed-wire fences which present a constant hazard to the net-draped angler. I have lately taken to leaving my net at home. Fishing netless has given me a freedom of movement I never enjoyed in the old, net-over-the-shoulder days. More important, catching small trout has taken on a little extra zest, for now I have the additional problem of how to land the little rascals.

When I first abandoned the trout net I beached my fish by swinging them ashore in the time-honored method employed by small boys with alder poles. But that proved ineffectual on the lunker fish of 12 or 13 inches that occasionally fell to my happy lot. I lost the big ones and landed the small ones, which didn't make sense. When you get down to 5X tippets, along about mid-June, you can't horse your fish around the way you can in the early, or 1X, part of the season. And, perversely, as the tippets get finer the chances of hooking a holdover fish increases, the April fishermen having cleaned out most of the fresh hatchery stock.

Next to eels, trout are the slipperiest of all God's creatures. You draw them up close to you, close your hand around them and lift them from the water, whereupon they squirt from your fingers like a wet watermelon seed. Wrestling small trout in this manner often injures them so badly they cannot survive release. It's far better for the trout and easier for you to slide your fingers down to the hook, grasp the shank with thumb and forefinger, and twist it a time or two. The hook almost always comes free. Should it be too deeply imbedded, lift the fish by the hook or lower jaw, tuck the rod under your arm, and use both hands.

If the fish is of keeper size and you drool for fresh-caught trout rolled in corn meal and sizzled to a golden brown, slide your hand down the leader and then either pinch the trout's lower lip between thumb and forefinger or grasp the fish firmly around the middle while keeping tension on the leader. That's the trick, keeping the leader tight. It prevents the fish from thrashing about while you get a grip on him.

But back to Moosehead Lake and the far nobler fish that Tom hooked in the lee of Cranberry Island. As I said, it rose up and clamped its jaws around Tom's streamer fly and then bored off into deep water, leaving a boil such as a startled swordfish might make.

"Another squaretail, and bigger than yours," Tom said. "You'd better start looking for a beach where we can land him."

"I've already looked," I told him. "Nothing but rocks."

"Maybe we can borrow a net. Any boats around?"

"No boats, either. We'll have to dent his squash with a paddle, like we did mine."

Ten minutes later Tom pumped the huge trout to the surface where we could see it. The red spots on its side glowed bright in the sun. Its body was easily 20 inches long, and it was a broad, deep fish that would look handsome on a walnut plaque over a fireplace.

"Six pounds easy," Tom said.

"Four."

"Six," Tom insisted.

"Well, five maybe."

Tom guided the trout toward my end of the canoe. "Careful now," he said. "I want this fish real bad. Ready?"

I licked my thumb and ran it along the edge of the paddle blade. "I'm ready."

Tom lowered his rod, letting the leader fall slack. Gripping the paddle like an axe, I raised it, took careful aim, and chopped down hard. Just as the blade started downward, the trout gave a mighty lunge. The leader straightened and stretched tight over the boil he made at the exact instant the paddle blade hit the water, and we paddled back to the boat landing in silence.

106

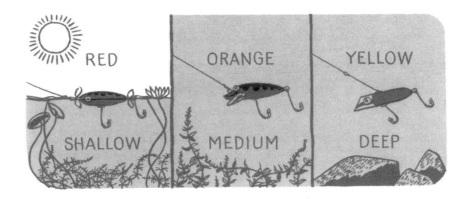

LURES

Lucky Lure Colors

EVERYONE KNOWS by now that fish can distinguish colors, and most fishermen are convinced that fish prefer one color over another. That's why the Eppinger people sell so many red-and-white Dardevles.

When you have a good day with a particular lure it's only natural to suppose that the color had something to do with your luck (your skill is something else again, of course). And when you are fishing close to the surface, but under it, color doubtless does have a lot to do with the way fish respond to your offerings.

But when you fish deeper, color becomes less and less important, because colors begin to lose their identity as the lure sinks. Ironically enough, the favorite color—red, naturally—is the first to go. Red darkens rapidly as the lure goes down, and at around 25 feet the fish can't distinguish it from black!

The reason for this is simple. Red, like all the other colors, reflects light rays of one particular wave length. The rays which reflect red have the least ability to penetrate water. Orange holds its color much longer, and does not darken noticeably until around 100 feet. Yellow lasts even longer, and can still be distinguished at around 200 feet.

So now let's speculate a bit. If you believe that color is important, and of all colors red appeals most to fish, then perhaps you could improve your luck (actually, when you get as scientific as this you're on your way to ruling luck out of fishing entirely) by using red at or near the surface. At around 25 feet of depth you could change to an orange lure, and at 100 feet or so switch to something yellow. The tactic might really pay off if you tried it often enough—and if you are one of those who believe that fish really like one color better than another.

TAP'S TIPS

(The fact that fish can distinguish colors does not necessarily mean that they like bright colors best. All-black and all-white lures often interest fish that ignore red, orange, and yellow lures. Gray and brown are the basic colors of most standard dry fly patterns.

(To change or brighten the color of a lure, touch it up with fingernail polish, now available in almost every conceivable shade. The paint job can be removed easily with polish remover. You can probably find everything you need on your wife's dressing table, along with lipstick for painting stripes and spots on spoons and plugs.

(To make lures glitter and sparkle, coat the underside with clear fingernail polish and before it dries sprinkle it with silver chips, which are called "sparkies" or "flitters." The lure will be easier for fish to find in muddy or stained water.

The Mighty Midgets

I have a friend who consistently catches more trout than I do. As a matter of fact, I have several friends who embarrass me that way, but this particular one does it with a gimmick. His gimmick is a miniature streamer or bucktail, and if you have never tried one, I entreat you to do so at the earliest opportunity.

By "miniature" I mean really small—not more than an inch long, quite sparse, and tied on a No. 10 or 12 hook, regular shank or medium long. Most sporting goods stores sell them, or you can tie them yourself with the tip ends of hackle feathers or bucktail over a tinsel-wrapped body. If you tie your own—they're very simple to make—I suggest that you make them even smaller and sparser than the commercially-tied

108

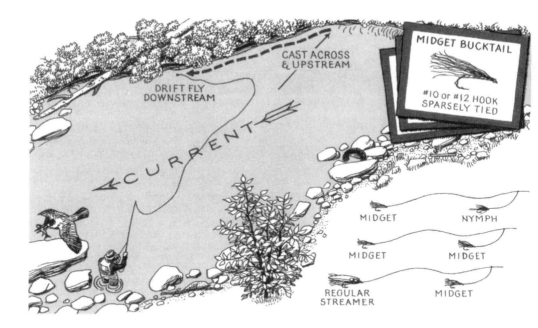

patterns, which must first catch fishermen before they can catch fish.

Pattern doesn't seem to matter much. I have my best luck with red-and-yellow and brown-and-white bucktails, but that may be due to the fact that those are about the only patterns I tie now. My friend, the one who catches more trout than I do, uses white marabou a lot.

When you fish the orthodox, or feather-duster, streamer you probably use a fairly heavy leader and cast cross-stream, pumping the fly as it swings down and around with the current. With the midgets, you can and should use finer tippets, down to 3X and even 5X in extremely low, clear water. You will find that you can fish a midget at more of an upstream angle, even directly upstream, and you will get strikes while the fly drifts back toward you on a slack line, like a nymph.

If you like to fish two flies, the midgets give you several easy-casting combinations, such as a regular-sized streamer with a midget as the dropper fly, two midgets, or a midget and a nymph. I use the latter combination quite a lot.

In fishing, as you well know, nothing works all the time. The midget streamers are virtually useless in high, discolored water, and are not generally as effective for trout fishing in ponds and lakes as the regular-sized patterns. But after the snow water runs off, give them a try. When you do, you may discover that they are just a wee bit more attractive to browns and rainbows than to brookies. My friend thinks they are, and I'm inclined to agree with him.

TAP'S TIPS

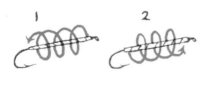

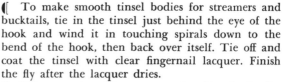

❪ To make smooth tinsel bodies for streamers and bucktails, tie in the tinsel just behind the eye of the hook and wind it in touching spirals down to the bend of the hook, then back over itself. Tie off and coat the tinsel with clear fingernail lacquer. Finish the fly after the lacquer dries.

❪ When you buy flies or a supply of hooks for fly-tying, test the temper of the wire. Occasionally a batch of hooks will be either too soft or too brittle, and one or the other may cost you fish—perhaps the big one you've always dreamed of catching.

❪ Thread one or two small glass beads on your leader tippet before tying on the fly. The beads add a flash of color and help to sink the fly. Try them ahead of spinning lures, too.

Stunts with Streamers

Usually, a streamer fly or bucktail will take fish for you with no dressing except maybe a little saliva for luck. Cast or trolled, it's the ticket for trout and landlocked salmon, and a better lure for bass, pike, and pickerel—yes, and for walleyes too—than many fishermen realize.

Sometimes, though, the streamer needs a little help. Running a small spinner ahead of it often speeds up the action. But the spinner's weight and air resistance make it awkward to cast. Tom Nixon, who fishes out of Maplewood, Louisiana, uses an ingenious means of adding glitter to a streamer fly without noticeably increasing its weight. Tom cuts aluminum cooking foil into strips about 2-inches long by ¼-inch wide, and folds a strip, shiny side out, tightly around the leader just ahead of the fly. In the process, the foil becomes crimped and uneven,

110

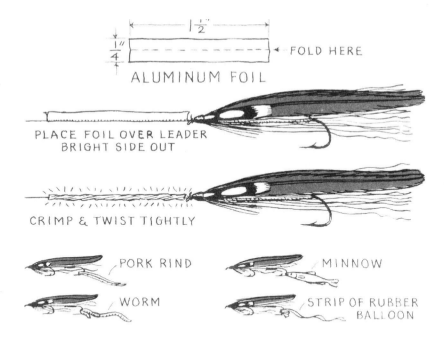

$1\frac{1}{2}"$

$\frac{1}{4}"$

FOLD HERE

ALUMINUM FOIL

PLACE FOIL OVER LEADER
BRIGHT SIDE OUT

CRIMP & TWIST TIGHTLY

PORK RIND

MINNOW

WORM

STRIP OF RUBBER
BALLOON

which creates a multitude of light-reflecting surfaces that sparkle as brightly as any spinner blade. The foil adds very little weight and no air resistance, so the streamer casts easily.

Tandem streamers, tied with a small trailing hook or fly, offer unlimited opportunities to dress the fly for extra fish appeal. You can hang almost anything on the trailing hook—a sliver of pork rind, a worm, or a small minnow hooked lightly through the lips. If you want to cast the streamer, cut a small pennant from a yellow or white balloon, fold one end a couple of times and jab the trailing hook through the folds. You won't notice the extra weight, because there isn't any, hardly.

Here's still another way to make walleyes and bass sit up and take notice. Bind a short length of light monofilament to the base of the tail treble of a deep-running bass plug and tie a streamer fly to that, so it follows a few inches behind the plug. The side-to-side motion of the plug sends little shivers down to the trailing streamer, giving it the appearance of a small minnow trying frantically to catch up with a larger one. I don't know for a fact, of course, that it looks like that to a fish, but it certainly does to me.

In general, use large, heavily-dressed streamers for bass, walleyes, pike and pickerel, as these species all like a mouthful. The red-and-yellow Mickey Finn bucktail is an excellent pattern for this fishing. Trout and landlocked salmon seem to prefer the sparser flies. My own favorites for landlocks are the Nine-Three and Green Ghost, which imitate smelt, and for trout my pet is the Dark Edson Tiger, a yellow-brown bucktail that looks quite a lot like a chub.

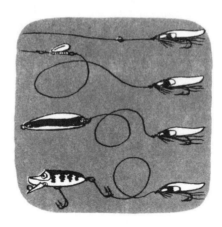

TAP'S TIPS

⟮ Painted eyes dress up streamer flies and probably make them more visible to fish. To do a neat job of it, dip the head of a 1- or 1¼-inch wire brad in cream enamel and press it lightly to each side of the fly head. After it dries, put a dot of black enamel in the middle.

⟮ When you have trouble casting streamers on a windy day, cut the leader back to a heavier diameter. A large streamer builds up air resistance that prevents a long, light leader from straightening out at the end of the cast.

⟮ If you examine the point of a new hook under a microscope you may be surprised to discover it isn't as sharp as it feels. Dull points make it necessary to strike harder to set the hook, and that results in broken leader tippets. So touch up new hooks with a whetstone, being careful not to hone the points so fine they break when they tick a rock or meet gristle in a fish's jaw.

⟮ Instead of attaching split shot to the leader above a streamer fly, leave a short whisker of gut when you tie on the fly, and squeeze the shot to that. It casts easier and the fly has better action. Also, the shot can be stripped off quicker than when it is clamped to the leader.

112

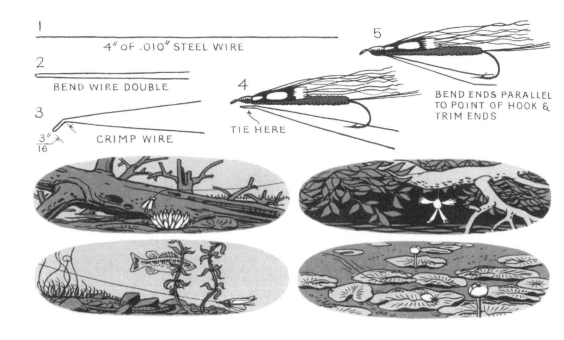

Snag-Proof Bass Flies

An apt definition of good bass cover might be: "Any spot where you're sure to get snagged on your first cast." Bass, and especially large-mouths, love to den up in thick tangles of brush, weeds, and stumps, and under overhanging foliage. Putting a lure into these places is much easier than getting it out again, but you can lick that by tying bass bugs and flies with wire weed guards.

Get some polished steel wire about .010 in diameter, such as is used for control line on gas-powered model airplanes. Cut a piece of wire about four inches long, depending on the hook size, and bend it double. Crimp about 3/16 inch of the doubled end and tie it firmly to the under-side of the hook, just behind the eye. Due to the crimping, the two lengths of wire will flare out beyond the point of the hook, one end on each side. Bend the end of each piece parallel with the point and snip off any excess. The fine-diameter wire adds so little weight that it can be used with floating lures, even deerhair bass bugs, without sinking them.

Now you can plunk your bug or fly right in where the bass live. If you see a log several feet off shore, drop your lure on the other side of it and drag it over the log in a creepy-crawly way and twitch it off into the water again. Any bass lurking in the shade of the log will snap to attention when that sort of thing goes on overhead.

When you're casting to the shoreline from a boat, drop your fly or bug up on the bank and make it jump off into the water. Or drape it over the limb of a bush or tree and dance it just above the surface. Bass are suckers for that sort of thing.

Lily pads reach their heaviest growth in hot weather, just when bass use them most. With a weed-guarded fly or bug it's easy to get right into the thickest growth and take bass even in the heat of midday.

The weed guard lets you go bottom bumping, too. This pays off especially in smallmouth water. The wire sinks the fly quicker, and you can drag it over rocks and sunken logs without fear of snagging.

In fact, the weed guards help you to take bass under almost any conditions—pike, pickerel, and walleyes, too. Once you've tried them you'll use them often, and discover that they give your fishing more tingle with less tangle.

TAP'S TIPS

⟨[Streamer flies and bass bugs are less likely to snag in weeds if they ride through the water with the hook up. To tie them this way, simply put the hook in the vise with the hook point on top. This reverses the dressing. Be sure to leave plenty of "bite" between body and point when making deerhair bugs.

⟨[Small rubber bands can be used to make a fly or bug semiweedless. Force the band through the eye of the hook, pass one loop through the other and pull tight. Then catch the band under the barb.

⟨[If you tie your own streamers and bucktails, make a few on ringed-eye hooks, for use with spinners. Flies with turned-up or turned-down eyes don't ride well behind a blade, as they have a tendency to cock up or down.

Please Pass the Pork

Pork rind is truly wonderful stuff. It comes in all shapes and sizes and colors, it is tough and wigglesome, and fish seem to like the feel of it in their mouths. You can stick a strip of it on a bare hook and catch fish, or you can hang a tiny morsel of it on a fly, spoon, spinner, or plug and catch even more fish. You can cast it, troll it, or jig it.

You can crawl a big chunk of it over the lily pads in bass and pickerel

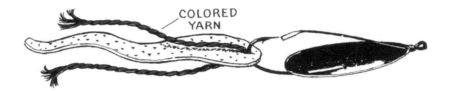

COLORED YARN

water with explosive results. You can add a small piece of it to a trolled streamer fly and catch trout, landlocked salmon, walleye, and bass.

Even a mere flick of it on a wet fly can make all the difference in the world when you're stream fishing for trout or casting over panfish water. And as practically every fisherman knows, a weedless wobbling spoon looks stark naked without a pennant of pork fluttering behind it.

Deadly as it is, a strip of pork rind can be made even deadlier by striping it with a piece of brightly colored yarn run through the head, so the ends hang free on each side.

But what I like best about pork rind is that it is so convenient. It gives a fisherman a reliable bait that he doesn't have to dig or catch with a net or pursue on his hands and knees. Anyone who carries a bottle of it in his pocket or tackle box will never want for a way to catch fish. *Any* fish.

TAP'S TIPS

(For the benefit of do-it-yourselfers, here's how pork-rind baits can be home-made. Using a razor blade, cut strips from salt-pork rind. Bleach them by soaking about three hours in a 15% solution of hydrochloric acid. Then pickle the strips by leaving them a couple of days in salt brine strong enough to float a raw potato. Rinse thoroughly and pack in screw-top bottles containing a 20% solution of formaldehyde (one part formaldehyde to four parts water).

(Here's a trolling trick worth trying when strikes are few and far between: Tie a three-way swivel to the end of the line or leader. To one ring of the swivel hang a short leader with a deep-diving plug; from the other, a longer leader with spinner and pork rind. The plug swims below the spinner, so the two lures seldom become entangled.

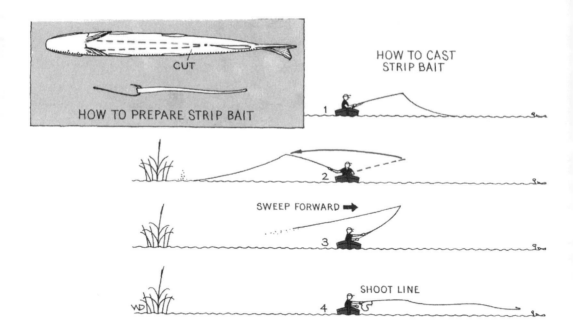

HOW TO PREPARE STRIP BAIT

CUT

HOW TO CAST
STRIP BAIT

1

2

SWEEP FORWARD ➡

3

SHOOT LINE

4

Fishing with a Stripteaser

No, not that kind. I mean a strip bait, a long, thin slab of skin and meat cut from the belly or side of a fish. And that brings up an interesting question. Should a strip be called a bait or a lure? You could argue it both ways. On the one hand, it obviously imitates a small fish, and we always think of imitations as lures. On the other hand, it is edible, so it could just as logically be called a bait. Well, whichever you call it, there's no argument about one thing. A strip of fish belly has the effect of a depth charge when thrown out into water inhabited by pike, pickerel or bass, even crappies and walleyes, trout, or 'most any fish-eating critter you can think of.

The traditional strip bait has always been a chunk of yellow-perch belly with the ventral fins attached. Perch belly makes a tough and colorful bait (lure?) but it is rather stiff and does not give you the sexy wiggle you can get out of a strip sliced from the belly or side of a pickerel. So the way I usually do it is to first catch a perch, which is generally pretty easy, and use a strip from the perch to catch a pickerel, and then cut up the pickerel to catch more pickerel.

116

In cutting a belly strip, start at the V where the gills meet. The skin and flesh are very tough there and the strip stays on the hook very well. Trim the rest of the strip in a long taper ending with a shaved tail of bare skin. Strips from the side of a pickerel are less durable, but the dark skin gives it a nice two-tone effect. Push the hook through the head end from the meat side, and use a big one—long-shank 2/0 for pickerel and bass, about 4/0 for pike. Be sure to use a heavy leader or shock tippet of 20-, 30-, even 40-pound-test nylon. Not wire; it's too stiff.

Strip bait can be cast quite easily with either spinning or bait-casting gear, but nothing beats a fly rod for slapping a strip bait around. It should be powerful, and preferably made of glass. The work is a bit too rough for an expensive bamboo rod. But you don't actually cast a strip bait anyway; you throw it. Starting with a couple of rod's lengths of line, swing the strip behind you and let it rest on the water. Then before it has time to sink lob it forward with a sweeping side-arm motion, releasing line at the same time to lengthen the cast. With a little practice almost anyone can heave a strip bait 40 or 50 feet with considerable accuracy.

No other lure is quite capable of giving you the teasing, tantalizing motion you can get with a strip of fish. It dips and darts and curls its tail, it skitters over the pads and crawls along the bottom, it looks like a lazy minnow one second, a terrified minnow the next. To me, that's a large part of the fun of fishing a strip bait, seeing how much action I can give it.

Pickerel and pike usually hold a bait where they take it, but bass almost always run off with it before stopping to work on it. So when you get a hit you can usually tell what kind of a fish has taken it. However, a strip bait is almost invariably seized in the middle, so the fish must be given time to twitch it around in his mouth and get it in position to swallow. This may take only a minute or two if it's a pickerel or bass, but if you are gunning for pike with a 10-inch strip you may have to wait four or five minutes. When you think the fish has played with the strip long enough, wait just a little longer, then gather in the slack and hit him hard enough to break his neck. If the hook digs into solid meat, plan on being busy for the next few minutes.

TAP'S TIPS

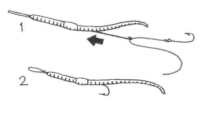

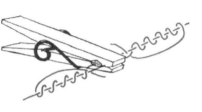

❪ Instead of simply jabbing a hook in and out of the head end of a plastic worm, try this method. First, snell the hook with braided nylon bait-casting line—not monofilament, which is too stiff. Then force a barbed steel crochet needle into the large end of the worm and push it out where you want the hook to come through, about a couple inches from the head. Pick up the snell with the barb of the needle and draw it back. Tie a loop in the snell to hold it snug against the head of the worm.

❪ If you're "all thumbs" when tying Blood knots in monofilament, try holding the crossed ends between the jaws of a wooden spring-type clothespin. First flatten the jaws by filling the notches with plastic wood and filing the surfaces smooth. The clothespin will hold the leader or line firmly while you make the necessary number of turns around the two standing ends.

118

Helpful Hardware

Stop and think—do you have a few spinners in your fishing kit? Because I warn you, the time will come when you'll need them.

A flashing spinner blade improves almost any natural bait you can use. Nightcrawlers, for instance. Naked, the worm that walks in the dark makes an indifferent trolling bait. But when you dress him up with the flashing blade of a spinner you have one of the deadliest trolling baits ever devised for walleyes, trout, landlocked salmon, bass, panfish, and, yes, for the pike family too.

Whatever it is a spinner does for a worm, it does even more for a trolled minnow. Landlocked salmon and lake trout fishermen shoot the works, with a string of large blades ahead of a sewed shiner, chub, or smelt. But for most trolling a single blade proves more satisfactory. The large willow leaf spinner is ideal for pike, pickerel, and musky fishing with trolled minnows. For smallmouths use a shorter, broader blade and nip on enough weight to keep your lure close to bottom.

Spinners combine just as nicely with other fishing methods. If you hit a trout stream running bank-full and cloudy following a heavy rain,

a small spinner will make it that much easier for the fish to find your bait. Cast it across and downstream, twitching the spinner slowly against the current to keep it fluttering, every so often letting your bait or lure drift back before you twitch it again. Most strikes will come when the bait is drifting back, but you can be sure the fish were attracted to it first by the glittering blade of the spinner.

The spinning rod greatly increases your chance of taking advantage of the beguiling spinner. With it you can heave light baits adorned with a small blade, and cover all the water you want to reach. In trout and smallmouth water the worm and minnow are just that much deadlier when you have the casting weight and the attraction of a small blade to dress them up.

Bucktails and streamers take more bass when you hang a spinner ahead of them, and small wet flies often need that added flash to stir up the panfish. Or if you want to go to seemingly ridiculous extremes, try running a spinner ahead of a wobbling spoon. It might surprise you!

TAP'S TIPS

⟨[Don't throw away spinners because the blades are too badly tarnished to be restored. Often a dull or dark blade attracts fish better than a bright one, especially when the water is clear and the day sunny.
⟨[Swivels and split rings have an annoying habit of

120

running off and hiding when they are needed. To make sure you can always find one when you want one, string a dozen or so on a safety pin and fasten it under the flap of your fishing shirt pocket.

《 Keep the lure in the water till the last possible second when casting for pickerel, pike, or muskies. These three have an odd habit of following a lure right up to the side of the boat and waiting until the lure is directly under your rod tip before striking.

《 Occasionally a snap swivel is forced open by the weight of a heavy fish. To avoid this possibility when fishing for pike, muskies or lake trout, file a notch in the clasp and bend the tip of the snap arm to fit into it. This locks the snap firmly so it can't come free.

FILE NOTCH → BEND

BEND → BEND

Fishing with a Bubble

Like most fishermen, I always associated spin fishing with metal lures, and used the fly rod for feathers. Then one day Joe Bates, Jr., the well-known spinning expert, introduced me to a small plastic bubble-shaped ball. The ball has put some extra fish in my creel, now and again.

I still prefer the fly rod for fly fishing, but there are times when the spinning outfit comes in handy for throwing flies, particularly when an extremely long cast is needed to reach choice water or when there isn't room for a back cast.

121

To fish the bubble, tie a dropper strand into your line a foot or two from the end. Attach the bubble to the end of the line and hang the fly of your choice on the dropper. Open the little port hole in the bubble and let in enough water to provide the needed casting weight, leaving air space for flotation, and close the hole with the attached plug. When the bubble comes to rest on the water, out there farther than you could hope to cast with a fly rod, it looks exactly like a water bubble, and the shyest trout will come under it to take the fly.

The bubble is also useful for bait fishing. Fasten the partially-filled ball to the end of the line and add an extension of monofilament leader. Attach your hook and, if you want to fish your bait deep while using the bubble as a float, nip on a split shot or two for casting weight. This works wonderfully well on big water, both lake and stream.

TAP'S TIPS

⟨ When a spinning lure hooks bottom, let the line hang loose for a minute before trying to yank it free. As the lure sags down it may drift off the snag, or the current may pull it away. Applying force usually results in a broken line and lost lure anyway.

⟨ To make longer casts with small spinning lures, use the lightest monofilament that is practical and reduce drag tension on the reel. Four-pound test line is amply strong for trout and bass if the fish is played properly.

⟨ River smallmouths love hellgrammites, especially if these large, ugly dobson larvae are native to the stream. To find out, turn over flat stones and hold a net in the current below. The smaller nymphs will pass through the netting, but the hellgrammites will cling to it long enough to let you pick them off.

The Amazing Trout Bug

Fishing below the flood control dam on the Blackwater River in New Hampshire one afternoon last spring, I caught four trout almost on successive casts, and each of them in a completely different way.

The first, a 12-inch brown, rose confidently in a glassy slick and took a drag-free float inches away from a natural. The second fish, another brown, chased my lure halfway across the tail of the same pool and boiled under it like a tormented largemouth lunging at a popper. In the riffle below the pool a rainbow plucked at my lure as it drifted like a loose caddis just under the surface, and held it barely long enough

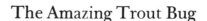

122

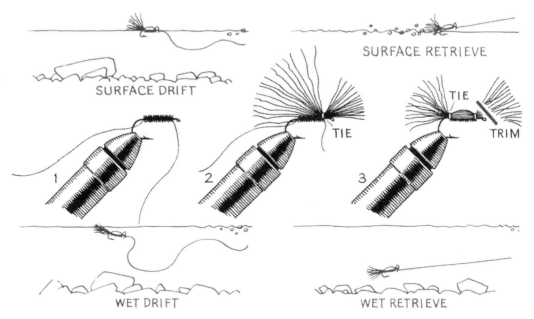

SURFACE RETRIEVE

SURFACE DRIFT

TIE

TIE

TRIM

1

2

3

WET DRIFT

WET RETRIEVE

to let me ease the barb into him. The fourth trout, a small brown, hung himself solidly on a deep quartering retrieve through a run of broken water.

If you assume, as any fisherman naturally would, that I changed from a dry fly to a nymph and then to a wet fly or streamer to take these fish, you are wrong. They all came—and quite willingly, note—to the same lure, and it wasn't any of these. It was, in fact, a bug, just a pinch of deer hair tied down over a peacock herl body, a lure any novice tyer could make in a couple of minutes.

On the rivers hereabouts we call the thing a Cooper Bug. It bears a little resemblance to the famous Tuttle Devil Bug, and it also has some of the characteristics of the equally famous Muddler Minnow. However, it is not a copy of either, and in my opinion it is a more versatile lure than both. Nearly every fisherman I know who has given the Cooper Bug an honest chance to show what it can do says it is the greatest thing that has happened to trout fishing since someone thought of putting barbs on hooks.

You can hang on one of these little bugs and catch trout at the surface in almost exactly the same way you take bass with a popping bug, except that the Cooper Bug doesn't pop. If you spot a fish rising, you can drop the bug above him and as often as not he will come to it as willingly as he would come to a match-the-hatch dry fly. When the bug soaks up a little water you can fish it as a nymph, drifting dead just under the surface. Or you can simply throw it out and twitch it back like a wet fly or streamer. That's what I like about the Cooper Bug: one way or another, it will go out and round up some trout for you.

If you would like to try these amazing little trout bugs yourself—and I can almost promise you will have some fun with them—you probably won't be able to buy them in a store. However, the sketch shows you how to tie them. First fasten winding silk at each end of the hook shank and build up the body with peacock herl. Tie a hank of deerhair to the head end, just behind the eye, then tie it down tightly at the bend of the hook, so it forms a hump over the body. Clip the hair close around the head and push back the short ends so you can poke your leader through the eye. That's all there is to it.

I use mostly 12's, but I carry a few 16's for low-water fishing and also some 8's for the big rivers and for casting into the lakeshores for landlocked salmon. Color seems to be of little consequence. I carry a few Cooper Bugs made with white and yellow hair and have fooled around with different body materials, but if the fish are inclined to take the funny-looking thing at all, they usually come readily to a bug made with natural gray hair and herl body.

TAP'S TIPS

❪ A set of muffin tins makes a convenient storage bin for the fly tying bench. Use as many sections as needed for hooks and small bits of material, the others for keeping flies separated according to patterns or sizes.

❪ Never put moth repellent in a plastic fly box. The crystals or balls soften and discolor the plastic and ruin not only the box but sometimes the flies as well. If flies are stored over the winter in a plastic box, seal the edges with tape.

❪ To make sure that wet flies will sink readily, tie them with materials that absorb water—wool bodies and feathers from crows, hawks, owls, grouse, or barnyard hens, and use heavy wire hooks. Some fishermen hold the fly flat in their mouth for a moment before tying it on, to let it soak up a little saliva.

One Fly for Every Hatch

Smoke-colored mayflies were hovering over the pool as I dropped my fly on the slick at its tail, where a trout had shown himself a moment before. As the fly drifted easily into the quickening current, the fish rose again and took it down with him.

Whether I landed this particular trout, and how big it was, has no

124

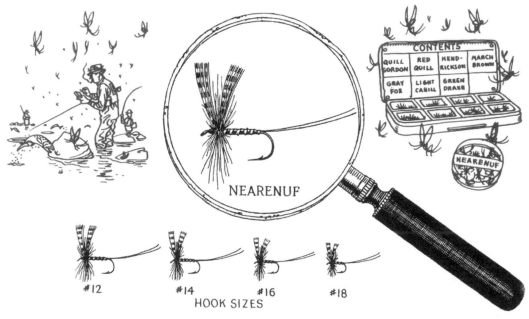

NEARENUF

#12 #14 #16 #18
HOOK SIZES

bearing on this report, although I did land him, and estimated him at 13 inches before turning him loose.

What does matter is that the brown had been rising steadily to a hatch of Quill Gordons in clear, shallow water where it could easily spot a phony. Yet it had taken a different pattern without the slightest hesitation.

During the trout seasons of '59 and '60 the same thing happened to me many times on several hard-fished rivers, and during hatches of many different species of mayflies. Throughout these two seasons I used only one dry-fly pattern, regardless of what fly was hatching, without ever making an effort to match the hatch. Yet I think I caught as many trout as I ever did in two seasons, and apparently as many as other fishermen who were trying to match whatever fly was coming off the water at the time.

Meanwhile, reports coming in from Harold Blaisdell, fishing the transparent trout rivers of Vermont, and from Len Putnam, on the heavily pounded streams of coastal New England, tallied with my own experience. A single dry-fly pattern can take trout in almost any mayfly hatch.

Our idea in putting the pattern together originally was to blend elements of the standard flies that best imitate the hatches most common to our section of the country. These are the Quill Gordon, Red Quill and its female the Hendrickson, March Brown, Gray Fox, Light Cahill

125

and occasionally, Green Drake. The fly wouldn't imitate any of these patterns perfectly, of course. We just hoped that it would be near enough to fool the fish. We now think it is, and that's what we call it, the Nearenuf.

It would be foolish to say that the Nearenuf will take fish better than any of the standard imitative patterns. But if the experience of three dedicated dry-fly fishermen over several full seasons means anything, the fly will raise fish in any of the common hatches, and offers an acceptable substitute for many of the popular dry-fly patterns found in most fly boxes.

When I give you the dressing for this fly you will see that its body, hackle, and wings are similar to many of the most popular imitative American dry-fly patterns. Only the tail is different, to give it a buggier look and to keep it riding high on the water.

If you use the Nearenuf, your only problem will be to match the size of the hatching flies, a much simpler matter than trying first to identify whatever those things are that are dancing over the water, and then to match them in both pattern and size, which generally involves much fumble-fingered tying on and snipping off of flies the fish don't seem to want.

Sizes 14 and 16 have been the most useful for us, and we tie most of our Nearenufs in those two sizes. However, we carry a few 12's for heavy-water fishing and in the hope of finding the Green Drakes hatching, plus some 18's for the low-water half of the season when the smaller flies show up. With this range of sizes, and relieved of the worry about what pattern we should tie on, we can concentrate on the important matter of fishing the fly properly. And for all we know, perhaps that's the real reason we have been so successful in taking trout with it.

Here's the dressing:

Wings: Woodduck side feather, split and upright.

Hackle: Mixed dark ginger and grizzly.

Body: Quill from peacock eye.

Tail: Two stripped grizzly hackles, flared and tied extra long.

As you see, the Nearenuf is actually a mongrel that looks a little like a great many old reliable dry fly patterns—near enough, at least, to fool the trout.

TAP'S TIPS

⟨ Wet flies and nymphs improve with age. The more chewed-up they get, the better the fish seem to like them. This is not true, however, of dry flies. As soon as a dry becomes matted and no longer stands up on its tiptoes, take it off and tie on a fresh one.

126

❮ Which is more important in trout flies, pattern or size? The answer depends on whether the fly is a wet or a dry. Most fishermen agree that the pattern of a sinking fly is more important than its size, the size of a dry fly at least equally as important, if not more so, than its pattern. However, that is a broad generality, and at times the reverse is true. Smart fishermen try to find a fly that looks good to fish in both size and pattern.

Fly Tying Tricks

Most beginning fly tyers have trouble setting wing and tail material in proper position on top of the hook. Until they get the hang of it, the materials twist around the shank or lean drunkenly to one side or the other. But here's a simple way to make things sit up where they belong:

Pinch the material—matched wings for a wet fly, for example—between the thumb and forefinger of the left hand and bring the fingers, still pinched firmly together, down over the shank of the hook at the point where the material is to be tied in. You are now pinching both the material and the hook shank, with the material in correct position.

Now pick up the tying thread with your right hand (southpaws please reverse these directions) and bring it up between your thumb and the material without relaxing the pinching fingers. Carry the thread over the material loosely and force it down between forefinger and material on the other side of the shank. Then draw the thread down tightly. This closes the loop and binds the material down snugly to the top of the hook shank. Continue pinching, and repeat the process. Then relax the pressure enough to slide the pinching fingers back just a bit to expose the two windings, and make two or three tight turns in the same place. This anchors the material permanently in position. Throw a half hitch over the winding to prevent it from loosening, or let the weight of the thread bobbin hold it while you get ready for the next step.

Although I have tied flies for nearly 30 years, and once even wrote a small book about it, I always had trouble setting the wings on fanwing dry flies until Harold Blaisdell showed me this trick. Bind waxed thread to the hook at the point where the wings should go, and select a matched pair of duck breast feathers. Strip the down and surplus fibers from the quills. Place the feathers back to back and grasp them with thumb and forefinger of the left hand pointing *down* the feathers—not across them, as would seem more natural. Then straddle the quills over the hook shank just ahead of the thread.

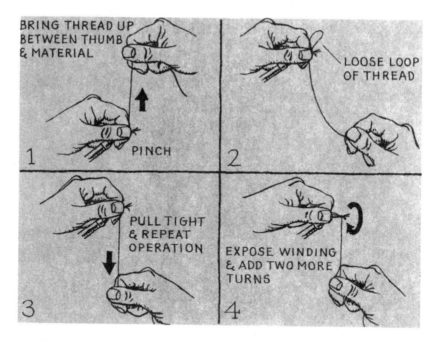

The trick to setting the fanwings in correct position is to take four turns of thread without moving the left hand. The first two turns are made by bringing the thread up from behind the quills and sliding it between the thumb and the quill on the near side of the hook, looping it loosely in front of both quills, and then carrying it down between the forefinger and the quill on the far side. Draw this loop down firmly without relaxing the grip on the feathers. Then bring the thread behind the quills at the bottom and make another turn in the same manner.

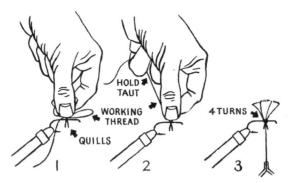

The next two turns are a little more difficult, as they are made ahead of the quills under the hook, and behind them on top of the hook, while still holding the wing firmly in position. But there's a helpful trick to this, too. When the thread is brought up behind the wings, curl the little finger of the left hand around the thread to hold it taut. Reach under the hook with the right hand, grasp the taut section of thread, and bring it down in front of the quills at the bottom to complete the turn. Repeat with another full turn, hold the thread under tension, and release the wings. If the left hand didn't move while the four turns were made, the wings should sit perfectly erect. If they do, draw the quills back along the bottom of the hook shank, bind them down with thread and trim off the surplus. If they don't, try it again, and this time try to hold them more firmly in position while making those four turns.

Many fly tyers finish off the head of a fly with a series of half hitches. That is the easy way to do it, but sometimes the last half hitch comes loose, and then the next to last hitch lets go, and soon the head of the fly starts to come apart. That's why all skilled tyers use the whip finish. It looks tricky to tie, and sounds even trickier when the step-by-step directions are set in type, but it is really quite easy.

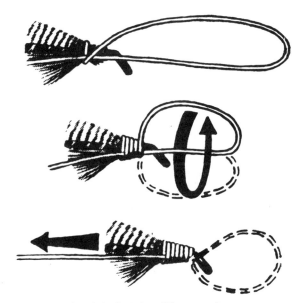

Hold the end of the tying thread in the left hand—still assuming you are right-handed—and form a loop in the thread with the middle and forefinger of the right hand, and then turn the loop to make the thread cross itself close to the hook. Lay the thread that you are holding in your left hand parallel with the hook, and keep it in that position, under slight tension. Then use the two fingers of the right hand to rotate the loop several times over the head of the fly, guiding the turns with the forefinger. The sketches show how this buries the standing part of the thread under several of its own turns. To complete the finish, pinch the loop and draw it tight.

TAP'S TIPS

HACKLE FEATHER

STRIPPED QUILL

{ One of the best materials for dry-fly tails is the quill of a hackle feather from which the fiber has been stripped. Use two or three of the slightly curved tips, tied so they spread out. They help to support the fly and give the pattern a more lifelike appearance.

{ Use the green-and-gold quills from the peacock eye (not from the bronze-colored plume) to make striped quill bodies. The fuzz can be removed by scraping the quill with a razor blade or by soaking it briefly in Clorox, but most tyers favor rubbing it off with an eraser. A thin coat of clear fingernail polish makes the body more durable.

{ Many fly patterns call for spun fur bodies, made mostly from the fine underhair of muskrats and other animals that live near water. Spin a pinch of hair on doubled, heavily-waxed thread, roll it between the palms and wind it tightly along the shank of the hook. There's something about it that fish like.

{ All wobbling lures will spin if retrieved too fast. They should be fished very slowly, so they just flop and flutter. Be sure to use a swivel, preferably tied into the leader about 6 inches above the lure. It not only prevents line-twist, but gives the lure freedom to turn and twist freely.

{ When metal lures become stained or tarnished, their original flash can be restored with household silver polish. To preserve the sparkle, coat them with thinned clear fingernail lacquer. It chips, but can be renewed quickly and easily.

{ If your rod doesn't have a keeper ring to prevent the lure from catching in the brush while you are moving from one fishing spot to another, fasten it to the shaft with a pipe cleaner. The pliable wire goes on and off easily and quickly.

{ As a general rule, big fish spend most of their time in deep water. This is undoubtedly the most important single factor in fishing for the big ones. A small bait fished on bottom can take more large fish than a big bait fished in shallow water or close to the surface.

{ To prepare a fish for mounting, measure its length and then its girth at 1-inch intervals, marking the measurements on an outline drawing. Slit the skin from gills to tail along one side. Remove eyes and gills and separate skin from flesh carefully. Keep the skin in a glass jar, with some salt to preserve it, until you can get it to the taxidermist.

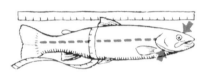

TACKLE AND GEAR

The Deadliest Rod

MANY FISHERMEN seem to think that the fly rod is the most "sportsman-like" rod to use because, being primarily an implement of light tackle, it theoretically gives the fish a better chance to escape.

Personally, I feel that the rod a fisherman uses has nothing whatever to do with his stature as a sportsman. That is something that lies entirely within the fisherman himself, and it has no relation to the way he fishes or to the tackle he uses. A man can be a fish hog with a fly rod as easily as he can with a cane pole. Easier perhaps.

Most experienced fishermen agree that the fly rod is an extremely efficient tool, even a deadly one in the hands of someone skilled in its use. With a fly rod he can cast small lures that imitate a tremendous variety of fish foods, and use such fine terminal gear that he can interest fish which would shy away from coarser tackle used by bait casters, spinners, and trollers. Obviously, the ability to hook a greater number of fish does not enhance the fly fisherman's stature as a sportsman. Quite the opposite, in fact, if he injures many of them or stuffs them in his creel.

After a fish has been hooked with a fly rod, the length and resiliency

131

of the shaft tire him quickly. Merely by holding the rod upright the fisherman can force the fish to exhaust itself by fighting the spring of the shaft.

Other types of rods are springy, too. But being shorter and relatively stiffer, they provide a smaller margin of safety when a heavy fish throws his weight and strength against the shaft. A sudden hard surge can tear the hook loose or break the line. Jumping fish are more difficult to handle with a short rod.

If the fisherman handles every fish perfectly, it doesn't much matter what kind of a rod he uses. But all fishermen make mistakes in the excitement of wrestling with larger-than-average fish, which accounts for the great number of stories about the big ones that get away. Mistakes made with a fly rod simply are not so costly as those made with stiffer, heavier gear.

A fly-rod fisherman with plenty of backing on his reel should be able to lick any fish that can be played and landed with a spinning, bait-casting, or trolling rod—and, in my opinion, some that couldn't.

TAP'S TIPS

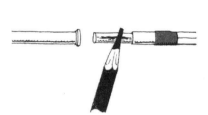

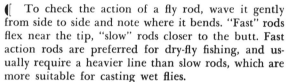
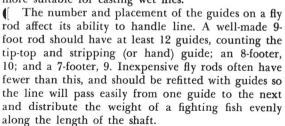

⟨[To check the action of a fly rod, wave it gently from side to side and note where it bends. "Fast" rods flex near the tip, "slow" rods closer to the butt. Fast action rods are preferred for dry-fly fishing, and usually require a heavier line than slow rods, which are more suitable for casting wet flies.

⟨[The number and placement of the guides on a fly rod affect its ability to handle line. A well-made 9-foot rod should have at least 12 guides, counting the tip-top and stripping (or hand) guide; an 8-footer, 10; and a 7-footer, 9. Inexpensive fly rods often have fewer than this, and should be refitted with guides so the line will pass easily from one guide to the next and distribute the weight of a fighting fish evenly along the length of the shaft.

⟨[The graphite in a common lead pencil is an excellent lubricant for sticky rod ferrules. However, if ferrules come apart reluctantly, first make sure they are clean and that the female end is not dented out of round. Ferrules that fit properly should not need lubrication.

What's Your Line?

Most fishermen agree that a double-tapered fly line is the easiest for a beginner to handle, and I agree, but not completely. A great many Saturday fishermen will find a level line just as satisfactory, and some

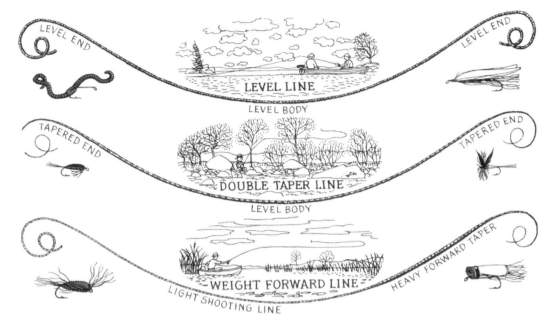

LEVEL END   LEVEL LINE   LEVEL END

LEVEL BODY

TAPERED END   DOUBLE TAPER LINE   TAPERED END

LEVEL BODY

WEIGHT FORWARD LINE   HEAVY FORWARD TAPER

LIGHT SHOOTING LINE

might feel justified in splurging on a weight-forward line. Like so many things in this uncertain world, it depends.

As you know, a double-tapered line is really nothing more than a level line with tapered ends. A weight-forward line has a heavy belly out near the front so the caster can shoot it more easily. That's oversimplifying the matter, but those are the essential differences.

Now keep in mind that you can buy a level line for a great deal less than a tapered line of comparable quality. My purpose here is to save you needless expense when you put together a new fly fishing outfit, if I can.

Selecting the right fly line can become pretty complicated because, unlike a spinning or bait casting line, it must not only fit the rod but it must also be suitable for whatever kind of fishing you want to do. You must decide whether it should be level or tapered, whether it should sink or float and, most important, you must find out what size (weight, really) will match the power and action of the rod.

The simplest way I know to fit a fly line to a new rod is to borrow lines of different sizes from a well-stocked friend and cast with them until you find one that feels right. Or better yet, if your friend is an experienced fly caster, ask him to do it for you.

Whether the line should sink or float depends on what kind of fishing you plan to do. If you're not sure, play it safe and get a floater. You can always sink a floating line—with a couple of split shot if necessary—but you can't always make a sinking line float.

Level or tapered? Here's where you may be able to stuff a few bills back in your wallet. The reason for tapering the end of a fly line is to make it roll out smoothly, turn over, and then drop lightly to the water. That's why the tapered line rates the odds-on favorite with dry-fly fishermen and fine-and-far-off nymphers.

A level line is entirely suitable for trolling flies and bait fishing. If you think you might want to use it occasionally for more delicate work you can soften its delivery by making a tapered leader for it. Start with a very heavy butt piece of 30-, even 40-pound monofilament and tie on graduating strands of 20, 15, 10, 6, and 4 pound, down to any point you want—1X, 3X, 5X. The heavy end of the leader will form coils from being wound on the reel, but you can straighten them out pretty well by stretching the leader or pulling it through a doubled piece of rubber cut from an old inner tube.

The weight-forward line is designed primarily for distance casting and throwing heavy bugs. It isn't difficult to cast, once you catch on to the timing, but it isn't any easier for the beginner, either. Also, it doesn't roll out quite as smoothly as a double-tapered line. Unless you're very careful, it has a way of slapping the water and putting down rising fish.

However, the weight-out-front line may be just the ticket for a very light rod—say, a stick of about 7 feet that weighs between 2 and 3 ounces. Such rods don't take kindly to a lot of false-casting, being neither long enough nor gutty enough to carry the load. But you don't have to wave a forward-taper line back and forth very much. Once you get the heavy belly section going you can just slam the line out hard and it will carry the lighter shooting section right along with it.

So as you see, choosing the right fly line for a new rod can become a bit complicated. But you can save yourself some money and have more fun fishing if the line you choose fits your rod and suits your method— especially if you can get along without those expensive tapered ends.

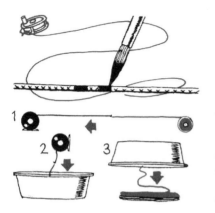

TAP'S TIPS

《 If you'd like to know how much fly line you are casting, mark it at 20-foot intervals with narrow bands of paint—two bands at 20 feet, four at 40, and so on. To mark braided bait casting line, sew in colored thread, using a small needle. Marking the line helps you to find and maintain the right trolling depth, too

《 Instead of guessing how much backing you will need to make a new fly line fill a reel, wind the line on the reel first and then add the necessary amount of backing. Then strip backing and line into a dishpan and turn the pan upside down. This reverses the lines so the backing can be wound on the reel first.

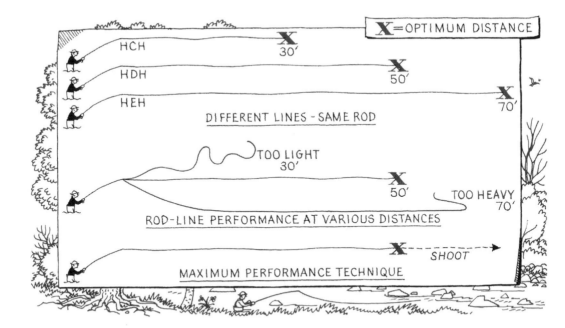

How to "Match" a Fly Rod and Line

If you think you could become a better fly caster if your rod and line balanced perfectly, you are probably right. I think I could, too. But unhappily, there is no way to match up a line with a rod so they will perform at peak efficiency every time you cast. In a vague sort of way, an expert caster is conscious of this imbalance, and compensates for it. To the beginner, it can be a problem.

When a rodmaker recommends the line size that should fit a fly rod, he can base his recommendation on only one thing, the rod's action. The length and weight of the stick have little bearing on the matter. A soft-action rod performs best with a light line, such as an HEH, while a rod that is stiffer, and hence "faster," needs the extra weight of an HDH or even an HCH. But the rodmaker has no way of knowing whether the man who buys his rod is an expert caster or a novice, a long-line fisherman or a short-line fisherman, a false caster or a line shooter. So if he recommends an HDH line—or a DT6, as it is called now—that size may or may not fit both the rod and the fisherman's style of casting.

The chief reason, of course, is that no one always casts the same length of line. An HDH may have just the right amount of weight to cast well at 50 feet, but the same line on the same rod will feel wispy

135

when it is cast only 30 feet, and noticeably heavy when the fisherman tries to drive out a 70-footer.

The difference in line weight at these distances is greater than many fishermen realize. The first 30 feet of D in an HDH line weighs about 160 grains; the first 50 feet weighs about 265; and 70 feet of D line weighs about 370. Obviously, a rod that can throw 160 grains of line easily would labor under the burden of 370 grains.

Since a rod and line will be out of balance when the fisherman shortens or lengthens his casts, he will have to settle for a compromise of balance by fitting the rod with a line that performs satisfactorily at his average casting distance.

If he is not an expert caster, he may be wise to use a line one size heavier than the rodmaker recommended. The extra weight will develop the power in the rod at short distances without danger of overloading it.

The average-good caster can safely follow the rodmaker's advice. Then if he finds that the line doesn't snake out as easily as he thinks it should, he can get a little more weight out front by trimming back the front taper. If you try this with a new fly line, just be sure you don't cut off too much, because you will need some of that light line out there when you drop a fly over a scary fish.

After shortening the H end of the line a little you should discover that the rod feels especially good in your hand when you have a certain amount of line out—probably somewhere between 30 and 50 feet. That's because the weight of the line balances the action of the rod at that point. Remember where it is. Then, when you want to make a long cast, work out line by false casting until you reach the point of balance, and shoot more line to gain the extra distance. That is how an experienced fly caster compensates for the imbalance of his rod and line. He simply finds the line length where they do come into balance, and shoots as much additional line as he needs—up to a point, of course.

So anyone who learns how to shoot line can stop worrying about whether his line fits his rod, and get on with his fishing.

TAP'S TIPS

⟨[When rod ferrules refuse to part company, call your fishing partner and have him place his hands on each side of the balky joint, put your hands over his and exert steady pressure. If you are alone, clamp the rod under your knees, squat, and spread your legs slowly, keeping your hands braced against the outside of your knees. If that fails, pour a drop or two of carbon tetrachloride in the shoulder of the female section and let it soak overnight.

❡ A wooden nail keg, free at most lumber yards and building supply houses, can be made into a useful and decorative rod-case holder. Clean the keg, bend over nail ends, and paint it flat black, using a contrasting color for the hoops. A second keg, similarly painted, can be used for a matching wastebasket.

❡ If you want to "balance" a fly rod with a reel, remember the old rule-of-thumb that says the reel and line together should weigh about 1½ times as much as the rod. This is a fairly reliable rule, and you can test it by putting a light reel on a heavy rod. You will be surprised to find how much heavier the rod will feel in your hand.

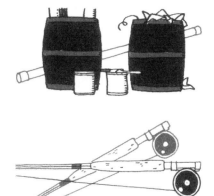

Line Loops and Splices

There are several ways to attach leader to fly line and fly line to backing—with a knot, a splice, a metal eyelet, or with interlocking loops.

Ideally, the connection should be smooth so it can pass easily through the rod guides, and simple so that a new leader can be attached with a minimum of fuss and bother.

Most leader-to-line connections made with knots and wraparounds have a way of rattling as they go through the guides, and if the connection is the least bit bulky it may hang up on a guide just long enough to allow a good fish to break free.

When the eyed metal pins first came on the market I swore I would never use them, because I felt sure they would not hold a heavy fish. I have since changed my opinion of them. However, I have never completely trusted the barbed shanks to hold, so I whip a few turns of thread tightly around the line where the shank of the pin is inserted. This snugs the fabric core of the line around the barbs so tightly they can't possibly pull loose.

Even so, I prefer the spliced loops. I hope that some day one of the line manufacturers will produce fly lines with ready-looped ends, even if they have to add an extra dollar to the price of the line. In the meantime, we who prefer loops to knots and metal pins will have to make them ourselves. This is how to do it:

Scrape the finish off the last ¼ inch of line and fray the core fabric by picking the threads apart with a needle or pin. Bend the end of the line back to form a small loop and scrape the finish off the line where the frayed section lays against it. Taper the frayed end with sharp scissors and work soft wax into the threads. Re-form the loop, placing the waxed threads against the spot where the finish was scraped off, and wind No. 0000 silk or nylon thread tightly over the joint, covering the tapered end. Complete the winding with a whip finish, roll the splice over a flat surface to make it perfectly smooth, and give it two coats of varnish.

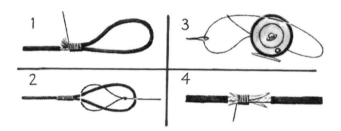

People born with three hands could do this without help, but I find it necessary to have my wife hold the loop while I make the winding. She hooks one end of an opened paper clip through the loop to give me room to work. A buttonhook would be ideal, but since women stopped wearing high-button shoes, buttonhooks have become scarce items.

To connect a leader to a looped line, poke the leader loop through the line loop, thread the leader through its own loop, and draw the two loops together. This forms a connection that looks like a square knot. Line backing is attached in the same manner, except that the loop in the backing must be large enough to pass over the reel. This connection slides smoothly through the rod guides when a running fish takes line into the backing, and also makes it possible to reverse a line, or change from one line to another, quickly and easily.

Splicing two sections of fly line is just as simple. Scrape the finish back for a ¼ inch at each end, fray the threads and wax them. Split the ends to form three-legged forks (see drawing on page 138), and taper them with scissors. Fit the forks together snugly and meld them to the line by rolling them between the fingers. Start the winding in the middle, where the crotches of the forked ends come together. Then wind 0000 thread from the middle of the splice over the forked ends to the main line, back over the splice to the other end, and then back to the middle. Complete the splice with a whip finish, or invisible knot. Roll the splice smooth, cover it with varnish, and after the last coat of varnish has dried hard and smooth, rub paste wax over the splice and buff it briskly. The resulting splice should be so close to the diameter of the line that it barely ticks when it slithers through the rod guides.

TAP'S TIPS

❲ White nylon thread turns almost transparent when coated with clear varnish or fingernail polish. Used for splicing lines, the thread makes a virtually invisible winding. However, it should be handled with perfectly clean, dry hands, else it will become discolored.

❲ To lengthen the life of a level or double tapered fly line, reverse it on the reel three or four times during the fishing season. Do not wind the line on the reel too tightly, as this forms wiry coils and could even produce flat spots in the finish.

❲ Fly lines don't take kindly to spending the long winter wound tightly on their reels. I strip mine into a suit box punched with holes for ventilation, separating them with newspaper and tucking in a written reminder of the size or type of each and the reel with which it belongs. Some fishermen coil their lines and hang them on a wooden peg, while others wind them on large spools or around an oatmeal box. A few tackle-fussy anglers soak their lines through the winter in mineral oil.

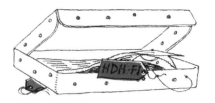

Floating-Sinking Fly Lines

Fish can be captious creatures at times, and trout more so than any. As a case in point, observe what so often happens when you gear up to fish a dry fly with a freshly-dressed floating line. The instant you draw the knot tight on your fly, the trout stop rising and begin grubbing stuff off the bottom. Conversely, if you have just finished stringing a sinking line through the guides of your rod, to fish a streamer or wet fly, every trout in the river promptly starts slurping at the surface.

Knowing that this can happen, and that it very probably will, many trout fishermen carry two fly reels, one loaded with sinking line, the other with a floater. Then whichever the trout take it into their silly heads to do, it's just a simple matter of switching reels. The only trouble with this arrangement is that the extra reel and line cost from $15 to $25 or more. It works out very well for line and reel manufacturers, but somewhat less ideally for indigent fishermen.

Here is how you can save money for both yourself and your fishing partner. Cut your double-tapered floating line and his sinking line— the same taper, of course—exactly in half and splice the floating ends to the sinking ends (see "Line Loops and Splices," page 138). Each of you will then have a complete tapered line that can be reversed for fish-

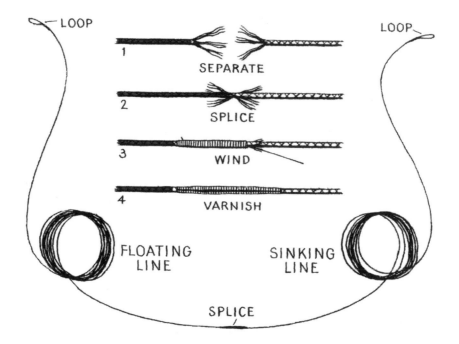

1   SEPARATE

2   SPLICE

3   WIND

4   VARNISH

LOOP   LOOP

FLOATING LINE   SINKING LINE

SPLICE

ing with either top-water or sunken lures. Splice loops in the ends, or insert eyed pins, so the line can be attached easily to backing and leader when you swap ends.

True, it takes a little longer to reverse a line than to change reels. Stripping the line out, detaching and reattaching leader and backing and reeling it back in again consumes about 2½ minutes (I timed it) if you don't dawdle. But I don't think you will dawdle much if you do it while trout are rising like crazy all up and down the river.

Author's note: Readers who recoil from the thought of cutting a perfectly good fly line in half will be relieved to learn that Cortland Line Co. now manufactures a reversible floating-sinking fly line. Sold under the familiar Cortland 333 label, this top-quality line is available in all double-taper sizes.

TAP'S TIPS

❨ Overdressing a fly line with floatant makes it sticky and prevents it from sliding freely through the rod guides. Apply the dressing evenly and sparingly, then wipe off the surplus with a clean cloth. The line will shoot much easier when you drive out a long cast.

❨ Cracks in the finish of a fly line can be repaired

140

by winding over them neatly with No. 0000 silk or nylon thread. Complete the winding with a whip finish and roll it over a hard, flat surface until it is perfectly smooth, then give it two or three coats of varnish.

Leaders

Nylon has now almost completely replaced silkworm gut as the material for making leaders. A few oldtime fly fishermen still prefer gut, and delight in proclaiming its superiority over the synthetic stuff the rest of us use, but their arguments are supported mainly by tradition and sentiment. Nylon is a far better material for leaders than gut ever was. It is cheaper, stronger, more uniform in diameter; it does not deteriorate from age, and it doesn't have to be soaked before it can be used. As far as the fisherman is concerned, the silkworm will just have to look around for something else to do.

However, we have retained the same general size designations that were used for drawn gut. When silkworm gut was drawn through holes in a die plate, it was called 1X, 3X, 5X and so on, according to the size of the hole and the number of times the strand of gut was reduced in diameter by drawing it through successively smaller holes.

Nylon is not drawn this way. However, the X sizes have been retained, doubtless because doing so made it easier to wean fishermen from gut to nylon when the chemical product was first introduced. So nylon marked "1X" is approximately the same diameter as 1X gut, although not necessarily the same pound test.

The manner in which a tapered leader is graduated, and also its length, have a great deal to do with the number of fish that find their way into the wicker morgue.

The purpose of the leader, obviously, is to form an invisible (to the fish) connection between your line and your fly or bait. Sometimes tying on a fine tippet—say, 5X or even 6X or 7X—will do the trick nicely. But sometimes it isn't enough.

Many fishermen use only one length of leader for nearly all their fishing. The popular lengths are 7½ feet (for some obscure reason) and "as long as the rod." These lengths are fine for fishing small streams or casting in a wind. You might even cut off a couple feet if the wind gets heavy or you move into cramped quarters where you haven't much casting room.

However, when you come to one of those long, flat pools of glassy water and find trout dimpling all over it, a 7½-foot or rod's-length leader may not be nearly long enough. Twelve feet is more like it, 15

feet even better. True, you may have some trouble laying it out, but the long flats give you plenty of room to cast, and you'll be throwing a long line anyway.

As you move from one kind of water to another, you will want to change the length of your leader to suit different conditions, and to improve your chances of taking fish in each. Changing leaders is simple if you carry a supply in different lengths—say, 6, 7½, 9, 12, and 15 feet or merely 6, 9, and 15. Personally, I find it easier to stay with one leader and simply to cut off or add tippets. The reason for this is that a leader should match the line to which it is attached. The butt of the leader and the tip of the line should be of approximately the same weight (not necessarily diameter) so the line-leader connection will roll out smoothly without breaking the curve of the line. Therefore, when I build a leader that performs well with the line, I leave it on permanently and lengthen it or shorten it by adding extra tippets or cutting it back.

One of the major advantages nylon offers over silkworm gut is that it does not have to be soaked before it can be used. However, there is also a disadvantage inherent in this. Dry nylon floats. Ideally the leader, or at least the last few feet of it, should sink so it will be less visible to the fish. I have given up trying to sink nylon, and try to reduce its visibility by using extremely light tippets and by casting curves, so the fly drifts over the fish ahead of the leader. But before I gave up I tried

142

many different ways of encouraging a leader to sink. All of them worked to a degree, and perhaps I would catch more trout if I tried harder to get my leader under water, instead of putting my faith in cobweb tippets and curve casts.

Here are some of the methods you can try to sink a nylon leader: Soak it before use between felt pads moistened with water, glycerine, or household detergent; rub it with soap, toothpaste, mud, or fish slime (don't ask *me* where you can get the slime. Perhaps you can borrow some from a spin fisherman); dress it with a commercial preparation such as Lo-Leader; split a No. 9 shot and clamp it above the next-to-the-last leader knot. Or you might like to try the nature's remedy my friend West Jordan, the Orvis rod-builder, told me about: Mash some alder leaves between your fingers and rub the pulp into the leader. It works about as well as any of them.

TAP'S TIPS

❮ Limp monofilament is wonderful stuff on a spinning reel, but not on the end of a dry-fly leader, as it is too soft to turn the fly over properly. Use nylon sold as "leader material" or "tippets"; it is worth the extra cost.

❮ If the knots you tie in nylon tend to slip, touch the end of the strands to your pipe or cigarette. The heat swells the tips, which jam when you tighten the knot.

❮ To take the kinks out of a leader, pull it through a tightly folded square of inner tube rubber. If the kinks prove stubborn, warm the leader first by placing it on a sun-baked rock or, even better, in warm water—or the thermos coffee.

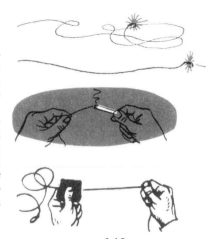

143

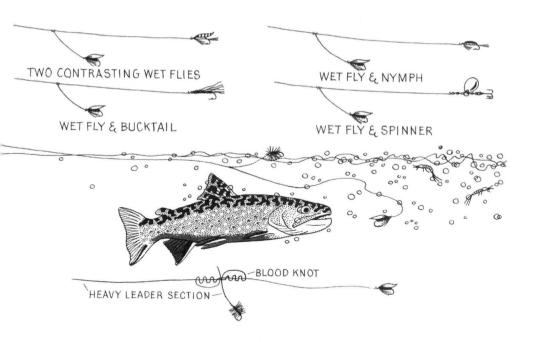

TWO CONTRASTING WET FLIES

WET FLY & BUCKTAIL

WET FLY & NYMPH

WET FLY & SPINNER

BLOOD KNOT

HEAVY LEADER SECTION

Dropper Fly Dope

If you're like me, you probably start to lose faith in a fly almost as soon as you tie it on, and by the time you have made a dozen casts with it you begin to think you ought to take it off and try something else. First you change to a different pattern. Then you try a nymph, and immediately start wondering if a small bucktail wouldn't work better. Or a marabou, or a Muddler Minnow. If the water is running low and clear, you may even consider the idea of trying to pound up some fish with a big bivisible—or if the stream is up a bit, digging into a muddy bank for some worms.

Obviously, this is no frame of mind to get yourself into when you want to enjoy an afternoon on the river. The human mind recoils from making decisions. So if you are as incapable as I am of simply tying on your old reliable and leaving it on, I recommend my own solution to the problem: fish with two flies. Three, if it makes your mind any easier.

With more than one fly on your leader you can offer the fish a number of interesting combinations—two contrasting patterns of wet flies, a wet fly and a nymph, a small bucktail and a wet fly, or whatever

144

suits your fancy. A particularly deadly combination is a small Colorado spinner with a wet fly or bucktail tied above it. Fish may ignore the spinner but, no doubt attracted by the flash of its blade, come readily to the dropper fly, and stop coming to it when you take off the spinner to try something else.

As you know, you miss a great many light strikes when fishing a single wet fly or nymph. The dead-drifting fly is so difficult to locate in broken water you fail to see the glint of fish that come up to it, take it briefly, and let it go. Try fishing a white-winged wet fly or bushy floater as a dropper fly. It not only helps you to keep your tail fly accurately located, but also serves as a signal to tell you when a fish nips at it.

Occasionally you will hook two fish at a time when fishing with a dropper. When you do, it is strictly plumcake, like scoring a clean left-and-right double from a covey rise. Sometimes the flurries of a struggling fish attract a second fish, and if you prolong the fight a little he may grab the loose fly. This has happened to me more than once while trolling a brace of streamers for landlocked salmon, and many times when fishing for wilderness brook trout.

Back in the day when flies were tied on gut snells, the flies were attached to the leader by means of loops. The native-born squaretails of that era didn't seem to mind the loops, but the more sophisticated trout of the present day would dive for cover at the sight of one. However, even a cagy brown will come to an eyed fly tied neatly to a short whisker of nylon. To make the dropper strand, simply retie the leader two or three feet from the end with a Blood knot, leaving one end about 3 inches long—the shorter the better. If the knot joins two diameters of leader material, use the heavier one for the dropper. The short, stiff strand coming from the Blood knot at a right angle holds the fly away from the leader so it won't tangle quite so often.

TAP'S TIPS

❲ To get the most out of a brace of flies, choose contrasting sizes, patterns, colors. If the fish take one fly and ignore the other, change the neglected fly for one that is more like the fly the fish are taking.

❲ Here is a convenient way to store and carry fly line dressing. Cut the bottom off an empty toothpaste tube, open the end and wash out the inside. Then warm the dressing and pour it into the tube. Fold over the cut end twice and crimp it tightly with pliers. You will find it easier to squeeze the dressing out of the tube than to wrestle with the friction lid of a can, especially when your hands are cold.

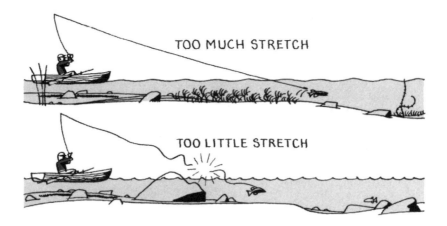

TOO MUCH STRETCH

TOO LITTLE STRETCH

Nylon Nonsense

Buying a spinning line should be a very simple matter. All nylon monofilament is produced from the same basic ingredients and by essentially the same methods. Therefore, one manufacturer's line should be just about as good as another's—unless you happen to believe everything you read in the ads. In that case, you may tend to fret about such things as stretch, limpness, uniformity of diameter, and whether you dare trust the knots you tie in the stuff.

After using many, if not most, of the various brands of spinning line sold in sporting goods stores today, I have come to the conclusion that all of the name-brand lines have as much strength and limpness as I will ever need for making long casts and horsing heavy fish, and that any of them will hold even a granny knot if the knot is drawn together carefully enough.

I don't mean to imply that all monofilament is exactly alike. Machine testing reveals small differences in elasticity, in strength related to diameter, in limpness and knot-holding ability. What I do mean is that for practical fishing purposes these differences are so small you can safely forget them. If you recognize the name on the spool, go ahead and buy it.

But as you shop for the cobweb diameters needed for ultralight spinning, these differences become a little more important. For example, if a UL line stretches a bit more than it should you could have trouble digging your hook into fish that strike at the far end of a long cast. If the line doesn't stretch enough, you may pop it when a fish belts your lure close in, or when you come up hard against a nearby rock. Knots may slip or even cut themselves unless you use only those recommended for nylon, and tie them with extra care. One maker's line may mike just a fraction of a hair's breadth fatter than another's of the same pound test, although that would be nothing to worry about. A 2-pound line that registers .0055 on a micrometer won't cast noticeably better than one that mikes out at .006.

If you owned a micrometer, some testing gear, and had a lot of free time, you could probably find the one line among all lines that might be considered the best line for ultralight spinning—or everyday spinning too, for that matter. Otherwise, you will simply have to rely on what the manufacturers tell you. That is the system I use, and it works just fine for me.

There is, however, one bit of nonsense about buying a spinning line that annoys me. That is the apparent necessity for buying twice as much of it as you need.

When you buy a new spinning machine you always find a little folder in the box that tells you how much line the spool holds. In fact, the manufacturer makes the enormous line capacity of the reel sound like a major advantage to the fisherman. To take a case at random, the Orvis 100, a very fine medium-sized open-faced reel, holds 250 yards of 6-pound line, which is as heavy a line as any knowledgeable fisherman would want to put on a reel of this size. Yet not one fisherman in a hundred would ever use more than 100 yards of it. The rest of the line represents waste, in both the cost of the unused line and in the time it requires to wind it on the spool.

To save the cost of using expensive spinning line as filler, simply fill about half of the spool with backing—old line from another reel if you have it, or several turns of plastic tape cut to the width of the spool—anything to fill the gaping recess of the spool and provide a smooth foundation for the hundred yards or so of line that will be used.

Winding line on the reel spool is a tiresome job if you follow the old method of making ten turns right handed, then ten left handed, to cancel out the twists. A much simpler and quicker way is to use a hand drill of the "egg beater" type, with a twist drill slightly smaller than the hole in the reel spool. Wrap a rubber band around the drill to make

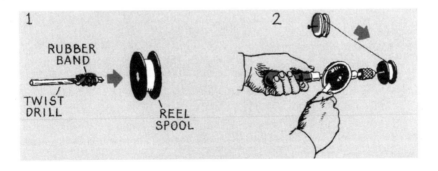

a nonslip fit and also to protect the spool from damage. Force the spool gently over the end of the drill, attach the line, drop the line spool over a nail, and crank the egg beater. The line goes on faster than the eye can follow it, with never a twist or a kink.

While you are at it, think seriously about buying an extra spool for your reel and filling it with much lighter line—say, 2-pound test. The light line will permit you to fish ultralight lures when very low, clear water rules out the larger spinners and wobblers. The tiny thumbnail-sized sparklers weighing between $\frac{1}{8}$ and $\frac{1}{16}$ ounces are deadly during gin-water conditions, and it takes a very light line to throw them out.

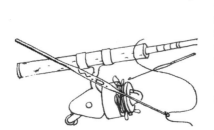

TAP'S TIPS

⟨[Many spin fishermen handicap themselves by using monofilament that is heavier than necessary. The finer the line, the farther and easier you can cast with it. Four-pound test is amply strong for trout and most other fresh-water fish. Carry an extra spool filled with 6-, 8- or 10-pound line for bass fishing in weedy waters, or for pike and muskies.

⟨[To reduce line-twist when fishing with spinning lures, tie a small barrel swivel into the leader about six inches above the lure. This controls twisting better than two swivels fastened to one another immediately ahead of the spinner.

⟨[Tuck some round wooden or plastic toothpicks or, even better, a steel crochet hook, in your pocket when you go spin fishing. Then if your line becomes snarled or underwound on the reel spool you can pick it out in a jiffy—much faster than you could with your fingers.

Knots for Nylon

Every time you tie a knot in your leader or line you weaken it. How much you weaken it depends on the knot you use and how carefully you tie it. For example, when you join two strands of nylon leader material with a Blood knot, you may reduce the strength of the monofilament as much as 20%. If you tie the knot carelessly or incorrectly, you may cut its strength by twice that much. And if you use any other knot, the leader may pop the first time you set the hook in a six-inch bluegill.

So it's worth a little time to learn the basic knots that hold best in nylon monofilament. Fortunately, there aren't many. Any fisherman can get along nicely if he can tie only these four:

148

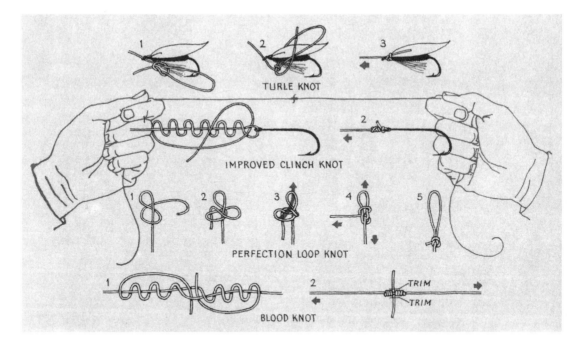

TURLE KNOT

IMPROVED CLINCH KNOT

PERFECTION LOOP KNOT

BLOOD KNOT

TRIM

TRIM

The *Turle knot* (please, not "turtle"; it was named for a Major Turle) is used to tie a leader to a hook that has a turned-up or turned-down eye—never to a ringed-eye hook. This knot grips the hook shank behind the eye and should not be tied directly to the eye itself. The leader passes through the eye in line with the shank, so when you strike a fish the hook moves in a straight line and improves your chance of driving the barb in hard and deep.

To make the Turle knot completely slip-proof in nylon, tuck the end back through the loop before drawing the knot tight. Doing this also bends the short end back so it cannot pick up weeds and grass.

The *Clinch knot,* also called the Jam or Twist knot, is the one most fishermen use to tie a leader or line to a ringed-eye hook or to the eye of a swivel or lure. When used in monofilament this knot should be formed with at least five turns and the end tucked back through the loop before the knot is drawn tight. The end can then be clipped off close without danger that the knot will slip or come apart.

The *Perfection loop,* also known as the Fisherman's loop or Compound knot, is the standard knot for forming a loop in the butt end of a leader. It is also used to make a nonslip loop in bait casting line. The diagram looks complicated, but this is really a simple knot to tie and one every fisherman will use often.

The *Blood knot,* often called the Barrel knot, is used by every capable angler I have ever known for tying leader material and spinning

149

line together. It is not a difficult knot to tie, except when a middle-aged, foggy-eyed fisherman like me tries to tie on a 5X tippet just as dusk settles over the river.

I learned how to tie the Blood knot before the days of nylon, and I was taught to tie it with exactly 3½ turns on each side—never less, never more. The habit has been difficult to break, and I still tie 3½-turn Blood knots today, even in the finer diameters of nylon. The Blood knot as I tie it seems to hold pretty well, but according to my friend Reg Ellis, who works for the Du Pont Company, it shouldn't. Each time I make printed reference to the 3½-turn Blood knot Reg sends me another copy of a Du Pont booklet that tells, among other things, how to tie knots in Du Pont's "Stren"—and, I presume, in other brands of nylon as well. According to the booklet, a Blood knot should be tied with at least five turns around the standing parts of the line. In fact, Du Pont's electronic tensile tester has revealed that a 4-turn Blood knot reduces the strength of 10-pound "Stren" to 8½ pounds, a 3-turn knot to 7½ pounds, and a 2-turn knot to 6 pounds, or a loss of 40 per cent.

So perhaps it would be better to play it safe by tying the Blood knot with a minimum of five turns, as Du Pont suggests—at least in the end tippet of a tapered leader. Always remember to draw the knot together slowly and firmly. Then clip off the ends as closely as possible so the knot won't stutter going through the rod guides.

TAP'S TIPS

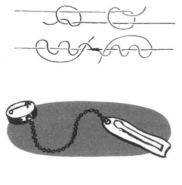

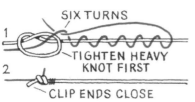

SIX TURNS

1

TIGHTEN HEAVY
KNOT FIRST

2

CLIP ENDS CLOSE

([The Water knot, while not as satisfactory as the Blood knot for tying strands of leader material, is an excellent knot for splicing breaks in braided bait-casting line. It is tied by making two slip knots, each around the standing end of the other. To make the knot doubly secure, add a couple of turns as if it were a Blood knot.

([Check spinning line occasionally where the fore-finger picks it up for casting. The line often shows sign of wear at this point, particularly in ultralight diameters.

([A pin-on recoil spring is just the ticket for keeping leader clippers out of the way but easy to get at. The one I use came from the five-and-dime, and had a small pencil attached to the end of the chain.

([A composite knot—half Water knot, half Jam knot—must be used to tie heavy nylon to light nylon when making a "shock leader" for pike and pickerel fishing. A Blood knot will not hold when used to join two strands of greatly different diameter, but this one will.

Sinkers

The humblest item of fishing equipment is the sinker. Yet the size of the chunk of lead you use often determines whether or not you catch fish, even whether you catch big fish or little ones.

In general, the best rule is to use as little sinker as possible, or none at all if you can get away with it. When you fish with bait, the important thing is to present the bait to the fish in a manner that looks natural and convincing. In still water you can let the bait sink slowly of its own weight, without a sinker. In moving water, use the smallest amount of weight that will carry your bait close to bottom. The faster the current and deeper the water, the more weight you'll need, of course. But by lobbing your bait well upstream and letting it sink as the current washes it into the hole or pocket you want to fish, you can usually steer it into the deep places with only one or two split shot nipped to your leader.

Sometimes you have to add a little extra weight to your artificials, too. Bucktails and streamers generally do their best work when they are fished deep. A slightly weighted artificial nymph is deadly for trout in ponds and deep, still pools. The trick in deadwater nymph fishing is to inch the nymph along close to bottom, and you need a bit of weight to take it down there. If you tie your own flies, you can wrap the hook shank with strip lead (cut from a flattened toothpaste tube) and dress your nymph on the weighed hook.

You can spin-cast streamers, bucktails, and even wet flies quite easily with a small sinker clamped to the line a foot or so above the fly. All minnow-eating warm-water game fish can be taken with weighted streamers if you can get your fly to them with some action in it. And as everyone knows, that's the way to take big trout that can no longer satisfy their gluttonous appetites with flies and nymphs.

So keep a supply of different-sized sinkers on hand and use the smallest one that will take your bait or lure to the fish. You will find that the right-sized sinker, used right, can be worth its weight in lead.

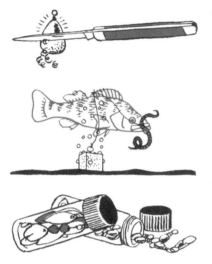

TAP'S TIPS

❴ When you tie on a dipsy sinker for ice fishing, scrape it first with your knife to make it shiny. It will attract fish to the bait or jigging lure.

❴ To make a sinker that will dissolve after it has carried the bait to bottom, mix 4 parts of sand with 1 part ammonia sulphate (fertilizer), and 1 part water. Pour the mixture into an ice cube tray to mold it into squares. Insert U-shaped pieces of wire (don't close the ends) to serve as loop eyes. Bake till hard. The fisherman who told me about this says that the cube gives off bubbles as it dissolves, and that the odor of the fertilizer, plus the bubbles, attracts fish.

❴ Small plastic pill boxes are ideal for carrying such small, easy-to-lose items of gear as sinkers, swivels, split rings, and bait hooks. Your doctor or druggist will probably make you a present of all you can use.

Wading Gear

The framed original of the drawing on the next page hangs on the wall over my writing desk. My eye rests on it every time I glance up from my typewriter, and although I have looked at it hundreds of times, I still consider it a very funny drawing. Significantly, all of my friends who fish in waders chuckle when they see it, while those who don't wear waders, or who don't fish at all (a rare breed around here), seldom discover much humor in it.

Everyone who fishes in high waders knows how it feels when the depth of the water threatens to exceed the height of his waders. Even so, waders are as essential to a serious trout fisherman as his rod and reel. Rubber boots are perfectly adequate for slopping around a meadow brook or wading the shore of a bass pond, but when you fish big water for big trout, waders become a necessity.

Choosing the kind of waders that best suits your need is largely a matter of deciding how much you feel you can afford to pay for them and how you will use them. Plastic waders offer many advantages. They are inexpensive, compared with most fabric waders, light in weight,

152

Drawing by Walter Young

comfortable to walk in, and much improved in quality over those of only a few years ago. If you decide that plastic waders will suit your purpose, be sure to get those with a seamless seat and 30-gauge molded stocking feet.

Fabric waders are much heavier and more expensive than those made of plastic, but they are also more durable and considerably more resistant to briars and other perils of the path that leads to the trout stream—except, of course, for barbed wire. If weight and comfort are prime considerations, get the stocking-foot style; if you lean toward convenience, you will find the boot-foot waders easier and quicker to get on and off.

Waders are made in two heights, waist and chest. While the waist-high waders are somewhat lighter and a couple of dollars cheaper than the higher model, most fishermen prefer long waders so they can wade deeper and, therefore, cover more water. If the waders don't have a draw-string around the top, it is wise to get a canvas belt so the top can be snugged tight to your chest when you are wading in deep, heavy water. Then in case of a minor mishap very little water will slop inside the waders and the captured air will provide ample flotation if you should suddenly go bottoms-up in water over your head.

Perhaps the most important part of the waders—certainly not the least important, anyway—is the bottoms. Rubber-soled waders give the

153

longest wear and are quite satisfactory for wading on mud or sand. But most trout streams have rocks in them, and it is a characteristic of rocks in trout streams to be slippery. Rubber skids on them like an automobile tire on a patch of ice.

Wading chains, made to wear over the wader foot, grip a little better than rubber. But, like tire chains, they are not completely skid-proof either. In addition, they are uncomfortable and awkward to walk in.

Many fishermen prefer wading brogues with soft iron hobs. The hobs bite into rocks quite well—actually, the rocks bite into the hobs—but, being soft, they wear down fast and must be replaced quite often. Also the brogues are quite expensive.

Felt bottoms, on the other h—— foot, stick to slime and moss, sunken logs, rocks, and even to ice. They give the wearer a sure-footed feeling that allows him to forget his footing and devote his full attention to the more important matter of fishing. Felt wears down quickly, but the manufacturer will take them back for re-soling, or the fisherman can do it himself with a resoling kit, listed in my Orvis catalog for $5.95. Felt-soled wading sandals which can be strapped over boot-foot waders cost around $6, canvas wading shoes average about $15.95, leather and canvas shoes, $26. With reasonable care, the felt bottoms on any of these should last through two or possibly three seasons of weekend fishing.

One objectionable feature of high waders is that they must be peeled down to the knees when it becomes necessary to respond to one of nature's urgent calls. I have often wondered whether the genius responsible for the electronic computor, nuclear fission, and orbiting space craft could, if it tried, invent a waterproof fly zipper for waders. It seems such a simple, useful thing in comparison.

While there is no direct connection between this paragraph and the one immediately above, it should be mentioned that waders may become wet inside even though neither the waders nor the fisherman sustains a leak. This is the result of condensation, which occurs when heated air inside the waders comes in contact with the water-cooled fabric. Moisture collects on the inner surface just as it does on the inside of a window pane on a cold day. If the fisherman inside the waders is hot and the water outside them is cold, condensation is inevitable. However, it can be controlled to some extent by loosening the wader tops to let air circulate inside.

Finding a leak in waders is sometimes more difficult than patching it. The hole may be virtually invisible, caused by the merest prick of a briar, but as the icy water seeps through it can dampen not only your skin but your enthusiasm for fishing as well. Usually you can locate the hole by lowering a trouble light inside each leg. In a darkened room the hole will reveal itself as a pinpoint of light.

If that doesn't work, try the water test. Dry the outside of the waders thoroughly and fill the legs with water—one at a time, of course. When

154

a damp spot forms, the hole will be located at the very top of it. Draw a circle around the area with chalk so you can find it again after the waders have dried. To find a leak north of the crotch, seal the legs by binding them tightly with strips of cloth, and hold them above the crotch while you fill the seat with water. Check seams carefully, as a slight imperfection here can cause a slow leak that's very hard to find.

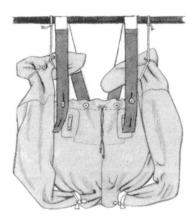

Because waders often engender a feeling of overconfidence and tend to lure a fisherman out into reckless depths, a wading staff can be a great help, especially if the water is heavy and the fisherman's legs aren't quite as nimble as they used to be. True, the staff is another encumbrance, and most of us carry too much gear anyway. But for fishing big water in the early spring when the rivers run high, strong, and cold, it can be a comforting thing to have along. With its aid you can brace yourself against the hard-shoving current while casting, or force your way back upstream through a deep, fast-moving stretch you couldn't possibly navigate without it. Be sure to attach the staff to something strong, such as your wader belt, so you can let go of it while casting or playing a fish.

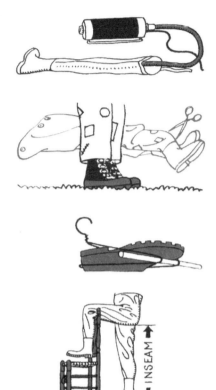

TAP'S TIPS

❲ To dry the inside of wet boots and waders quickly and easily, blow warm air into them by attaching the vacuum cleaner hose to the exhaust outlet. An electric hair dryer does a fast job, too.

❲ Save old waders and hip boots, even if they are beyond patching. Cut off the feet and wear the tops when washing the car or the dog, hunting in the rain, or sitting in a muddy duck blind.

❲ Hang boots and waders bottoms up to allow air to circulate inside and prevent creasing. A bent coat hanger is just the thing for this. Form the wire so the heel fits snugly and use dowelling to hold up the toes. Store the waders in an airy spot removed from artificial heat.

❲ Always insist on a perfect fit when buying new waders. Length of leg is most important for walking comfort and long wear. Test the inseam length by swinging the leg over the back of a chair. If you can do it without feeling crotch-bound, you won't have any trouble crossing fences or climbing steep embankments.

Tackle Tinkering

Long and drear are the evenings of winter, and distant the opening day of another fishing season. A fisherman could come down with cabin-fever at this time of year if he couldn't find something better to do with his time than watching the boob tube or re-reading old copies of his favorite sporting magazine.

Personally, I can kill off a winter easily just tinkering with my fishing tackle. Some of my friends make crude jokes about this harmless pastime (example: "What do you do if you can't find anything to repair —break something?") but I find it a pleasant and profitable way to occupy myself while waiting for spring to come.

Here are a few projects that can make the clock hands spin during a long winter's evening:

Empty the tackle box, clean it thoroughly, sort out lures, make a list of favorites that must be replaced. Brighten spoons and spinners with silver polish; touch up plugs with high-gloss enamel or fingernail lacquer; straighten, sharpen, or replace hooks.

Fluff up flies and bugs with a teakettle steam bath. Rewind frayed

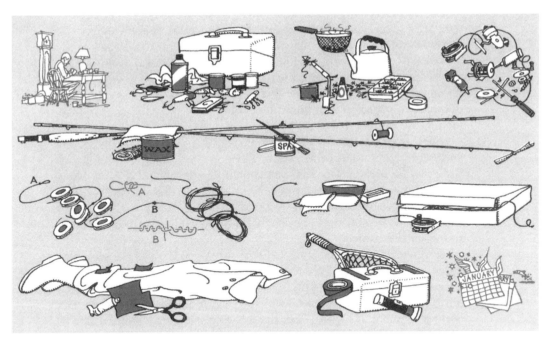

head windings. Sort out by size and/or pattern, put each in a separate fly box compartment and seal the box with masking tape.

Clean and oil reels. Wash parts, except nylon gears, with kerosene or lighter fluid. Daub just a smidgen of graphite grease on metal gears, put a drop of light machine oil in oil holes and level wind. If you need replacement parts, order them from the manufacturer now.

Check your stock of leaders. You can tie up a season's supply in half an evening. Start with a butt of 20-pound nylon and taper it down in 18-inch steps to 15-, 10-, and 6-pound, then 1X, 2X, 3X. This makes a serviceable basic leader to which you can later add a heavier butt or finer point if you wish.

Examine rods for frayed guide wrappings. Rewind and varnish. See if guides show signs of line-wear; it appears first in the guide immediately above the reel and in the tip-top. If the grooves are too deeply worn to smooth out with a strip of emery cloth, replace them.

Clean fly lines with line cleaner or soap and water, wipe dry and store loosely coiled in a ventilated box. Bait-casting line and nylon monofilament can spend the winter on the reels without harm, but fly lines should be allowed to stretch out and relax.

Have you ever fumbled around in the dark for your net, flashlight or tackle box when fishing at night? Mark them now with strips of reflector tape.

And how about that slow leak in your boots and waders that defied detection all during the last fishing season? You can probably find it now, when you have plenty of time on your hands. While you're at it, better replace old patches that have started to curl at the corners.

Perhaps your favorite bamboo rod has begun to look beat-up after all the line-throwing and fish-fighting it has done. You will probably never take time to repair it properly during the fishing season, so why not make a project of it in the winter, when you can lavish some tender, loving care on it?

First, make a note of the distances between the line guides so you will know where to put them back. Then strip off the guides by slicing the wrappings carefully with a razor blade. Check the ferrules and reseat any that have developed a knock. Next, strip off the old varnish with paint remover or a flat-edged knife blade and buff the surface lightly with fine steel wool, working on the flats and taking extra care not to round off the corners.

If the original guides were bent or scored, replace them with new guides of the same size. Wrapping a guide is a simple job, but there is a right and a wrong way to do it. The wrong way is to start the winding on the guide and wind down onto the rod. It is impossible to do this without leaving an open space in the winding at the point where it steps off the foot of the guide. Water can collect in this crack and in time the winding may become rotten. Besides, it doesn't look good.

To do the job right, bind one foot of the guide firmly in place (make sure it lines up perfectly with the other guides) with thread or Scotch tape. Start the winding on the rod about six thicknesses of thread below the guide foot. Wind toward the guide, being careful to place each turn so it touches but does not overlap the previous one. This results in a smooth, solid wrapping that completely covers the end of the guide. If the metal tip of the guide is rough or too high to permit the thread to climb over it without leaving a crack, taper it down with a file.

To finish the winding, make the last half-dozen turns over a loop of thread, pass the end of the winding thread through the loop, and pull the loop out. This buries the end of the thread under the last turns. Cut off the surplus flush with the wrapping, burn off the fuzz with an alcohol or gas flame, and coat the winding with color preservative or thinned fingernail lacquer.

Now to varnish the rod. This can be a little tricky, as the varnish must be applied evenly so that it covers the surface completely without forming thick runny spots. Ignore anything you may have read or heard about applying the varnish with your fingers. It just sounds like a good idea. Use a soft, flat brush about a quarter-inch wide, which will enable you to varnish one rod flat at a time. As varnish flows more evenly when it is warmed, pour a little in a clean saucer and place it on a radiator, or set the bottle in a shallow pan of warm—not hot—water. Hold the rod section upright by one of the ferrules and brush on the varnish with long, even strokes, rotating the rod with your fingers so that each flat is covered separately. Watch for bubbles and brush them out immediately or blow on them. When the section is completely covered, hold it up to the light and inspect it thoroughly for drips, bubbles, specks of dust, or "holidays." If it looks perfectly smooth and glassy, hang it upright in a dust-free room or closet and allow it to dry for at least twenty-four hours.

When the first coat is dry and hard, buff it very lightly with a fine abrasive, such as powdered pumice, and apply a second coat. The abrasive roughens the surface just enough to prevent the second coat from running, or slipping.

Whether you give the rod a third coat is up to you; some do, but I don't. Instead, I rub a thin, even film of hard paste wax, such as Simoniz, over the varnished surface and buff it briskly with a soft cloth. Then the rod really shines.

Perhaps the tip of a rod has suffered a simple fracture or has been broken off. Rod tips are notoriously accident-prone. The damage rarely results from anything as dramatic as playing a wild, heavy fish, however; more often it occurs when a door slams behind you or someone's foot crunches down on the rod.

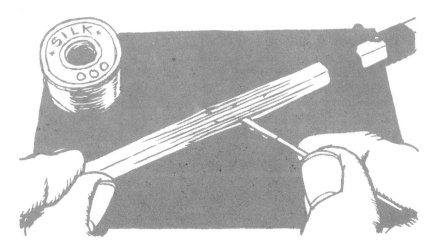

Most broken tips can be repaired, although it is too much to hope that they will be as good as new again. If the tip has sustained a compound fracture between the last two guides, the best way to fix it is to cut off the broken part, and fit the end to a new tip-top. The short tip will give the rod a "clubby" feeling, but it can be used in an emergency.

If the sections have only been forced apart, the damage can be repaired by prying the sections open still more and forcing glue among them with a toothpick. Work the glue into every crack you can find, applying it evenly but not too heavily. Before the glue has time to set, cross-wind the break tightly with thread or rubber bands and hang the rod section upright with a weight tied to the bottom to hold it straight. When the glue has hardened, scrape off the surplus, wind white thread evenly over the entire length of the fracture, and coat it with varnish. White thread becomes almost transparent when varnished, so the repair will be nearly invisible.

It is even possible to repair a clean break in a bamboo rod if you take your time and work very carefully. First, shave the broken ends to a smooth taper at least four inches long. Shape the flat sides of the tapered sections so they match perfectly when laid together. Score the faces of the two flat surfaces by crisscrossing them lightly with a knife. Then smear the touching sides with a thin film of glue. Wait until the glue becomes tacky-dry, then press the glued sides together and place them in a vise under just enough pressure to hold them in position, but not quite enough to make them slide apart. When the glue dries, scrape away the surplus that has oozed out, wind over the splice with white thread, and give it two coats of varnish. I can't promise that the tip will be as good as new, but it may prove to be stronger than you think.

A favorite bamboo rod can be a very personal possession, even an object of some affection. It becomes even more personal if it has your name on it—and possibly, if you should lose it, the name might bring it home to you.

Pick a clean flat on the butt just above the grip and carefully scrape the varnish off a section about three inches long—less if you have a

160

name like Poe, more for one like VanValkenburgh. Then buff the bared surface with fine steel wool to polish it and feather off the edges of the varnish.

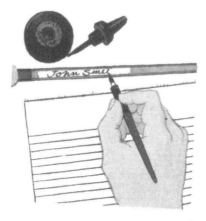

Write or print your name carefully with a fine-pointed pen and black India ink. If your handwriting is shaky, ask a commercial lettering artist to do it for you. However, your personal signature is preferable if it is distinctive and legible. You will find it easier to work on the raised surface if you rest your writing hand on a pad of paper or piece of wood about the same thickness as the rod section.

Allow plenty of time for the ink to dry, then varnish over the signature. If the overlapping varnish forms a high spot at each end of the section, cover the overlap with a wrapping of thread.

Here is just one more project to help you while away an evening or two in the winter. After this you are on your own. As you have probably discovered by now, as soon as you have acquired the number of reels you think you need, it becomes a problem finding a place to keep them. You just can't dump them in a box or pile them on a shelf in the closet. I hang mine in an orderly row from cup hooks screwed into the edge of a shelf. Harold Blaisdell, my Vermont fishing partner, built a special rack for his reels, and I think his method is better than mine.

Harold's rack consists of a wooden rod with reel bands, supported between two wall brackets. The rod can be made from dowel stock or a length of broom handle, planed flat on one side to permit the bands to slip over the feet of the reels. The length of the rod depends on the number of reels it will hold. Allow at least six inches for each reel.

To make the reel bands, buy a short length of 1-inch brass tubing and slice off the required number with a hack saw. Make them about a quarter-inch wide and smooth the rough edges with a file.

Cut the brackets from 1-inch stock. The dimensions aren't important, as long as the brackets hold the rods far enough from the wall to

161

leave room for the largest reels. Bore holes halfway through the brackets to hold the ends of the rod. Then screw the brackets to the wall with the rod in place. Varnish or stain the rack to match the woodwork in the room.

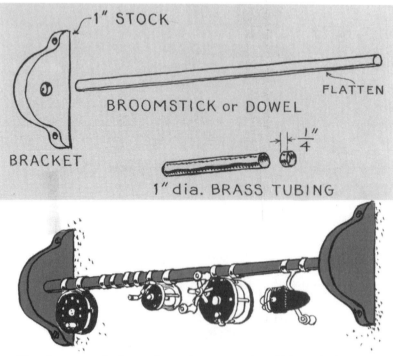

Hanging securely from the rack, your reels will be safe from harm and out of the way till you need them. A glance at the orderly row of reels as you leave to go fishing will avoid the possibility of rushing off with the wrong reel or, worse yet, with no reel at all.

TAP'S TIPS

⟮ Oiling the male ferrule of a rod by rubbing it against the side of the nose or through the hair is an old stunt. However, it shouldn't be necessary if the ferrules fit properly, and the oil may allow the rod sections to twist out of line. Instead, clean both the male and female ferrules with gasoline, lighter fluid, or petroleum jelly, using cotton batting twisted around a toothpick as a swab. If the metal is pitted or discolored from corrosion, apply silver polish sparingly; to reach the inner surface of the female section, use a wire rifle-cleaning brush.

162

Wooden runners attached to the underside of a tackle box keep it off the wet bottom of a boat and also silence the noise it makes when it is pushed around. Fasten ½-inch wood strips to the outside edges of the box with cement or screws and round the corners with a file.

Your name on items of sporting equipment may help you to get them back if you lose them or leave them behind at the end of a fishing trip. Type or print your name and address on gummed labels and stick them on rod cases, tackle box, net handle. Waterproof the labels by coating them with varnish or clear fingernail lacquer.

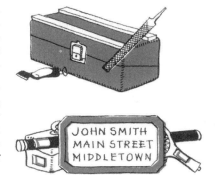

Laying up the Outboard

The old kicker started first pull last spring. That's pretty good, considering she's 12 years old. I've got a dollar that says she'll start first pull next spring, too.

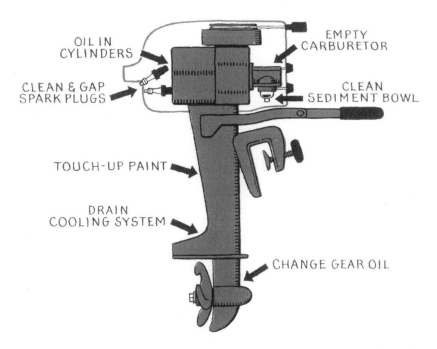

Any motor that operates efficiently when it is put away for the winter should operate just as efficiently when it is clamped to the transom the following spring. Spending a half-hour on it at winter layup time will make sure that it does.

163

First, flush out the cooling system if the motor has been run in salt water or in water that might contain chemical pollutants. Then drain off the remaining water by turning the flywheel a few times.

When flushing the cooling system, run the motor with the gas line closed to empty the carburetor. Remove and clean the sediment bowl.

Check, clean and regap spark plugs or discard them if you plan to buy new ones in the spring. Squirt lubricating oil in the cylinders and turn the flywheel a few times to work it in.

Drain and refill the gear housing. Examine the propeller for damage and smooth nicks with a file. Sandpaper scratches in the exterior finish and touch up with matching spray paint.

Then clamp the motor upright in a dry, dust-free corner and cover it with canvas or an old blanket. When spring finally gets here, the old boat-pusher will be ready and rarin' to go again.

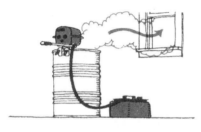

TAP'S TIPS

❲ Beware of exhaust fumes when you test-run your outboard motor in the garage or basement. The gases are just as deadly as those from an automobile exhaust. Always run the motor near an open window.

❲ When you carry your outboard motor in the back of the car, place it on a half-inflated inner tube. The tube cushions the jounces and prevents the motor from being dented or knocked out of adjustment.

❲ Every time you buy a gallon of gas for your boat you pay Uncle Sam a two-cent tax. This can amount to a sizable sum over a year, so be sure to keep a record of your purchases. File your refund claim before September 30 on Form 843, available at the nearest Internal Revenue Service office.

❲ An oil barrel with one end knocked out with a cold chisel is ideal for test-running an outboard motor or flushing it out after it has run in salt water. I got my barrel from the local filling station.

164

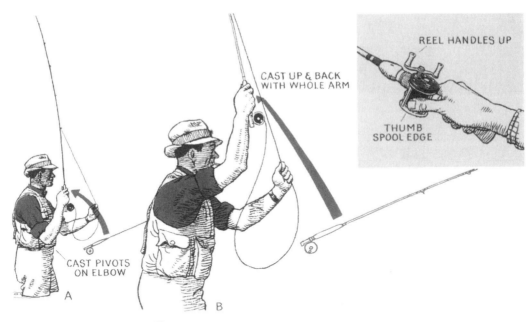

CAST UP & BACK WITH WHOLE ARM

REEL HANDLES UP

THUMB SPOOL EDGE

CAST PIVOTS ON ELBOW

A

B

CASTING
AND PLAYING FISH

Casting Clinic

ACCORDING TO some observations I made during the past fishing season, there appear to be a few fishermen around who still can't drop a lure into a teacup at 50 paces.

Those who can do it shouldn't fritter away their time reading this. If the others will settle for hitting a washtub at 50 feet, maybe this will help a little.

Fly casters will please forget all the twaddle they've heard about keeping the elbow pressed firmly against the hip bone. You need that elbow to perform the really important part of the fly casting motion, which is not the forward cast, but the back cast.

That's the secret of fly casting—the back cast. You've gotta lean into it. Heave the line behind you as high and as hard as you can, with a definite lifting motion and a grunt. If you put enough beef into it, your elbow will be a long way from your hip at the top of the cast. In fact, if you peek out of the corner of your eye, you'll find it at about the level of your shoulder. From that Statue-of-Liberty position, and with the line tugging hard at your rod tip, you just push the rod forward. Whoosh!

REACH

The trick to bait casting, if "trick" is the word, is to cast with the reel handles *up* and with your thumb riding gently on, and *in continuous contact with*, the edge of the spool. The thumb acts as a soft brake to control the speed of the spool and prevent it from over-running into a backlash. Just don't take your thumb off the spool from the time you take aim till you start reeling in. It's really as easy as that. Easier, if you stick to short casts.

Spin casting is so beginner-proof there's simply no trick to it at all. At first the lure may display a tendency to fly straight up or down, but it soon flattens out as the forefinger learns when to release the line.

Most of the spin caster's early troubles result from heaving hardware that is either too heavy or too light—usually the latter—for the rod. The average spinning outfit will handle lures from $\frac{1}{8}$ to $\frac{1}{2}$ ounce nicely. Anything lighter than $\frac{1}{8}$ ounce should be cast with ultralight gear, and lures heavier than $\frac{1}{2}$ ounce belong on the end of a bait-casting line.

If your casting still gives you trouble, maybe you should try a heavier or lighter line. Make it a size heavier if you're having trouble laying out a fly line, a lot lighter—say, down to 4-pound test—if you're spinning or bait casting. Makes all the difference in the world, sometimes.

166

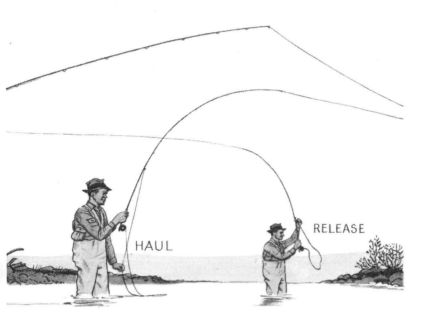

HAUL

RELEASE

Fly Casting for Distance

Want to add twenty or thirty feet to your casts with the fly rod? You can. All it takes is a little pull.

The pull, or line-haul, is old stuff to tournament casters and to any meat-and-potato fly fisherman who consistently lays out more than sixty feet of the tapered. With a little practice you, too, can reach the trout that rolls so tantalizing 'way over there against the far bank.

The purpose of the line-haul is merely to add speed and leverage to the cast—to give the rod something solid to push against. Properly executed, the line travels faster, farther, straighter. Here's how you do it:

First, work out a comfortable length of line and lay it out on the water in front of you. Now reach forward with your left hand and grasp the line close to the stripping guide. As you lift the rod to start the back cast, pull the line you are holding in your left hand downward with a smart sweeping motion. This overcomes the inertia of the line and greatly increases its speed as it snakes out behind you. Then by letting the line slide through your fingers you can shoot extra distance into the back cast.

As you.start the forward cast, hold the line again with your left hand, just a bit below the casting hand, and drive the rod forward. When you feel the rod bite into the weight of the line, bring the left hand

167

down with a long, smooth yank, just as you did in starting the back cast. This increases the leverage exerted by the rod on the line and drives the line forward hard and fast in a narrow loop. At some point in the forward cast you will sense that the rod is no longer pushing solidly against the weight of the line—that the line has received all the force it is going to get from the rod, and is traveling forward on momentum. At that instant, release your grip on the line. This is the shoot that adds extra footage to the cast. If you time it perfectly, you may see every inch of line go whistling out through the guides. That's the way 100-foot casts are made.

This, of course, is only an elementary description of a procedure that requires a great deal of practice, particularly in developing timing and coordination. But once you get the knack of it, you will find that your fly is reaching out and taking fish that were safely out of your range before you starting using a little pull.

TAP'S TIPS

(If you have trouble shooting fly line, it may lie in the guides on the rod. They may be too small, too far apart, or both. Replacing them with larger guides spaced closer together could add yards of extra distance to your casts by reducing line-drag.

168

Short-Line Casting

You can't judge a fisherman by his casting skill alone, any more than you can measure a grouse hunter by his ability to break clay targets on the skeet field. The stylist who can throw a hundred feet of line may be a good fisherman, and in all likelihood he is. But a much better fisherman may be a guy who just pecks away at close range with short little pinpoint casts. In fact, if you wanted to bet with me on which one might have the heavier creel, I'd be tempted to put my dollar on the short-line fisherman. If we made enough bets I'm pretty sure I would win more than half of them by letting my money ride on the peck-and-punch caster.

Of course, you have to whale out a long line sometimes to reach fish beyond wading range, and it's nice to know how to do it. However, the long cast has its disadvantages too. It is less accurate, more likely to be blown off target by the wind. If you are fishing with a dry fly the long line increases the chance of spoiling the float with drag. It is more difficult to set the hook in the fish if you get him to rise. And long-line fishermen are forever getting their backcasts hung up in the bushes.

As a practical matter, it's not so much where you cast *to* that counts, as much as where you cast *from*. For example, if a fish shows himself seventy feet upstream, you can lengthen line and make a dramatic bid to collect him from where you stand. But you will give yourself a much better chance to take him if you move to a position close enough to make a clean, accurate cast that will put the fly right over his nose first time. Choosing the shorter cast doesn't label the fisherman as a dub; on the contrary, it proves that he knows what he is doing.

When you find fish rising to a hatch of insects or nymphing just under the surface, remember that their cone of vision is quite small. You can wade close to them without being seen, particularly if you bend over a little to shorten your silhouette. You can also get surprisingly close to fish lying in fast, choppy water, because they can't see through the broken surface easily. Therefore, there is no need to shoot at these fish from eighty feet away—and at that distance you would probably miss the spot anyway, due to wind and other factors. With a short line you can fish the pockets, even different parts of the pockets, carefully and thoroughly, making every float count.

If you're afraid that you will look like a dub as you flick a short line at the pools and pockets of a trout stream, don't give it another thought. Anyone who failed to recognize a really good trout fisherman at work would have to be a dub himself.

TAP'S TIPS

⟨ Lots of fish are caught on imperfect casts. So when the line doesn't roll out as smoothly as you would like, or go in the direction you aimed it, fish out the cast anyway. Ripping the line off the water to make a better cast only scares the fish.

⟨ If you have difficulty casting a short line, the trouble may be with the taper, which makes the end of the line too light. Cut it back a foot at a time until you begin to feel line weight when you cast. If the line is double tapered, cut only one end, so the line can be reversed for making long casts over big water.

⟨ After fishing out a cast with a bass bug, lift both the lure and the line to the surface before picking it off the water, and start the backcast with a definite upward motion. This prevents the bug from nosediving if the tip of the line has begun to sink.

⟨ When a part works loose on a reel you may have to stop fishing—unless you have a small screwdriver with you. Keep one in your fishing jacket or tackle box. Some day you may be glad you have it.

⟨ To cast accurately, move the rod through a vertical plane on a line with your sighting eye and the target. Sideswiping, even from only a slight angle, makes pinpoint accuracy difficult with any rod.

⟨ Check the guides on your fly rod occasionally to see if they have collected dressing from the line. The gunk will prevent the line from sliding easily through the guides. Make sure you haven't skipped a guide in stringing up the rod, too.

⟨ You may be able to coax a little extra distance from a cast by holding the coiled slack near the stripping guide, and in line with it, when you release it for the line-shoot. This reduces friction as the line enters the guide.

Pitching Curves

Casting a curved line is one of the trickiest—and most useful—stunts a fly fisherman can learn. While used mostly by dry fly fishermen, it is often helpful in wet fly, nymph, and even bass bug fishing as well.

The purpose of the curve cast is to put the fly over the fish ahead of the leader. Suppose, for example, a trout rises directly upstream of where you are standing, and you cast your fly over him with a perfectly straight line. As it drifts down to him the leader, and perhaps also the tip of the line, must pass through his "window" before the fly drifts into it, and no trout worthy of the adjective "wily" will stand for that sort of thing. The splash of the falling leader, its motion or its grotesquely magnified shadow will either put the fish down or send him scurrying for cover. But if you curve the leader and line away from him so the fly comes over him first, he will be waiting and willing when it drifts into his view.

The curve cast is also useful for bending leader and line around an obstacle. Suppose you spot a rising fish that is lying directly above a rock. You can't cast directly to him, for the leader and line would drape themselves over the rock. And while we're supposing, let's suppose you can't wade to one side to avoid the obstruction. No problem, really; just throw the fish a curve that drops line and leader above and away from his feeding lane.

172

This suggests another use for the curve cast—to avoid drag. Often you will see fish rising in the glassy slick at the very lower lip of a pool, where it rolls over the edge into a run of fast water immediately below. You stand in the quick water facing the pool and lick your lips with relish. But if you make a straight-line cast to the rising fish the quickening current will snatch your fly off the slick and scare every fish around. That's when the curve cast comes in handy; the deep bend in the line and leader above the fly will require a little time to straighten with the pull of the current. In those few seconds of time your fly floats naturally over the fish—and a two-second float is probably all you will need.

The curve cast is also helpful when you are fishing a nymph or wet fly upstream or up and across. Here again it is important to drift the fly to the fish without drag and without letting them see the leader first. Many fishermen who claim they have poor luck fishing nymphs and wet flies would find these lures deadlier than they thought if they fished them with the same care they use to fish a dry fly, free of drag and with leader and line behind the fly.

In casting a curve the line can be made to bend either to the right or to the left. Some writers call the left curve a positive curve and the right curve a negative curve, but I think these terms are needlessly confusing. A right curve bends to the fisherman's right and a left curve bends the opposite direction; that seems simple enough.

The right curve is by far the easier of the two casts to learn. Actually, it is nothing more than an incomplete or underpowered cast which allows the line to drop to the water before it can straighten out. Start it by lowering the rod to the side so it travels roughly parallel with the water, and make the cast side-arm. In delivering the forward cast, apply less than the usual amount of force, so the line loses momentum and drops to the water with the loop still in it. The loop is the curve. To anyone watching, it looks like a pretty sloppy performance—unless the witness is a dry-fly fisherman himself, in which case he will nod his approval.

The left curve starts the same way, but the forward cast is overpowered. As the line straightens, check the rod tip sharply. This causes the fly to snap around to the left of its line of flight and drop to the water with the leader falling above it in a deep bend. At least, that's the way it is supposed to be done. In actual practice, the air resistance of the fly may prevent it from whipping around. Also, the timing of the left curve cast is more difficult to master than the much simpler right curve. Personally, I find it easier to cast the left curve by making an underpowered cast backhanded, that is, with the rod across my body. The result is the same, although it is difficult to achieve quite as much accuracy and distance with the backhand cast.

TAP'S TIPS

(Here's a stunt to try when stream fishing after dark. Hang a flashlight from a tree limb so it shines above (not on) the water of a likely pool. The light attracts insects, which in turn attract fish.

(A simple diary of fishing trips can contain an enormous amount of valuable information—the emergence dates of insects on various streams, the lures that worked best for you, the relationship of weather conditions and water temperature to fishing success, the number of fish you caught, the places you fished and when you fished them, and with whom. Many fishermen carry a notebook and jot down this information for later use—and use it often.

Handling Loose Line

Fly casting is a sloppy sort of operation, when you think of all that line waving back and forth in the air, slapping rocks and nearby fisher-

174

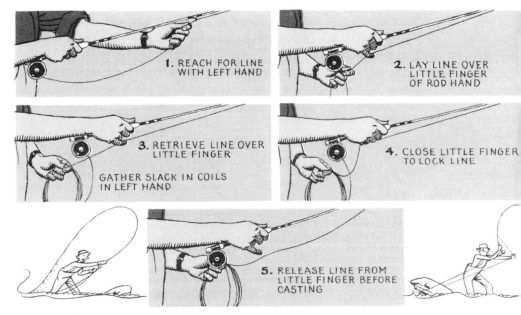

1. REACH FOR LINE WITH LEFT HAND

2. LAY LINE OVER LITTLE FINGER OF ROD HAND

3. RETRIEVE LINE OVER LITTLE FINGER

GATHER SLACK IN COILS IN LEFT HAND

4. CLOSE LITTLE FINGER TO LOCK LINE

5. RELEASE LINE FROM LITTLE FINGER BEFORE CASTING

men, and every so often falling in disarray upon the water, and still more line hanging between the stripping guide and reel, entangling the angler's feet or drifting off downstream in long loops and coils.

The line beyond the rod tip can be controlled by matching its weight to the action of the rod and then learning how to cast it properly, mainly a matter of timing. It's the other loose line, the stripping line, that makes a nuisance of itself.

I have observed, and not without some satisfaction, that many fairly expert fly fishermen have trouble with their stripping line. And even the best of them can't agree on the proper way to handle it.

As long as the experts have their troubles, you may not think me too presumptuous if I try to tell you how *I* think it should be done.

When you've made your cast, reach forward with your left hand (or your right, if you're a southpaw), grab the line below the stripping guide and drape it over the little finger of your rod hand. Now, by bending your pinkie, you can lock the line any time you want to. To retrieve your cast, just twitch the line through the little finger, which opens and closes to release or hold the line as you strip it in.

This procedure creates an accumulation of line below your rod hand, the slack that causes all the trouble. If you let it fall free, it will wrap itself around a rock or drift away in the current. So cultivate the habit of gathering it in neat coils in your left hand, keeping the coils in order so they will come off your hand in the same sequence they went on.

Now if you get a strike, you have complete control of the line. If the fish demands line you can let him take the coils off your hand until all the line is out and you can put him on the reel, which is where a heavy fish belongs.

If you don't get a strike, lift the line off your little finger and cast again. False casting and then shooting the line will carry the coils off your hand easily, adding extra feet to every cast.

TAP'S TIPS

(Cement a pad of sponge rubber, felt, or plastic foam inside the cap of your metal rod case to protect ferrules and tip-top from damage and prevent the rod sections from rattling. A wad of cotton batting forced into the bottom of the case will protect the other ends of the rod, too.

(Which type of bass bug takes the most fish, cork or deerhair? Some fishermen prefer one, some the other. Bugs with cork, wood or plastic bodies float higher and longer and create more disturbance on the water. Hair, on the other hand, casts farther and easier; also, striking fish are more likely to hold a soft hair bug if the fisherman is laggard with the strike. I carry both kinds in my box of bugs, but find that I use deerhair lures more than those with solid bodies.

Southpaw Reeling

Most fly fishermen cast and reel with the same hand. This results in passing the rod from one hand to the other and back again while casting, retrieving line and playing fish—an awkward and inefficient procedure.

For most of us who were born right handed, the starboard flipper is somewhat stronger and more dexterous than the left. We use it to hold the rod while casting and stripping in the fly. Then when we hook a heavy fish that must be played off the reel, we shift the rod from the strong right hand to the weaker left hand, and use the right hand for the simple task of cranking in line. Thus the strength and skill of the right hand is wasted on a purely mechanical function, while the left hand takes over the more difficult and tiring job of fighting the fish.

Anyone can learn to reel left handed in a few hours. Simply put an empty fly reel on the butt section of a rod and turn it while watching a couple of television programs. In a surprisingly short time the action becomes automatic. Once you have taught the left hand to operate the

176

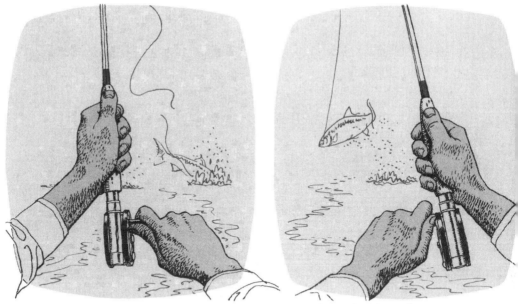

reel, you can use the stronger and more capable right hand for the tasks that require strength and skill—casting and playing a fish—without shifting the rod from one hand to the other as if it were a hot potato.

TAP'S TIPS

(Rough fish offer real sport if you scale the weight of your tackle to their size. The abundant fallfish, for example, takes wet and dry flies readily and puts up a fairly respectable scrap on light gear. Carp and suckers have the weight and strength to give you a tussle. More important, these fish often keep on biting when more desirable game fish are playing hard to get.

(An empty toothpaste tube will provide you with a generous supply of wrap-around sinkers. Squeeze the tube as clean as possible and cut it into ⅛-inch strips with heavy scissors. Leave the strips attached at one side, so they can be detached one at a time. The strips can be used doubled or single thickness, according to the amount of weight needed.

Hits and Misses

The trout came up to my dry fly with a splash and I set the hook quickly—into nothing.

177

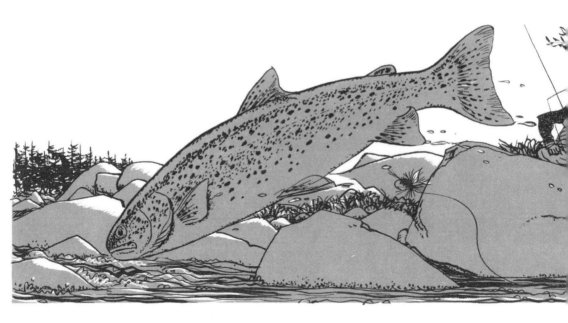

My partner, watching from the embankment above, made a cluck-ing noise and then observed helpfully, "You took it away from him."

A few minutes later another fish came up to the fly. Once again I struck and missed.

"See?" said Old Helpful. "You're striking too quick."

Three or four rises later—they were coming good that day—I felt the hook dig into something solid. But when I lifted the trout from the water I discovered that my fly was buried to the hackle in its chin.

What did that prove? Perhaps, as my companion suggested, that I had my rod set on a hair trigger—or, just as likely, that the trout didn't like the size or pattern of my fly and were refusing it at the last split instant, or that the hook point was dull or bent (although I had checked it, and it wasn't), or possibly that the trout were in a playful mood that day. Maybe it didn't prove anything at all except that you shouldn't expect to get your hook into every fish that makes a pass at your lure.

Out of a given number of fish that come to your lure or bait, you will hook only a certain percentage of them anyway, and it will never be 100 percent. The actual percentage figure would depend on a great many different factors, such as the species of fish, the lure, the size and sharpness of the hook, even your own experience and skill with a rod. Whatever the figure might be, if you could raise it just a notch—say, from 50 to 60 percent—obviously you could put a lot more fish in your creel over the course of a season.

Your reflexes play an important part in your ratio of fish raised to

178

fish hooked, of course. You've got to punch the button fast when you raise a rainbow to a dry fly in fast water. But I think experience is even more important than the sharpness of your reflex. That same rainbow would rise much more deliberately in a slow current, and if you knew it, and expected it, you would be less likely to snatch the fly away from him or bust him off by hitting him too hard.

One day while fishing "five fish and out" with small poppers on bluegill water, my son and I counted the number of strikes we needed to hook each series of five bluegills (after catching five you pass the rod over and take up the oars). The number ranged from a low of nine to a high of thirty-one! The average, we figured, was close to twenty, which meant that we were getting the barb into about one bluegill in every four that came to the popper. Bluegills, mind you.

The first time I fished a dry fly for Atlantic salmon I whisked the fly away from the first four fish that came to it. Sea salmon are classic examples of slow-rising fish. You can take all day to strike them; in fact, they usually hook themselves if you let them.

Bass, on the other hand, generally hit a lure as if they were angry with it, and your hook usually hangs up in some part of their big kisser. However, smallmouths seem to use the hit-and-run technique more than largemouths do, and smallmouths in fast water sometimes act as flighty as trout.

You will never hook every fish that takes a crack at your lure, no matter what you do. But you can raise your average if you remember to strike slower in slow water, if you change to a smaller hook size, check the point of the hook to make sure it is needle sharp, and remember that you can control a short line better than a long one. Add them all up and they may fatten your hitting average and cut down the strikeouts.

TAP'S TIPS

❨ Cork rod handles are shaped to fit the average hand—but yours may not be average, or perhaps you hold the rod a little differently from the way most fishermen do. In either case, you can custom-fit the grip to suit your fancy. Use a fine, half-round file to hollow out a spot for your thumb and smooth it carefully with fine sandpaper. You can also alter the taper of the grip. But use the file sparingly, for you can't replace the cork you have filed away.

❨ Here's a rule that sometimes helps when you don't know what fly to try first. When imitating natural foods—hatching mayflies, nymphs, terrestrial insects—match the color with drab patterns in brown, gray, even black. If you don't see anything on or in the water to imitate, use a bright-colored pattern to attract the fish's attention. The Royal Coachman is an excellent "fancy" pattern to try when you are stuck for a fly to start with.

Lost Lunkers

It's trite, but true: it's usually the big ones that get away. The reason? Maybe because the brute simply out-fought or out-maneuvered the fisherman. More likely, because the fisherman was careless.

Let's face it. Most of us are careless, to a degree. Not you? All right, then, tell me: Do you test all your leader knots after you tie them? How many times do you stop fishing to see if the point of the hook has been bent or broken after ticking a rock on the back cast? I thought so—yet it's a sure bet that the knot will slip or the hook will fail to penetrate just when you keep your rendezvous with the biggest fish of the year.

Bait-casting lines and even monofilament become worn where they bear against the rod tip. Do you check it frequently, or do you always make just one more cast first? Sure as fish have fins, that's the cast you will spend all year wishing you could have back.

Fishing writers are forever shaking fingers in your face and warning you what will happen if you don't keep your hooks needle sharp. If you think it's just because they can't find anything more interesting to write

180

about, try setting a hook by hand into the jaw of a fish you've caught. You'll be surprised to discover how much force it takes to drive it in over the barb. Dull hooks have saved the life of many a good-sized fish, yet points can be freshened in seconds with a small carborundum stone.

There are other booby traps in the path to fishing fame, such as the loose reel seat that lets go of the reel at the critical moment, the scored tip-top that cuts the line, the torn landing net that dumps the fish back into the drink. Behind almost every sad tale of the big one that got away, you'll find an act of carelessness or a simple repair job postponed.

Who fusses with such time-wasting details as testing knots or sharpening hook points? The guys who *don't* lose the big ones, that's who.

TAP'S TIPS

⟨ Round labels punched out of masking tape are ideal for marking items of fishing gear—the pound test or diameter of the monofilament on a spinning reel, the size of the fly line on a fly reel, or the contents of a lure box. Waterproof the labels by covering them with a thin coat of clear fingernail lacquer.

⟨ The barometer is a helpful (but not infallible) guide to good fishing. Fish ordinarily become active when the glass rises or remains high and steady, lay off feeding when it falls or stays low. As a rule-of-thumb, the dividing line between high and low on the barometer is 29.90. The pressure reading is much less important, however, than its trend. All you really need to know is whether the glass is rising or falling.

⟨ The last foot of bait casting line, which constantly saws and flexes against the top guide in casting, sustains more wear than any other part. To strengthen the line at this point, double it by forming a long loop, using either the bowline or perfection loop knot. If line visibility is a factor, use a short monofilament leader instead.

Pump and Reel

It seems odd that a method used to bulldog big game fish with the heaviest of gear should also be used by light-tackle fans. That's the pump-and-reel method of moving a stubborn fish.

Just so we'll know what we're talking about, pump-and-reel means lifting a fish with the rod and then cranking in line as the rod is lowered. When you hang a really big fish, something like a 500-pound tuna, you darn well have to pump and reel, or you will probably bust off your fish.

The same is true of spin fishing with hairline tackle and, to a lesser extent, of fly fishing with 5X tippets or bait casting with tournament braid. By pumping and reeling you can lift a fish you couldn't budge —safely, that is—just by cranking line through a half-circled rod.

With a bait-casting or fly rod you can recover line simply by holding the reel handle as you pump. Not so with the light spinning outfit. When you spin-fish with hair-fine mono, you must set your drag very lightly. So holding the crank won't do any good, because the fish can turn the spool and thus prevent you from lifting him.

But on your rod hand you have a very useful appendage called the forefinger. By pressing this appendage against the lip of the spool, you can prevent it from turning or, by relaxing pressure slightly, permit it to turn as slowly as you want. This lets you recover line on the pump-up, and still give the fish line if he suddenly asks for it.

As a matter of fact, your forefinger is a more sensitive, quickly adjustable, reliable brake than any mechanical device yet invented for spinning reels. If you use it as such, you can set your reel brake as lightly as you wish, and thus give yourself an extra margin of safety

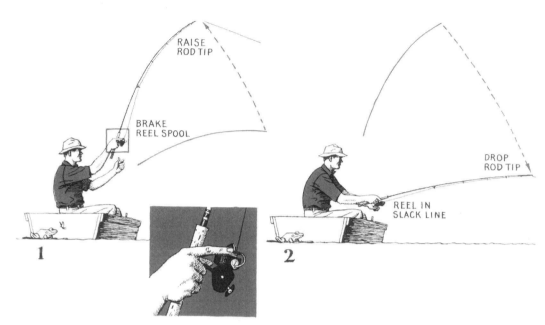

1

2

against sudden, heavy strikes or unexpected snags that could part your line against a hard-set mechanical drag.

The pump-and-reel method of playing a frolicsome fish offers another advantage. Monofilament spooled under great tension comes in stretched. It can sink into the previously spooled line, causing a jam when you cast. If the tension is great enough, it may even crack the reel spool. Pumping and reeling brings the mono in relaxed so that it lays on the spool gently and peels off in orderly spirals without kinking or twisting.

TAP'S TIPS

([Spin fishermen can control the flight of their lures as easily as bait casters can—but with the forefinger instead of the thumb. When the spinning lure takes off too fast or threatens to overshoot the target, point the forefinger down and let the outcoiling line slap against it. After a while this becomes almost automatic, and accuracy improves greatly.

([Worms can be fished very effectively with spinning gear. Nightcrawlers cast easily with light tackle even without a sinker. To cast small worms (or large worms on heavy gear) clamp a couple of split shot to a whisker of nylon just above the worm. Add or subtract shot as needed to keep the bait close to bottom at all depths and current speeds.

183

((Although it is perfectly smooth, monofilament can wear grooves in rod guides, particularly the tip-top. If the grooves are not too deep, they can be smoothed out with 120-grit emery cloth, rolled to the diameter of a cigarette. Then buff the surface with jeweler's tripoli or rottenstone.

Fish out of Water

What should you do when a fish jumps? In the excitement of the moment it would seem that there's not much you can do but let him jump and pray the hook stays stuck. However, many a fish lost in mid-leap could have been saved by quick action on the part of the embattled angler.

What you should do when a fish lifts himself out of water depends upon whether you hung him on a weighted lure, such as a plug, or an unweighted one, such as a fly or baited hook. A sizable bass with a ⅝-ounce plug or heavy spoon rattling around its jaw will come out shaking its head and body violently, thrashing the lure from side to side. The weight of the lure often provides sufficient leverage for the fish to toss it away, especially if the hooks are not well seated. So when you find yourself hitched to a plug-hooked jumper, lean back on the rod when he bursts out of the water; tighten up on the line and try to tip the fish over, thus preventing him from tossing the lure around and perhaps flinging it free.

A fly or baited hook, on the other hand, has little weight, so there is small chance that the fish can shake it loose. The danger lies in the possibility that the fish may hit a taut leader with his tail or fall on it, and either break the light tippet or tear the hook loose. Therefore, when a fly-hung fish vaults out of water, lower your rod tip quickly, lean forward and throw as much slack into the line as you can, so the leader will lie loose should the fish fall upon it. After the fish plunges back into the water, lift the rod tip with a sweeping motion to pick up the slack again.

Should you try to prevent a fish from jumping and thus avoid the possibility that it will toss the lure or smash the leader? I think not; in fact, when I hook a fish I try to encourage him to jump—first because I

184

enjoy seeing a fish leap (especially when it is my hook that is stuck in its jaw), and second because jumping tires a fish. That is the object of the thing—to wear him out so he can be landed. Also, if I am going to lose the fish I prefer to lose him in the middle of a wild jump. It's more spectacular, and provides a fitting climax to the encounter.

TAP'S TIPS

⟨ I always carry a tube of liquid cement in my tackle kit, and use it often—for plugging boat leaks, patching canoe canvas or torn waders, tightening a loose rod ferrule or tip-top. And being flammable, it also serves as a quick fire-starter on rainy days.

⟨ Making deerhair bass bugs requires more patience than skill. Use the short, coarse body hair, not the tail. Cut off as much hair as you can hold easily in your fingers; lay it at an angle over the hook shank; and bind it in place with two turns of waxed tying thread. When the thread is pulled tight the hair, being hollow, flares up and spins around the hook shank. Force the hair back tightly and repeat until the shank is crammed solid, then trim to the desired shape.

⟨ Ever lose a tiny screw when taking a reel apart, or wonder which screw goes in which hole? Next time, stick the screws and other small parts on a strip of masking tape in the order in which you removed them. Prevents losing or mislaying a screw, and helps you to put each one back where it belongs.

185

Shooting Jumps

When you're lucky enough to get a good picture of a game fish in midleap, something must click besides the shutter in your camera. You need good equipment, lots of patience, plenty of jumping fish to shoot at, and a partner who doesn't mind losing a fish now and then to give you a chance for a good shot.

You can "stop" a leaping fish at 1/250 second, but 1/500 is better and 1/1000 ideal. Most photographers who specialize in making jump pictures use cameras with a shutter speed of 1/1000. But don't let that stop you.

If you haven't got a fast shutter, look for slow fish. The largemouth bass is the easiest fish to photograph in the air. Meaning no disrespect to our bigmouthed friend, he jumps more sluggishly than the smallmouth or trout and salmon, and he can be teased into jumping close to the boat.

Focus your camera at 10 at 12 feet, set your shutter at its fastest speed, and adjust the lens opening according to light conditions. Then wait for your partner to hook a willing jumper.

The first two or three jumps are usually too far away to give you a chance to make a good picture. But your partner can discourage the fish from jumping by holding the fish with light pressure, meanwhile teasing him slowly toward the boat. If the fish is still fresh, a sharp twitch will usually spur him into jumping right about where you want him. Otherwise, let the fish rest a while on a slack line and then lift his head and try to prod him into one last desperate jump. When he comes out, try to shoot him at the very top of his leap and you may get an action picture you'll prize more than any fish you've caught with rod and line.

186

TAP'S TIPS

(Before ordering enlargements of fishing and hunting pictures, examine the negatives or contact prints with a magnifying glass. This may save you the expense of blowing up negatives that are out of focus, blurred, or otherwise unsatisfactory. If you think the picture is good enough to be published, order a glossy-finish print; 7 x 10 is the ideal size for framing or for newspaper or magazine reproduction.

(When taking outdoor pictures, remember that you get more interesting light and shadow contrasts in the morning and afternoon, when the sun strikes objects from the side. Angled lighting gives the subject depth and perspective.

(Sun glasses can be used as a filter to photograph dramatic cloud effects on black-and-white film. Be sure the goggles are perfectly clean, and don't forget to open the camera lens one or two f stops to compensate for the light that the glasses filter out.

Hunting

UPLAND BIRDS

Food Means Game

LATE SUMMER is the time to check on the wild crops and start planning strategy for fall hunting. Game goes looking for food, so it's smart to know where food is abundant. That way you won't waste precious hours hunting in barren country.

Walk with your head up. If you see a bumper crop of acorns, make a note to hunt the oaks in October. You'll find grouse and squirrels for sure, quite possibly pheasants also, after the early bombardment drives them out of the swales and cornfields. Raccoons work the oak ridges, too, a matter of considerable interest if you're a houn' dawg man. In years when the acorn crop is only so-so, squirrels and coons invade the cornfields. That's worth knowing.

Walk along a beech ridge with your head still up. An abundance of beechnuts promises grouse shooting as soon as the frost cracks open the burrs. Deer feed on beechnuts, too, even after snow falls and they have to paw through it to get a meal. In an off-year a beech grove won't hold so much as a stray chipmunk. You'll get better hunting if you know about the beeches before the season opens.

Above all, check on the abandoned apple orchards. A big apple year promises top grouse hunting, for the fruit attracts birds for acres around. Deer feed on apples, too. Come deer season, you'll find them skulking in the nearby thickets by day, boldly munching the fruit by night.

While you're checking on apples, notice if any young trees are split apart at the first fork. That could be the work of a bear. A visit at dawn or dusk may pay off with a crack at bruin.

Thornapples, wild grapes, berries—mark 'em all down for future reference, because where you find feed you're practically certain to find game.

TAP'S TIPS

❲ Don't hesitate to work a bird dog on wild game during the last two or three weeks before the season opens, if your state's game laws permit it. The dog probably needs the exercise, after a lazy summer, and can use a refresher course in bird handling. As long as the young birds are old enough to fly strongly, no harm will be done by breaking up the broods. In fact, scattering the flocks often reduces loss from predators.

❲ Dry shooting at flying birds with an unloaded gun will regroove your swing and help you hit more birds after the hunting season opens. Burning up a few boxes of shells on clay targets is an even better way to get ready for the big day.

❲ Here's a way to keep hunting boots snug and comfortable throughout a long day's hunt. Lace the boots about halfway, keeping moderate tension on the lacings, and tie off with a square knot. Then finish lacing to the top more loosely. The halfway knot holds the boot snug to the foot and prevents heel blisters. Above the knot the looser lacing gives the ankles and calf muscles more freedom. Without the knot, tension on the lacings becomes equal from top to bottom and the boot may start rubbing at the heel.

SQUARE KNOT

Hunting by Map

My old gunning partner of revered memory used to call our favorite grouse and woodcock covers "a string of pearls" and on our topographical map, may it never fall into enemy hands, that's what they looked like.

Gorham and I could start out in the morning and drive from one cover directly and quickly to the next, spending a few minutes in one

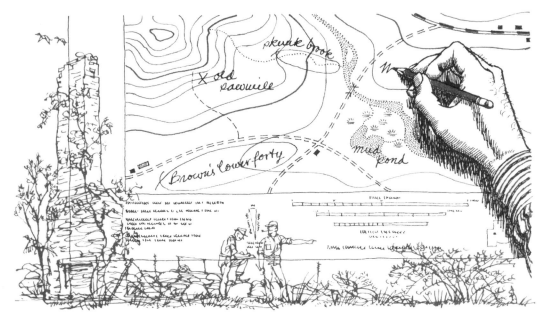

brushy little pocket, as much as an hour in a long "hunt around," and finish the day hardly more than a mile from our starting point.

Time is precious in the fall, and it's a crime against nature to waste the golden hours riding around in search of a place to hunt.

Suppose you're a pheasant hunter. A lot of pheasant hunters just drive around the farming country and prospect any promising swales or cornfields they see. But they spend more time riding than hunting and probably see more NO HUNTING signs than pheasants.

But suppose you've already done your prospecting and you know four or five places that generally hold a few birds. You've also spotted a pothole with mallard feathers floating on it, not far from an alder run where flight woodcock occasionally drop in to dig for worms. You put some time into finding these places, adding one or two new ones each season, but after you've found them you can start saving time, in big chunks.

First, you buy a U. S. Geological Survey topographic map* of the quadrangle you've scouted, and mark the location of your covers on it. It's a good idea to give each one a name that identifies it, like "Barking Dog" or "Old Outhouse." Your map shows old roads, farm houses long since fallen into their own cellar holes, streams, swamps and heights

---

* For quadrangle maps of areas west of the Mississippi, send 30 cents to Geological Survey, Federal Center, Denver 2, Colorado. East of the Mississippi, to Geological Survey, Washington 25, D. C.

192

of land, so it's easy to pinpoint your covers exactly. Then you just tie them all together by the highways and byways that run near them.

At the beginning there'll be some big blank spots between covers, but as time goes on you'll fill them in with places worth visiting—and that's the main idea. Eventually you'll put together your own string of pearls, looping around in a circle that brings you home in the evening feeling as if you'd done a good day's work—and with birds in the game bag to prove it.

TAP'S TIPS

⟮ Can you remember how many birds you shot last fall, or the year before? You would know the exact number of each species you collected if you kept a feather tally. Just pluck a tail feather off each bird you bring home and keep it in a handy container (I use a small flower vase). At the end of the season put all the feathers in a large envelope, mark the date on it, toss in some repellent to keep the moths out, and file it for future reference.

⟮ You may have noticed that a great many experienced hunters wear shooting glasses in the woods. The goggles protect the eyes from three common hazards: sun glare, stray shot, and getting "twigged." Any shooter can become used to wearing the glasses in a single day.

⟮ If your hunting trips take you over back roads, you may avoid getting stuck in mud or snow by carrying a few strips of asphalt shingles in the back of your car. Placed in front of the wheels, rough side down, they provide excellent traction.

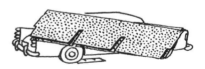

Easy to Hit, Hard to Find

One thing most upland hunters agree upon: The easiest bird to hit and the hardest to get a shot at is the ringnecked biddy with the long, long tail.

For all his sneaky habits on the ground, a cock pheasant offers a tempting target in the air, due to his large size, his relatively slow, straight flight, and the fact that he generally flushes out in the open where you can see him.

The man with a dog—practically any breed—can get shots merely by keeping close to the dog till it puts up a bird. But the dogless hunter has his work cut out for him.

However, if he knows how pheasants behave, where they are likely

193

to be at different times of day, and how to get them off the ground, he can occasionally enjoy a slab of white breast meat spiced with No. 6 shot.

As a rule, pheasants leave their roosts soon after daylight, go to water, then feed till midday. They like to spend a long noon hour dusting leisurely on a sunny hillside before reversing the procedure. So those are the places to start looking for pheasants, at those times of day.

Heavy hunting pressure changes the pattern, however. Then the beleaguered birds desert the gang-hunted areas and take to the woods, where they roost in trees at night and grub moodily for mast and berries during the day.

When flushed from an open field, pheasants try to get to the nearest woods if they can. A hunter can turn this habit to his advantage by stationing himself just inside such tongues of wooded cover while other hunters flog the fields. I once shot my two-cock limit within five minutes by finding just such a spot and acting as a reception committee for birds another party of hunters had flushed from a nearby corn patch.

The lone and dogless hunter couldn't do better than to look for brushy hedgerows separating cultivated fields and follow them to their end. Pheasants love to dawdle in hedgerows, and will pussyfoot ahead of the hunter till the cover thins. By looking ahead for such places and hurrying to get within shooting range of them before the birds flush, the gunner stands an excellent chance of cashing in on some easy shooting.

194

TAP'S TIPS

(Many hunters shoot behind crossing pheasants because the length of the tail fools them into shortening their lead. Whether you are a ride-'em-out wing-shooter or a poke-and-snap artist, try to concentrate only on the head and ignore (if you can) everything behind it.

(Pheasants like to crouch under a clump of weeds and let the hunter pass by if they think they can get away with it. So walk slowly when hunting without a dog, and stop frequently at patches of cover. Birds seem to panic when they lose the sound of the approaching hunter, and often burst into cackling flight almost from under his feet.

(Winter feeding stations often help the pheasants and quail to pull through prolonged periods of ice and snow. If you live near areas that hold game birds, you will enjoy watching the birds come to your station. Build it close to cover so they can get to it without exposing themselves too much. A roof of brush will be sufficient to protect the area from snow, but be sure to leave both ends open so feeding birds can escape from cats or other predators. Scatter cracked corn, mixed chicken feed and/or sunflower seeds on the bare ground beneath the shelter, and don't forget to include some gravel, which they need to grind the food in their crops.

Finding Grouse

Many a purple paragraph has been written in praise of the ruffed grouse, but not nearly so many about how to hunt him, which speaks well for the common sense of outdoor writers in general.

The princely "pa'tridge" dearly loves to make a monkey out of the most seasoned upland hunter, and I for one can offer no sure-fire way to put grouse in the game pocket. A good dog isn't necessarily the answer, because one of the most successful grouse hunters I know will not hunt with one—and another, just as successful, won't hunt without one.

Some grouse hunters like to sneak through the covers as quietly as possible, while others crash through the woods making as much noise as a rutting moose. Some gunners claim they take careful aim and calculate the exact amount of lead they should have before pulling the trigger, while others use the snapshoot method. About the only thing all grouse hunters have in common is this: They miss more birds than they hit.

One thing about grouse hunting you can depend on, though, is that

the more birds you flush, the more fun you have. And to flush birds you've got to know a lot of good covers and hit as many of them as possible before sundown. By working a planned circuit of closely-spaced covers you can move twice as many birds per day as you would hunting at random.

The typical grouse cover is usually just a brambly pocket with a few gnarled apple trees or a pasture corner grown to wild grape, black cherry, thornapple or alder, with a tumbled stonewall bounding it, and always close to some thick conifers where the birds can roost at night and find refuge in times of storm. In size the cover may range from a half-acre to five acres or more. One swing through it will usually move any birds that may be in residence at the time. Then get back to the car and drive to the next one. That's the way to move a lot of grouse in a day.

Most good grouse covers lie along country roads where you can spot them easily from the car, once you know what to look for. Watch for evidence of food—apple, thornapple, wild cranberry, grapes—and the places where such food is most likely to grow, around abandoned farms and old cellar holes, in clearings and forest edges. Remember the places where you've found birds in the past or, better yet, mark them on a topographical map, and when you've laid out a string of them fairly close together, you've got the makings of grouse hunting at its exciting best.

196

TAP'S TIPS

❲ Most upland hunters favor the walk-and-stop system for flushing grouse. However, I think grouse
sometimes lie better (for me, anyway) when I walk at
a steady, even brisk, pace and make no effort to be
stealthy. Grouse are set on a hair-trigger and often
flush too far ahead when they lose the sound of the
hunter's approach. Also, keeping on the move enables
me to scour an area faster so I can visit more covers
during a day's hunt.

❲ When you mark down a fallen bird in thick cover,
walk straight to the spot where you think it came
down and drop your hat or handkerchief there. By
making this marker the center of your search, and
hunting around it in ever-widening circles, you should
be able to find the bird.

Cock Grouse, or Hen?

A great many upland gunners insist that they can tell a cock ruffed
grouse from a hen bird in flight. Maybe they can—but their chance of
being right is only a little better than fifty-fifty.

With a bird in the hand, identification is somewhat easier. The

197

cocks, which average slightly heavier than the hens, have longer tails, the feathers measuring between 6 and 7½ inches as compared with 4½ to 6¼ for the hens. The black band on the hen's tail is *always* broken in the middle, while the cock's band is *usually* continuous. The cock's ruff is larger and more prominent, extending entirely across the breast. But the difficulty in making a sure-fire identification comes when you pick up a medium-sized grouse with tail feathers of medium length— say, 6 inches. Even if the tail band is broken, the bird *might* be a young cock.

Incidentally, the color of a ruffed grouse has nothing whatever to do with the bird's age or sex. Red and gray plumage are color phases which occur throughout the entire range of the species. However, red-colored grouse appear to be more common in the southern half of the bird's habitat, while "graytails" seem to occur more frequently in the northern states and Canada.

Just for the record, there are twelve subspecies of grouse, although they all look pretty much alike over the barrels of a fast-swinging shot-gun.

TAP'S TIPS

⟨ Ruffed grouse are not really partridge. The early settlers called them that because the bird resembled the European partridge. And our native bobwhite quail, which is also called a partridge in the South, is technically neither a quail nor a partridge.

⟨ The grouse is essentially a homebody and may live out its entire life on a patch of land hardly bigger than a square mile so long as the area continues to provide adequate food and shelter. So a productive grouse cover will almost always hold some birds, and can be hunted year after year.

(Have you ever discovered a grouse that has weathered out a severe winter storm by burying itself in a snowdrift? Look for a slight depression in the snow and prod it with a stick. If you're lucky you may get a faceful of exploding snow and feathers, along with an experience you will always remember.

Woodcock, High and Low

When a shotgunner starts acting like the cat that ate the goldfish, you can make up your mind that he has probably stumbled on a new woodcock cover. If you expect him to share his new-found treasure with you, however, it just goes to show that you have yet to learn one of the elementary facts of life. The devout woodcock hunter would as soon publish the balance in his bank account as disclose the location of his pet woodcock covers, even to his best friend. Perhaps *especially* to his best friend!

Since it's every man for himself, prospecting for new covers is one of the most important elements of woodcocking. The secret of successful timberdoodle sleuthing lies largely in looking for birds in several different types of cover. The popular notion that woodcock always prefer the low alder bottoms is false. Woodcock feed primarily on earthworms, and they'll move in wherever they find easy pickin's. This may be in the rich, black soil of the alder runs, but it's not always there by any means.

Look low, and then look high—on the sunny hillsides and even on the very ridgetops. A sidehill stand of young birch or poplar may be favored feeding grounds, so give cover of this type a thorough going over. Work sections of the hillside moistened by springs, and follow along brooklets that trickle down the slope. The damp earth holds worms and you may find woodcock, even though at first glance the cover seems much too sparse.

Sometimes you will find alders growing in really high country. Such covers hold golden promise. One small hilltop patch may hold more birds per acre than all the thick growths in the valley below. If anything, in fact, woodcock seem to prefer high ground whenever the all-important earthworm is to be found there.

When it comes to the go-bang part, woodcock aren't *too* hard to hit —after you have learned to wait 'em out.

They lie closer and fly slower than most game birds. This leads to the temptation to blast away at close range—and probably to miss. Let your bird get out where your pattern can open, then collect him.

If you mark the place where each bird falls you will rarely lose a

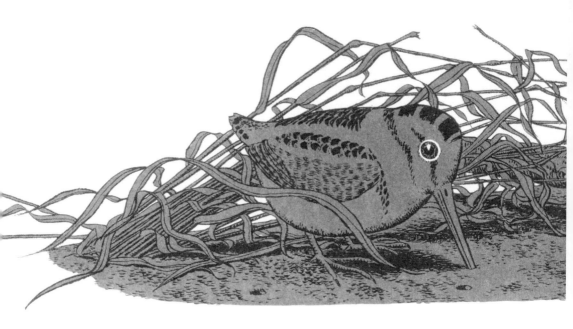

cripple. Woodcock, no matter how lightly wounded, seldom move from the spot where you drop them. Their protective coloration makes them hard to see on the leafy ground, but don't give up until you pick up your bird. If you brought him down, he's probably right there within a few yards of where he fell.

TAP'S TIPS

《 Woodcock "sing" when they stop at way stations on their journey north in the spring, and continue their prenuptial performance after they reach the nesting grounds, usually between mid-March and mid-April. If you have never enjoyed the show they put on with their singing and acrobatics, you can have a ringside seat if you sit quietly at a field edge close to cover just as the sun sets, or immediately after dawn.
《 Hunting shoes that seem to fit perfectly in the morning can become painfully tight by afternoon. Your feet may swell with walking, especially in warm early-season weather, so allow for it when you buy new boots by taking the next half-size larger than your street shoe size. Wear an extra pair of light weight or medium weight socks to make a snug fit, and take them off when the boots start to feel tight.

200

Woodcock Facts, Plus a Few Fancies

"A woodcock," my old gunning partner once said, "is a funny dang bird. He ain't hardly ever where he oughta be and he don't stay where he is after he gets there. I dunno's I'd enjoy hunting woodcock at all, except they're such a lot of fun to shoot at."

But he did enjoy it, and for more than twenty Octobers we chased woodcock up, down, and across the four northern New England states. In the process of doing so we learned almost enough about woodcock and their ways to qualify as junior-grade experts, or thought we did.

Among the things we learned about woodcock is that you shouldn't look for them only in alders. True, you will often find them there, and sometimes in great numbers when they are flighting through in the early fall. However, you will also find them in poplars and birches, in willows and overgrown apple orchards, and almost any place where cattle leave their noisome calling cards. On several occasions we found flight birds in pine groves—once in the middle of a harvested potato field.

One night when "laying over" in a New Hampshire inn during the gunning season we whiled away the evening hours by compiling a list of some of the things we knew, or thought we knew, about woodcock. Here are some highlights from the list, pretty much as we wrote them down that October night at the inn:

It is a waste of time to look for woodcock on mossy ground or in high grass.

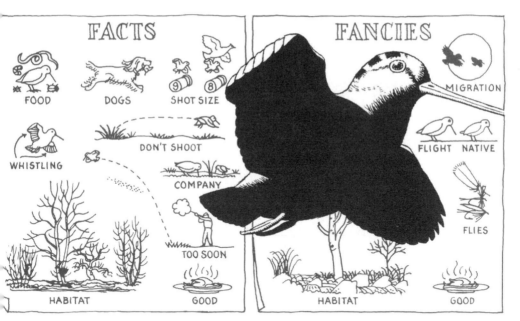

FACTS

FOOD   DOGS   SHOT SIZE

WHISTLING   DON'T SHOOT   MIGRATION

COMPANY   FLIGHT   NATIVE

TOO SOON   FLIES

HABITAT   GOOD   HABITAT   GOOD

FANCIES

You will find more woodcock near brooks with muddy banks than brooks with rocky beds.

Woodcock don't necessarily travel on a full moon, or on the dark of the moon either. They flight when the wind is blowing their way, or whenever they happen to feel like it.

The whistling sound is made by the woodcock's wings. Sometimes they fly without whistling at all.

Woodcock feathers don't make especially good trout flies.

Light loads of No. 9 shot are ideal for woodcock. However, 8's are better if you expect to put up some grouse, too.

Hunting woodcock without a pointing dog takes most of the fun out of it.

Flight birds aren't bigger or smaller than native birds. All native birds become flight birds when they head south.

Dogs that dislike picking up woodcock can become good retrievers if you just make an issue of it.

Most woodcock are missed because the gunner shot too soon.

Woodcock don't feed entirely on earthworms. They also eat grubs, beetles, and many other varieties of insects.

Where you find one woodcock you're almost sure to find another nearby.

Shooting at ground-skimming birds can place your partner or your dog in danger. Always try to take your shot against the sky.

Woodcock broiled with bacon strips are delicious. (This was written at the insistence of my old gunning partner.)

Woodcock taste awful. (This was written by me.)

202

TAP'S TIPS

❴ While woodcock are capable of flying at a smart turn of speed, they seem to be moving faster than they really are, due to their small size and their habit of lying tight and flushing close to the gun. Of all game birds, woodcock give the gunner the longest time to get off a shot. If you take advantage of this fact you are almost certain to improve your shooting score.

❴ One of the many peculiarities of the woodcock is that the hen always incubates four eggs. I have never seen, nor heard of, a woodcock nest—actually, just a depression in some leaves—that contained three eggs or five eggs.

❴ Northbound woodcock offer a wonderful opportunity to give a bird dog some out-of-season work, or to start a pup pointing. No bird lies tighter to a dog, and during the spring migration, woodcock are plentiful enough to provide plenty of action. Look for them as soon as the ground clears of snow. The spring flight continues for a couple of weeks or longer, depending on the weather.

How Fast Was It Going?

If it was a game bird and you missed it, it was probably going faster than you thought, and almost certainly much faster than you allowed for when you swung ahead of the bird and pressed the trigger. Because as every experienced wingshooter will surely agree, under-leading accounts for more than 90 percent of the misses, and it is a rare bird indeed that lives to fly another day because the shot charge crossed in front of him.

Most birds can zip along pretty fast when they open the throttle, but their flight speeds are not particularly impressive when expressed in terms of miles per hour. For example, the chart on page 204 shows that a pheasant can fly at a speed of about 50 miles per hour (actually, they can fly much faster than that; the figure is a typical flight speed, not the maximum). A cock clattering over a cornfield at 50 mph isn't loafing, exactly, but that rate of speed doesn't sound nearly as fast as 73 feet per second, which is the same thing. It seems incredible that a ringneck flapping away at that speed will cover eight feet in just the eyeblink of time it takes a charge of shot leaving the gun at nearly 1,000 feet per second to catch up to him at 30 yards range. Even a woodcock, bumbling along at only 25 mph, will clear the alders at the rate of 37 fps, and travel another three feet while the No. 9 shot is overtaking it.

SPECIES & FLIGHT SPEED	LEAD at 30 yds.
CANVASBACK · 65 mph	11 ft.
PINTAIL · 60 mph	10 ft.
GOOSE } MALLARD } 55 mph	9 ft.
PHEASANT · 50 mph	8 ft.
QUAIL · 40 mph	6 ft.
GROUSE · 30 mph	4 ft.
WOODCOCK · 25 mph	3 ft.

So while you may find the figures in the chart interesting, in an academic way, I'm afraid you won't find them very useful. You could hunt pheasants all season long and never get a shot at one flying exactly 50 mph at a 90-degree angle to the gun. Even if you did, you would probably miss him if you led him exactly 8 feet, due to the many variable factors that make an accurate calculation of lead impossible under field shooting conditions.

In addition to the bird's precise angle of flight, you would also have to know the direction and force of the wind and take into account even the size of the shot pellets and the amount of powder behind them. On top of that you might also have to know your individual reaction time—how long it takes you to pull the trigger after you decide that the time has come to do so. This varies greatly. A well-coordinated individual might do it in as little as two-tenths of a second—and that's faster than average—while it might take you or me twice that long. In two-tenths of a second a 50-mph ringneck will fly another 15 feet, and you or I could miss the bird by that much if we stopped swinging or failed to follow through as we let off the shot. That one factor alone can mess up any mathematical formula we try to apply to wingshooting.

So it won't do much good to know how much forward allowance a flying bird should be given under theoretical conditions. What can help, though, is to know and remember that it takes a measurable length of time to deliver a charge of shot to a moving target. The way to take care of that time lag is to develop a smooth swing, follow through after the shot, and, perhaps most important of all, give the bird a little more lead than you think necessary.

TAP'S TIPS

❦ One of the best ways to make a gunning partnership pay off is to hunt abreast of one another. Otherwise flushed game may cross behind the leading hunter or far ahead of the trailing hunter. Moving together at a matched pace is safer, too, because each partner then knows where the other is, even when he is hidden in thick cover.

❦ A dog doesn't enjoy taking pills any more than a human does, but he'll hardly realize he has taken one if it's given properly. Hold the dog's upper jaw with the cheeks pressed against his teeth so he can't close his mouth. Then place the pill 'way back in the throat opening, clamp his jaws together, and stroke his throat downward to make him swallow.

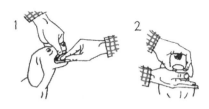

Hardest, Easiest Targets

Which game bird is the hardest to hit? Whenever you feel like touching off an argument, drop that bit of kindling among some hunters. You'll start a fire every time.

Some will insist that nothing in feathers is harder to hit than a ruffed grouse battering his way through heavy cover or diving headlong out of a pine tree. Others will tell you the toughest target is a dove, because of its great speed and darting flight. Somebody's sure to ask with a sneer if you've done much pass shooting at ducks, and someone else will mention quail in a reverent voice.

All right, then, which is the easiest to hit? Pheasant, you may say, because it's so big, usually gets up in open cover and flies straight. Uh huh. You ever missed one? Missed *more* than one? Well, me too.

Woodcock, maybe. Flutters up like a big butterfly, so all you've got to do, really, is wait till he clears the top of the cover and take him as he levels off. Just a simple matter of timing, that's all. Surprising, though, how many upland gunners never quite get the hang of it.

Ducks over decoys? They look easy, and should be. But there are more places where they ain't than where they are, and sometimes you wonder if the ammunition companies don't let some shells come through

HARDEST TO HIT

EASIEST TO HIT

the loading line without any shot in them. For one reason or another, you miss ducks more often than you like to admit.

The real key to wingshooting is timing, I think. Like a high-average batter timing his swing to a fast ball and then to a change-up, the wingshot must adapt his own timing to the flight of whatever game bird he's hunting. Once you get it, and for as long as you have it, birds will come down. Otherwise, any of them can be hard to hit.

Many shotgunners, I think, worry too much about which size of shot they should use for whatever species of game bird they happen to be hunting at the time. Actually, the biggest problem is not what to hit the bird with, but to hit it—period. Any load, from the souped-up high-base extra-long-range whoopee shell down to the standard field load, will do its job if the bird is in range when the pattern smacks it.

Seldom will any two gunners agree on the proper size of shot for a given game bird, mostly because their guns may handle some loads better than others—meaning that they throw smoother patterns at killing range. However, as a rule of thumb it's a sound idea to use shot in the smallest practical size, because the effectiveness of any load is due not so much to the penetration of the individual pellets as to their shocking power. Ballistics experts will tell you that shocking power increases as the square of the number of effective pellets. In everyday language, that means that two pellets have not twice but *four times* the shocking power of one. So the more pellets you plunk into your bird, the better your chance of seeing it come cartwheeling to earth.

The following table will serve as a guide to choosing an efficient load to throw at your favorite game bird:

206

	Size of Shot	Diam. in inches	Approx. pellets per ounce
Quail	9	.08	585
Woodcock	9		
Grouse (early season)	9		
Grouse (late season)	7½	.096	350
Doves	7½		
Pheasants (over dogs)	7½		
Pheasants (open fields)	6	.12	225
Ducks (over decoys)	6		
Ducks (pass and jump)	4	.13	135
Geese (over decoys)	4		
Geese (pass shooting)	2	.15	90

TAP'S TIPS

⟮ When you are stop-and-go hunting for upland birds, plan to "go" quickly through the thickets and "stop" in the openings. Birds usually flush during the "stop," so pausing when you are in a clearing puts you in a better position to get off a shot.

⟮ Cock pheasants almost always cackle when they flush, but it would be a mistake to depend entirely on this as a means of telling whether the bird is a legal cock or an illegal hen. Although it very rarely happens, hens can make a cackling sound too—and waiting for the cackle that doesn't come may cost you a shot at a cock. Let your eyes tell you whether the bird is a cock or hen; let the cackle serve as the alert signal.

⟮ To prevent briars and brush from tearing off your pin-on hunting license, first pin it securely through an unworn, untorn part of your jacket (preferably double thickness), and then squeeze the clasp tightly around the pin with pliers.

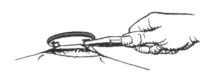

Split-Seconds Count

Gorham Cross, my grouse hunting partner during what may well have been the best twenty years of my life, used to grin sheepishly when I referred to him as "Old Bang-Mark."

Gorham was the courteous type who always called "Mark!" to alert his companion when a bird got up. But he was also an exceptionally fast man with a shotgun, so it would sometimes come out Bang! "Marrrk!" followed as often as not by "Fetch" to the dog, for Gorham was a deadly shot as well as a fast one.

Looking back, it seems that all of the top wingshots I've known had exceptionally quick hands. I don't mean that they always shot fast. But they could when they had to.

Have you ever figured how much time a game bird gives you from the instant it flushes till it gets out of range? You'd be surprised how little it is.

Let us suppose, for example, that you are hunting grouse, and a fidgety bird suddenly erupts from a clump of thornapple just twenty yards away. By rights, you should be able to pepper that foolish biddy with No. 8 shot before she gets decently clear of the ground. But you don't. Instead, she darts behind a hemlock and your load of shot spatters harmlessly into its trunk.

Now, it just doesn't seem possible that any bird can fly far enough, in the eyeblink of time it takes you to get off a shot, to remove itself from danger. But it can, and often it does.

Mounting and firing a shotgun is a much slower process than many hunters realize. It takes time for the human brain to flash hurry-up messages to muscles and for muscles to fit the gun to the shoulder, slip off the safety, adjust angle and speed of swing, and then to pull the trigger. And while all this is going on the bird is removing itself from the scene with frantic haste.

According to speedometer-clocked figures, a grouse can cover about 35 feet in a second, a quail as much as 75, a pheasant 90, a canvasback more than 100. So the faster you can get a well-aimed charge of shot to an outgoing target, the better your chance of hitting it while it is still out in the open and within range.

There's nothing you can do to hasten the flight of the shotstring, which uses up about 1/8 second in covering 40 yards. But you can save time simply by getting your gun to your shoulder quicker.

Most hunters carry a gun in one of three ways: from the hand, like a suitcase; cradled in the crook of the arm; or in front of the body with hands on fore-end and grip.

The other day I borrowed a stopwatch to see how long it took me to mount, swing, and shoot a shotgun from each of these carrying positions. Taking an average of a large number of dry firings, I found that I needed 1⅕ seconds to shoulder and shoot the gun from the crook-of-the-arm position, exactly 1 second from the suitcase carry, and ⁷⁄₁₀ second from the front-of-the-body, or port arms, position. And, lest you think I dawdled, I must state here as modestly as I can that I have flung lead at feathered game for more than thirty years, and am not considered the slowest gun in the East.

Now, getting back to the close-lying grouse that flushes at 20 yards, here's how the faster gun-carrying position can help you to gather her in—at least, in theory.

If you are cradling the gun in the crook of your arm when she takes off, she can fly about 42 feet before your shot charge catches up to her, assuming she's in high gear and it takes you as long as it took me—1⅕ seconds—to get off your shot from that carrying position. If you are holding the gun in your hand, hanging at your side, you should be able to cut her down 35 feet from where she flushed. But if you are carrying the gun in front of you with both hands, muzzle up and perhaps with the butt resting lightly on your hipbone, your shot charge can overtake her before she flies 25 feet. And with a little bit of luck, you may dump her before she reaches the hemlock.

TAP'S TIPS

⟨ Hunting is tough on the feet, but a change to dry, clean socks at noon can make you feel like a new man. Carry an extra pair in the car or in your hunting coat. And be sure they are made of wool.

⟨ When you start hunting birds after warming up on clay targets you may miss the first few birds you shoot at and wonder why. The reason may be that you have become accustomed to shooting at targets that are losing speed, and have forgotten that game birds gain speed after they flush. Once you adjust your swing to that factor you will probably start hitting birds.

⟨ Firm footing is important to good shooting. If the soles of your hunting boots are smooth and slip on leaves or pine needles, you can improve their traction by scoring them in a crisscross pattern, using a sharp knife or the edge of a grinding wheel.

Save Your Game

Almost any kind of upland game can furnish the makings of a meal fit for a—well, fit for a hungry hunter and his family. But it doesn't always work out that way. Too many game birds, rabbits, and squirrels end up in the garbage bucket because the hunter didn't deliver them to the cook in good condition.

Strictly from a hygienic point of view, what we call "clean" kills are anything but. A center-of-the-pattern hit almost always punctures intestines. The contents then drain into the body cavity where they may taint the meat or even make it utterly unfit for cooking.

You can avoid this by drawing your game in the field, promptly after it has been killed. Simply slit through skin and membrane, and you can remove most of the intestines with a couple of hard shakes. Drawing game is especially important during the warm weather of early gunning season. Heat, plus the confinement of a game pocket, can ruin neglected game quicker than you think. On such days, after field-dressing your game, stuff the body cavity loosely with dry grass. This holds the cavity open and allows air to cool and dry the exposed meat.

Unless you like your game "hung till high," finish the cleaning job promptly after you reach home. In addition to skinning or plucking, cut out and discard all badly mutilated and clotted sections. Remove pellets embedded in the flesh, along with the plug of feathers or hair that each one has driven into the meat. Then wash the carcass in cold water, wipe it dry, and pop it into the freezer or refrigerator. The next time you see it, sizzling on a platter, you'll be glad you took the time to dress it.

TAP'S TIPS

(A pair of small tin shears makes the job of cleaning game birds easier and quicker. They cut through bone without effort, making it simple to snip off wings, legs, feet and heads, and preserve the edge on your knife for more delicate work with skin and flesh.

(High-velocity loads don't belong in the upland gunner's pocket, unless he hopes to see a fox, bobcat, or something else larger than a game bird. Lighter charges not only kill most flying game as efficiently as the magnum stuff, but deliver a softer wallop at the butt plate. You will shoot better when you feel confident that you can pull the trigger without fear of being kicked out from under your hat.

(Here's a quick and easy way to pick the shot and feathers out of game bird meat. Hammer the point of a small nail flat so it forms a tiny spade with jagged edges. Insert the nail in the shot hole, twist, and out come both shot and imbedded feathers.

Keep out of My Grouse Covers!

"Wipe that feather off Mack's chops," George hissed, "and make like you haven't seen a bird all day. There's a feller comin' down the road."

"For the love of Pete!" I said. "He must have seen us coming out of the alders. If he can't add that to a couple of guns, two bird dogs and the silly look on your face, then he wouldn't know a woodcock if one pecked him in the eye. Besides, he hasn't even got a gun. Looks like a walking stick to me."

"Just the same, you never can tell," insisted George, lowering his voice and talking from the side of his mouth. "Lots of hunters just snoop around back roads like that, tryin' to steal other people's covers. You better let me do the talkin'."

I stuffed the two dogs into the back of the station wagon, laid my gun against the front seat, and slumped on the fender. "Carry on," I said.

The stranger came abreast of the car and stopped, a pleasant smile on his face. "Hunting?" he asked.

"Oh, just sort of looking around," George answered in an elaborately offhand manner. "Not many birds this year, you know. We're really out for the ride more than anything else." He cast an eye upward. "Foliage is lovely, ain't it?"

"Nice-looking dogs you've got there," the stranger said, peering into the car. "Setter—and what's that one without any tail? Some kind of a spaniel, isn't it?"

"Brittany," I told him, jumping up. "The best damned—"

"Dogs aren't good for much," George interrupted hastily. "They chase rabbits, about all. Wouldn't know what to do if they saw a—uh—pheasant." He turned to me. "Would they?"

"Yours wouldn't," I said.

George stared at me hard for a moment, then turned to the stranger again. "You do much hunting?"

"No, I—"

"Live around here?"

"No, I—"

"Own any bird dogs?"

"No."

"Just as well," George informed him. "Dog can't earn his horse-meat these days. Just no birds around this year, that's all."

"Yes, so you said." The stranger started edging away. "Well, good luck to you both."

He walked off quickly, swinging his stick at crimson maple leaves that littered the shaded New Hampshire lane.

"There, see?" George swung on me. "Notice all those questions? As if he didn't know a Brittany when he saw one! Are we hunting, he wanted to know! That feller'll be back here with a gun soon as our backs are turned, you mark my words. Dammit, look at the bulge in the back of your shooting vest! You should've hid those birds before he got here. He had a shifty eye, that fellow. I'll bet he heard us in there, with all that damned bang-banging of yours and screaming at the dogs. Let's get out of here before some other snoopy so-and-so comes along."

So we got out, with our five woodcock and our pair of grouse, and that night at the Valley Hotel in Hillsboro, where we "laid over" for the Sunday shooting, George unrolled the topographical map and spread it over the bed. With a pencil he drew a bold circle around the newly discovered woodcock parlor and beside the circle he lettered the following legend: Snoopy Stranger.

Most of the names we have given our grouse and woodcock covers betray their origin in similar manner—Woodcock Pasture, for example, where during the second or third week of October we sometimes find an almost incredible number of timberdoodles in residence; Gold Mine, Jackpot, Shellbox, T Corner, Deer Trails, Red Gate, Bear Traps.

One of our better covers lies in an otherwise undistinguished area of scattered popple and pine. We had driven by it many times over the years, never suspecting what treasure lay hidden there, and we might be driving by it yet had we not one day spotted a grouse running across the dusty road. George slammed on the brakes and, the day having been an unrewarding one, we boiled out in eager pursuit.

Mindful of our rule that road-birds must never be potted on the ground, we chased the biddy over the stone wall and into the popples, where she got up. George missed her on the rise, I missed her as she banked and turned, and we both failed to connect with our second barrels. As we stood there with smoking tubes watching her scale out of sight, five more grouse rose from the popples one at a time and thundered out, offering five straightaway shots on which any small boy could have scored with a slingshot.

The next day we went back and put a pair of them to the sword, and many times since we have visited the patch of popple with sanguinary results. Should anyone steal our map, he will find the cover identified thereon as The Traitorous Road-Bird.

Finding an unbroken brood in a tucked-away corner is something like digging up a chest of pirate gold in a garden plot. Not all our covers, however, are so well populated. We have one little patch of tangled grapevine wherein dwells a lone grouse; always one, never more. We know it can't be the same bird we find every time, but for all of us it may be, for we have never cut a feather in there. The bird is a constant challenge. On days when the pickings have been slim George is almost sure to say, "Let's go shoot at The Stinker."

We hardly ever fail to find her home, but each time we approach her tangled lair she gets out wilder, and each time she seems to know in advance the careful battle plan we have worked out. George, who is deadly on driven birds, posts himself in line with the clump of pines where she often seeks refuge—and she promptly squirts out of the side. We both pussyfoot around the edge of the cover, letting the dogs do the dirty work, and she hammers out of the far end, flirting her tail at us contemptuously.

Once we had her tightly boxed. Both dogs pointed from opposite sides and George and I moved in from each end, guns at ready arms, confident that at long last we had The Stinker dead to rights.

"Kick her up," George said evenly, "and wait till she gets out a way before you plaster her."

As I moved in to flush her a woodcock twittered up behind me and, in the silly fashion of a woodcock, swooped in front of my Bing pup. Bing broke point and took off after the timberdoodle. Staunch old Mack, tempted beyond all reason, whirled and joined Bing in the merry chase. While George and I cursed and screamed at the dogs The Stinker scuttled out to the edge of the cover and rumbled away, scot-free again.

George and I do not always agree on the names by which we call our covers. One such is a hidden pocket of alder and apple that lies—

well, never you mind where it lies. In southern New Hampshire, let us say, and not too distant from the friendly bulk of Mt. Monadnock. That's close enough. We stumbled upon it late on a golden afternoon in mid-October after noticing on our tattered map a dead-end road that wound among the hills to a farmhouse. We ground over the road in second gear and found only the cellar hole of the house, with an alder-fringed brook trickling through the valley and the ragged rows of an apple orchard marching up the slope beyond.

"How'll we hunt it?" I asked. "You want to clean the woodcock out of the alders and then hit the orchard, or shall we kill off the grouse first?"

George eyed me glumly. "Pretty cocky, aren't you?" he said. "Well, now, if I had a couple of birds stashed away today, like you have, I s'pose I'd feel that way too. You just wait till your eyes start to go back on you, like mine. Just wait"—he rubbed his right shoulder tenderly—"till you get the arthritis so bad you can hardly lift your gun. My legs are giving out on me too. They feel like I was walkin' on rubber bands." He sighed deeply. "Guess this is my last season in the woods with you, old friend. Well, let's try them alders first."

Dropping two shells into the open tubes of his gun, George strode forth toward the thicket. His Mack dog was already flowing through the alders like a white ghost. My Bing remained whimpering in the car, doing penance for having flushed and chased and—worse yet— barked at a woodcock.

"Mack's gettin' old too," George tossed back over his shoulder. "Five years ago he'd have had them alders scoured by now, and if there was a bird in—Whup! Point!"

We marched in abreast, one on each side of the pointing dog. The woodcock sprang toward my side, offering one of those ridiculously easy shots such as artists like to paint for sporting magazine covers. I slapped the barrels on him and pulled. Miraculously, the bird kept going. Hastily I covered him again and yanked the second trigger. Twittering with contempt, the woodcock banked over the alders and disappeared from my view just as George's gun spoke up.

"Fetch him in, Mack," he ordered in a matter-of-fact voice.

Mack laid the bird in George's hand. "Notice how Mack just trotted in with him?" George pointed out. "Sure sign he's gettin' old. He used to run in with his birds, so he could get back to huntin' quicker. Poor old feller. Hie on, Mack."

The big setter ran his vacuum-cleaner nose through the alders, hurdling the brook on each cast, and whirled into point directly in front of me. "Point!" I called.

"Take him," George called back. "And for heaven's sake, please

214

kill another bird for him. He ain't got many chances left in this world, you know."

The bird got up leisurely, lifting out of the alders like a free balloon. I let him get up against the sky, blotted him out with the barrels, and pulled the trigger. It flickered loosely. So did the one behind it. The woodcock climbed higher, and at the bark of George's gun it collapsed and fell almost at my feet. Mack picked it up, leered at me, and carried it to George.

Woodcock in hand, George stepped from the alders. "Wha' hoppen?"

"I forgot to reload," I told him lamely.

He grinned maliciously and burrowed back into the cover. I thumbed open the breech of my gun, slipped in a pair of fresh loads and moved on up the brook, feeling a bit grim.

"Point!" called George hardly more than a minute later. "This place is full of 'em."

I edged into an open spot and waited, thumb on safety. Dimly I heard the whistle of wings and then, drowning out the sound, a rumbling roar. George's gun spoke authoritatively twice, the two shots almost blending into one.

"Fetch," I heard George say. Then, a moment later: "Good dog. Now go bring me t'other one."

I moved in to witness the proceedings. George was standing at the edge of the run, a woodcock dangling from his fist, while Mack trotted up to him with a grouse in his mouth.

"Great balls of fire! You doubled!"

"Well," he said modestly, "a mixed double. The pat got up from under that old blowdown same time the woodcock went up. Now, then," he said, striking a judicial pose, "which one would you take first? Over there's the pat, bumblin' out of the blowdown. Yonder's the woodcock, a-twitterin' and a-twistin' in the alders. Well, said I to myself, that pat's goin' to get out of there fastest; so maybe you better—"

"Skip it," I said. "I'll hear about that all the rest of my life anyway. Where's Mack?"

George looked around. "Must be pointin' somewhere," he said mildly. "Maybe we better look him up."

We found Mack stretched out under an old apple tree, head and tail high, his eyes rolling back at us. George and I deployed, one on each side of the tree, and moved forward. The bird rose from behind a thornapple and bored into the alders on George's side. As the gray tail disappeared from view George touched off his shot, showering leaves and twigs through the thicket. We waited, openmouthed, and a moment later heard the welcome sound of wings beating the earth.

George flipped open the breech of his gun, spinning the empty shell over his shoulder. "Fetch, Mack," he ordered, cutting a glance at me.

"Do you realize," I said, trying to keep the awe out of my voice, "that you have killed five straight in here?"

George took the grouse from Mack's mouth. "Have I?" he asked. "Well, now that you mention it, I guess I have. Easy shots, though. And awful lucky. Most of the time I was just shootin' at the sound, on account of my eyes bein' so bad. And you know something?" He turned to me with a mournful expression on his face. "I don't think my hearing's as good as it used to be, either!"

We walked out of the cover through the lengthening shadow of old Monadnock while Mack skirmished fruitlessly through the orchard. At the car, while George unloaded his birds, I hauled out the map and marked the dead-end road with a circle. Beside it I wrote, "Five Straight." George peered over my shoulder, took the pencil from my fingers, rubbed out the two words I had written, and lettered in a firm hand, "Easy Pickin's."

We like to think that all our covers, like Easy Pickin's, are ours and ours alone, undiscovered and unhunted by others. This is pure fiction on our part, of course, and we know it. Some of our pet spots are familiar ones, and a hunter must get up early and drive fast to reach them before another party has a chance to get there first, and, as George describes it sourly, "scramble the birds all to hellengone."

Probably the greatest blow George ever suffered was the discovery that someone else was actually hunting Jackpot, his favorite cover. Upon many occasions George has driven miles off our course to taste the delights of this birdy pocket where, day in and day out, a well-ordered hunt can move three or four grouse and, in season, several times that many woodcock. I had observed some evidence that another gunner might be calling on George's sweetheart—an empty high-base shell here and there, and once a hatful of grouse feathers where neither George nor I had ever dumped a bird. But he refused to believe that our secret had been discovered, and blamed the empty shells on rabbit hunters, the feathers on a marauding fox.

One day, however, during the very best of the woodcock flight, we caught the interloper at the scene of his crime. There was his car parked in our barway, and there was the red-shirted scoundrel himself, just stepping forth. Furthermore, there was his dog, a bony pointer trailing a drag-rope from his collar.

George stopped the station wagon and eased himself out from under the wheel. "Goin' to give it a try, eh?" he asked in a hail-comrade-well-met tone of voice.

"Thought I might," the hunter replied, forcing a small grin.

216

"My partner here and I were in there once, couple days ago," George informed him jovially. "Never moved a bird. Not even a woodcock."

"Well," the hunter said, "long as I've stopped here, guess I'll look it over, anyway. Just happened to notice it, driving by."

"Sure, sure," George agreed heartily. "Never can tell when a stray bird might work in. Watch out for the bull, though. He's meaner'n a snake, and he won't like that red shirt you're wearin'. Keep your dog in close, too. Never saw so many porcupines in my life as I saw in there. Your dog broke on porcupines?"

"Well, no, I can't say he—"

"There's an old well in there, too, with only a rotten old board over it. Pretty dangerous if you don't know just where it is. Man or dog could go right through it, and it's twenty foot deep if it's an inch."

"Thanks," said the hunter. He took three high-base shells from his pocket and inserted them in the breech of his pump gun. "I'll watch for the well, and keep my dog in close, like you said." He swung a leg over the wall, then hesitated and added over his shoulder: "As for the bull, don't you worry a bit. I recognize that when I hear it!"

"Now what," George demanded, turning wide-eyed to me, "do you suppose he meant by that?"

COVER

DECOY

SMALL GAME & VARMINTS

Crows the Hard Way

BETWEEN THE middle of March and the opening of the trout season there isn't very much a man can do outdoors except take off the storm windows or try to call in some crows. It has been my experience that taking off storm windows produces by far the best results—I'm always sure of bagging 26—because crow shooting is as tough in the early spring as it can possibly get.

Until the trees grow some new leaves, cover will be sparse. And until the crows bring off their broods, there will be only birds a year old or older to call. Most of them have heard a call before, and it takes a good man with a tooter to fool them.

Cover can be found, though, by driving the back roads with an eye peeled for thickets of pine or spruce. In fact, it is actually more important to find cover than crows, for an expert caller can draw crows from a half-mile away, while without good cover it is almost impossible to coax birds into shotgun range.

Crows are notoriously keen-eyed, and when they respond to a call they are craning their necks to find what's causing all the hullabaloo. But if you keep well hidden and don't expose yourself while shooting,

218

you ought to get off several shots before the birds get wise and beat it.

One of the secrets of shooting crows is to divert their attention from you to something they can see, recognize, and hate. A stuffed owl —it doesn't seem to matter what kind of an owl—is just about one of the best crow decoys you can get. A fox pelt, curled atop a large boulder or on an exposed knoll, will claim the frenzied attention of any crows that see it. So, I've heard, will a live cat in a bird cage, but I like cats too much to try it.

The body of your first crow will make a satisfactory decoy if you hang it in plain sight, preferably from a limber sapling which will allow it to flutter and swing in the breeze.

Remember, the purpose of the decoy is to attract and hold the attention of the crows, so be sure to place it far enough from your blind so the crows can't see you and your decoy at the same time—but close enough so that the crows will be within shotgun range when they come swooping over your fox pelt or stuffed owl.

Keep calling excitedly as long as the crows show interest. Above all, keep hidden. The sound of gunfire, even the sight of their falling brothers, doesn't seem to alarm the crows nearly as much as a white eyeball gleaming out of a clump of brush.

When it seems hopeless to call any more, gather up the casualties, if any, for use as decoys, and drive on a mile or so before calling again. In the very early season you may do well to get some shooting at every third or fourth place you stop. But even that little bit will give you more fun than you'd have at home taking off storm windows.

Finding crows, and an abundance of leafy cover to shoot from, presents no problem during the late spring and throughout the summer. But crow hunting becomes difficult again in the winter, when snow blankets the ground and the crows, now older and wiser, have learned that man sometimes has evil designs on them. However, the winter-bound gunner who likes to do things the hard way will enjoy the extra challenge of shooting under these long-odds conditions.

So winter is the time to break out the night shirt—and I mean the big, flowing garment, size Extra Large, that Grandpaw used to wear to bed. I paid a buck-ninety-eight for mine at Sears Roebuck. It has been one of the best investments I have ever made. Just slip the night shirt on over your heavy clothes (that's why you need the Extra Large size) and you've got your blind right on you. Where you go, it goes. If you can't find a white hat, just pin a handkerchief on whatever you're wearing, being sure to anchor the corners so they won't flap in the breeze.

In my experience, the gun, dark against the snow as it is, doesn't alarm crows so long as it doesn't move. They say crows will take alarm at the sight of a man with a gun and ignore a man without one. I believe that's true. But if they can't see *you*, your motionless gun won't frighten them off. Some winter crow hunters wrap their guns with white tape, but the chief advantage seems to be that doing so merely covers careless movement.

So if you itch for a bit of shooting in the dead of winter, buy yourself a night shirt and go looking for crows. They'll come to a call nicely, and if you've never tried crow-shooting in the snow, you'll be surprised to find so many of them wintering around the piggeries and river-bottoms.

TAP'S TIPS

❨ If you are lucky enough to locate a flyway that crows use to return to their roost in the late afternoon you can enjoy some fast and exciting pass shooting. If possible, pick a spot on high ground directly in the path of the flyway. Build a blind of leafy boughs, get into it well before the evening flight begins—and be sure to bring plenty of shells.

❨ Bird-lovers should feel no pangs of conscience over shooting crows. Many that fall to the gun will have the stain of song-bird eggs on their beaks. Crows destroy literally millions of birds every year, and it has been estimated that they kill more than twice as many ducks as hunters do—as many, some naturalists claim, as thirty million during a single breeding season.

⟨ Many crow hunters consider June and October the two best months of the year for crow shooting. In June the young birds are off their nests, swelling the crow population to its season's peak, and these birds are not nearly so wary as their parents. In October, when the crows start to gather in flocks before migrating south, they occur in great concentrations and seem less cautious than they were during the summer months.

The Varmint That Isn't

Woodchucks could be called our biggest small game. Or maybe our smallest big game. Whichever, the pasture pig (actually, an Eastern marmot, and a member of the squirrel family) offers a tempting target to the man who fancies himself a hotshot with a rifle. As a friend of mine once observed, chuck hunting gives you a chance to hunt antelopes where there ain't any antelopes.

It is a fact, and perhaps an unfortunate one, that woodchucks are more vulnerable in the spring than at any other season of the year. Hungry after their long winter's sleep, they feed boldly on the tender new grass before it has grown deep enough to hide them. Also, spring is their mating season. Beguiled with love-making and later busy with family cares, the normally shy woodchuck becomes careless of danger. So during April and May the chuck hunting is at its best, if the sport is measured by the number of chucks that are shot, or shot at.

Although few people strongly dislike the woodchuck, a cleanly, inoffensive animal that does little more damage than a rabbit and far less than a weasel or a skunk, every rifle-owner dearly loves to shoot at him. In those farm areas where chucks are overabundant, some measure of control through spring hunting is no doubt justified. Personally, I would rather wait till midsummer, when the young of the year are old enough to take care of themselves if something happens to Mama, and the shooting becomes more challenging, before I set forth for the pasture hillsides with a rifle under my arm.

Many thousands of woodchucks are shot every year with the rimfire .22. True, the rimfire packs enough punch at close-to-medium range to stop a chuck dead in its tracks—if the slug fetches up in the head or heart. But for every chuck killed clean with a .22 rimfire, I will wager that another drags itself down into its burrow to nurse a wound or to wait till death finally ends its suffering. The rimfire's light shocking power, its lobbing trajectory, and the iron sights of the typical .22 rifle make a crippling combination.

Like any game animal, the woodchuck deserves the compliment of a clean-killing load such as the .220 Swift or .219 Zipper, with better than 3000 fps velocity at the muzzle. The rifle should be mounted with a quality scope of at least 4 power, and preferably equipped with a sling. With such a rifle, chuck hunting is truly a fine sport, and a challenging one.

If you have never eaten woodchuck, just remember when you dress out the critter to remove the two red, pea-sized musk glands which lie inside the upper front legs, and trim off the excess fat. Then follow your favorite rabbit recipe. You may enjoy a pleasant surprise when you sink your teeth into the first mouthful.

222

TAP'S TIPS

❲ Woodchucks are obliging creatures. They feed mostly in the late afternoon and early evening—just when it is most convenient for a 9-to-5 working man to hunt them. During the long summer days you can finish your work, eat a leisurely meal, and still have time for a couple of hours of chuck shooting.

❲ To get good woodchuck hunting in midsummer, plan to be on hand immediately after the local farmers cut their hay. As soon as clover or grass grows tall enough, many chucks move into the fields to dig new dens. When the mowing machines leave, you've got them where the hay is short.

❲ Although a chuck will dive for safety at the first sign of danger, he will soon poke his nose out again to see if the coast is clear. So even if you miss a shot, or drive the chuck underground by exposing yourself, stick around. Sooner or later he will come out and give you a second chance.

Nutcracker Suite

One of the easiest ways I know of to pick up some of the important fundamentals of stalking wild game is to go squirrel hunting.

Of course, no squirrel can equal a wily old buck when it comes to the finer points of making a hunter look silly. But our nut-crackin' friend is smart enough to teach any of us a few valuable lessons. For example, you can't flush him out of a thicket and pot him on the hop, as you can a cottontail. You can't simply walk up to him and shoot him, either, because, like a deer, a squirrel just won't stand still for you.

So when you want the chief ingredient for a squirrel pie, take a stand where "cuttings" are plentiful, and start making like you were a permanent part of the scenery. Soon you'll notice how awfully quiet the woods are. A little later you'll become conscious of tiny noises. You can't see anything yet, but now you're beginning to hear things.

Now, just what is making which noise? A rustle in the leaves would be a squirrel, of course. A heavier sound must be a deer feeding toward you. . . .

Well, your "squirrel" proves to be an inquisitive chipmunk, and what you thought was a deer materializes into exactly what you're looking for—a squirrel. You decide that your ears aren't quite as woods-wise as you thought they were.

But sitting and listening for squirrels is just the kind of practice they need. Before long they'll become properly attuned to the woods,

and begin sorting out the sounds for you. When that happens, you've become a better woodsman.

How to hide is another lesson you can learn from squirrel hunting. Keeping covered, you'll find, isn't nearly as important as keeping still. Then, if you force yourself to move s-l-o-w-l-y, you'll get the shots that ordinary movement would spoil.

So try it on squirrels; it'll help you when you hunt deer next fall.

TAP'S TIPS

⟨[When crossing a wire fence, always crawl under it instead of climbing over. If you're not careful going over the fence you may loosen staples or pull them out, perhaps even break the wire—and that's what makes landowners tack up No Trespassing signs.

⟨[Sit tight after shooting a squirrel from a stand. There are probably others around, and you may get more shots if you remain perfectly still. Make sure the squirrel is dead, mark it down carefully, and leave it there until you are ready to move on.

⟨[Squirrel meat is tasty almost any way it is cooked, but never better than baked in a pie with a flaky brown crust on top and lots of meat swimming in the pool. In many families, squirrel pie is traditionally the beginning of the "wild-meat season."

Everybody's Favorite

According to all the surveys, the rabbit is the most-hunted and most-shot-at game animal in the world. This only confirms what everyone already knows, that rabbits are without question our most popular game species. Despite the fact that 19 out of every 20 rabbits never live to celebrate their first birthday, they are abundant almost everywhere. The open season is long. The meat is delicious. And best of all, rabbits can be hunted by almost any method you like. Just name the game and the obliging bunny will abide by your rules.

If you enjoy hound music, then Molly and Peter will give you and your beagles a merry run anytime you wish. It takes real hound work to follow that twisting trail through briar patch and thicket, and you'll have to shoot fast and straight to rack up a respectable score on that bobbing, bouncing bundle of fur.

According to at least one popular notion, rabbit hunting with hounds is a cut-and-dried affair. The dogs invariably drive the rabbit in a circle and you bowl him over when he returns to where he was routed. That's what the script says, but a single hunt with a pair of fast, eager beagles will prove that rabbit hunting is not quite that simple.

Hound-driven rabbits usually stay within a fairly small area, but they do *not* run in circles. On the contrary, they weave such a crazy, patternless trail that you can't possibly outguess 'em—and smart hunters don't try. If you just pick a likely spot, sooner or later the rabbit will come to you.

Generally, you can't choose a worse stand than the place where the rabbit was jumped. Almost always he picks a dense thicket for his bed, a place where you'll have no chance for a shot should he scuttle through on his first swing—which he probably won't! Instead, find a place that gives you reasonable shooting space, but that a fleeing rabbit won't shun for lack of cover. An opening the size of a golf green surrounded by thick evergreens or briars would be good. Guard the opening from far enough back in the cover to give the pattern a chance to open.

Brushed-out power lines, patches of sparse hardwoods which poke into thick cover, and brushy corners of grownup fields make other excellent rabbit stands. An old woods roads is perfect if you can find a spot where the trail makes a sharp bend—the sharper the better. To cross the U a rabbit must clear the trail twice, and this often gives you a much-needed second crack at him.

If you wind up with a well-stuffed game pocket, the hard-working dogs will deserve the lion's share of the credit. But you'll rate at least a pat on the back for knowing a good stand when you see one.

For the same kind of sport but more of it, seek out the big, white snowshoe of the North. This long-legged and tireless hare can hold his own with the toughest hound ever whelped, when allowed to run his race to a finish. But like the cottontail, the snowshoe doesn't ramble far from home, so the shooting usually starts before the chase grows very old.

Walking up rabbits can be almost as much fun as chasing them with a beagle. Pick a day after a fresh fall of snow if you can, and work the covers where the tracks lie thickest. Remember that rabbits lie close, and often have to be literally kicked out, so don't pass up a single brushpile, cornshock, or hummock. And keep your thumb on the safety, because you may have to shoot fast at a bobbing, scuttling target that won't be in sight very long.

A running rabbit in thick cover offers a tricky target, even for the scattergun. When you hunt rabbits with a .22 rifle, as many do for extra sport, the odds against connecting become almost overwhelming. But rifle hunting adds spice to an already spicy game. And if you miss more than you hit (as you probably will), so what? Plenty more where they came from.

Of course, those with the greatest reason to feel grateful for the abundance of rabbits are the archery enthusiasts. Were it not for the cottontail population, the bowhunter would have little chance to exercise his skill on live game. As it is, the archer can enjoy excellent hunting almost in his own back yard. And whether you shoot a bow or not,

226

you can easily imagine the thrill of seeing a shaft fly straight and true to a target as challenging as a running rabbit.

TAP'S TIPS

❲ Heavy snow at night makes it difficult for a dog to start a rabbit the next morning. When he finally gets one up and running, let him drive it a while, even if you have to pass up a tempting shot. The dog's clamor will stir up other rabbits, so the next one will be easier for him to find.

❲ If you don't have all day to hunt rabbits, try short hunts from late afternoon till dusk. Because rabbits are largely nocturnal, that is when they start moving around. A quick check of the thickets and field edges may give you an hour of brisk shooting.

❲ Shooting rabbits at close range spoils the hasen-pfeffer. When the cover is open enough, let the rabbit get out 20 yards or so before shooting. The thin pattern will do less damage to the meat, and kill the rabbit just as dead.

Running Red

Back in what we now think of as the good old days, a prime fox pelt was worth about $25. That doesn't sound like a princely sum by today's standards, but it was then, when the hired man earned $30 a month, plus room and board, and a laborer worked nine hours for $3. As you can see, it is not surprising that many a Northerner made a serious business of hunting foxes during the fall and winter.

As a moneymaking enterprise, fox hunting was an easy business to get into. All a man needed was a hound, a shotgun and some free time. And one thing more: he had to be just a bit smarter than a fox. It was this last detail that made it impossible to get rich at the game.

Today a prime red fox pelt is virtually worthless, and the lone hunter and his hound have all but disappeared. But the sport didn't die with the dollar. A fox values his scalp as dearly as he ever did. Hounds still make the same glorious music. And on a pleasant winter's day there are far duller pursuits for a man to follow than the trail of a fox.

He's a smart one, the red fox. He knows, or quickly learns, what a good trail hound can do, and how to prevent him from doing it. He carries a full bag of tricks, and doesn't hesitate to dip into it when the going gets rough.

For example, the red fox seems to know instinctively that his scent clings better to some types of terrain than to others. Pressed in a hot chase, he will go out of his way to cross a ploughed field, where the raw earth will confuse the hound. Instead of crossing a dirt road, he may run down it for a quarter of a mile or more, and then spring back to the same side from which he approached it. I've been told of one instance, solemnly sworn to, when a fox actually leaped aboard a horse-drawn sled and rode it out of danger. Having hunted foxes myself, I can believe the story.

Many a fox has saved his skin by running atop a railroad track. Does he know that the cold steel kills his scent completely, or does he reason that a passing train may take care of his enemy for him? Whichever it is, the shrewd maneuver has cost the life of many a good bold hound, and saved the life of many a fox.

While he is busy outwitting your hound, he seems to know you're somewhere around, too. No matter how carefully you pick your stand, you'll often find tracks in the snow to prove that he guessed where you hid, and swung wide around you.

So if you'd like to try something more challenging than rabbit hunting next winter, the red fox is out there somewhere waiting for you. If you bring back his pelt, you'll earn it.

TAP'S TIPS

❬ If you feel dry-eyed and headachy after a sunny day in the snow, you may be suffering from the first stage of snow blindness. Wearing colored glasses will protect your eyes from the glare, and also help you to spot game against the dazzling white background of snow.

❬ Foxes can often be called close to the gun by sucking the back of your hand to produce a squeaking noise such as a mouse makes. The trick is to make a small squeak, about the size of a mouse. Foxes have sharp ears, and can hear the sound from an amazing distance.

❬ When a hound-driven fox comes by far out of shotgun range, take a shot at him just the same. The spatter of the pellets, whether one or two sting him or not, may make him change directions. "Turning" a fox is a trick oldtime hunters often used successfully.

DEER HUNTING

Deer Hunting on Bare Ground

MOST DEER hunters pray fervently for tracking snow, and well they might. Deer kill figures shoot up spectacularly after a fall of white stuff, especially if it's deep enough to hold tracks all day, but not quite deep enough to make walking a job of work.

I couldn't say *all* deer hunters, because I know of at least one conspicuous exception. He lives in Vermont, a state notorious for its abundance of snow, and he much prefers to hunt on bare ground.

I submit herewith his reasons to you, hoping that they will help you to accept the earth's nakedness with better grace.

When you get a good tracking snow, he says, you naturally use it to track something. You spend hours following the tracks of a buck, and when you finally jump him close enough for a shot, along toward sundown, you observe that the animal is bald. In Vermont, a state which insists on at least three inches of antler on every dead deer, this is a sobering discovery to make.

So on the next day you take a stand and hope that some obliging still-hunter will push a deer your way. And maybe one of them does, but you happened to be watching north and east when the deer came

through traveling west and south. Because the snow muffled the sound of his passing, you never heard him.

My friend also complains that it never seems to snow the right amount. The fall is either so light that tracks melt away on you by midday, or so deep that walking through it becomes hard labor, especially in up-and-down terrain like Vermont's. He does have a point there.

On the other side of the ledger, bare ground permits you to hear a deer whether you are still-hunting or sitting on a stand. True enough, the deer can also hear you, which immediately rules out still-hunting. So you take a stand like a sensible deer hunter should and let the deer come to you. That way you're quiet and the deer snaps the twigs and rustles the leaves, which often leads to a frypanful of fresh deer liver.

If hunters who sit still shoot more deer than hunters who move around (probably true), and if noisy underfooting gives the stand-hunter an advantage (undoubtedly true), then my friend presents a pretty strong case for bare-ground hunting. Anyway, it's worth remembering when your prayers for fresh tracking snow aren't answered.

TAP'S TIPS

⟨ Most hunters know that three evenly-spaced shots are a call for help, but some do not know that the signal calls for an answer. Two shots immediately following the distress signal mean that the call has been heard, and help is coming. This can snap a lost hunter out of his panic and encourage him to sit down and wait where he is for rescue.

⟨ Four words that may mean a shot at a buck: *Watch your back trail!* Deer often hide to let a hunter pass by, and then step out for a good look at him. Keep an eye peeled ahead and around you when still-hunting or following a track, but stop every once in a while and turn around very slowly. You may find yourself face to face with a freezerful of venison.

⟨ The big bucks don't move around much until late in the fall, when the rutting season makes them restless and their heavy winter coats begin to feel comfortable. So as a general rule, the later you hunt, the better your chance of bringing home a trophy-sized rack of antlers.

Sitters and Stalkers

Most deer hunters fall into one of two categories, the Sitters and the Stalkers. The Sitters like to hunker down in a likely spot and wait for a deer to come to them, while the Stalkers go looking for their deer. They both lug home a lot of venison every year, but their success is not so much due to the methods they use as to the time of day they use them.

Deer, as every deer hunter well knows, are nocturnal creatures. They feed mostly at night, and bed down in some hidden retreat during the day. The smart hunter keeps this in mind and sits when the deer are apt to be moving around, stalks when they're bedded down for the day. So in a general way the formula for deer hunting success is to find a well-used runway and sit where you command a good view

231

of it from daylight till the sun hits the ground. Then get up and poke along s-l-o-w-l-y through thickets and swamps till the sun starts to drop. Late afternoon should find you back at your runway again, sticking it out till dusk.

When you pick a stand, choose it carefully. The ideal spot could well be one where the deer (and the other hunters) can see you. Deer have poor eyesight, and a perfectly motionless object will not alarm them if they can't smell anything strange about it. Hunters, on the other hand, usually have excellent eyesight, and a hunting coat of fiery orange doesn't look much like a deer if it's out in plain sight where even the most trigger-itchy hunter can see it.

On the other hand, deer have keen nostrils, and hunters haven't. So place yourself downwind of the area where deer are likely to pass— that is, with the breeze in your face—and snuggle your back against a rock tall enough and wide enough to cover your outline and thick enough to stop a .30-06.

That's all there is to it, except just one thing more: *sit still!* And that's what separates the men deer hunters from the boy deer. hunters —the ability to sit without moving. It's hard work, but it pays off in venison.

TAP'S TIPS

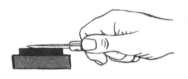

⟨ The edge of a new hunting knife is usually too wedge-like for easy cutting, and needs tapering. Grind at a flat angle on a coarse stone until you have carried the taper well up into the blade, then hone to a fine edge. To preserve the edge, avoid bearing down hard on bone when dressing out a deer.

⟨ Buck deer normally grow their largest antlers in their fourth or fifth year. After that the antlers are smaller each year. A very old deer, aged ten or twelve, may carry only spikes. So it is impossible to tell a deer's age simply by counting antler points.

⟨ Toss a roll of cheesecloth or cotton mosquito netting into your duffel when you pack for a deer-hunting trip. If the weather turns warm after you have shot your deer, cover the carcass with the netting to protect it from blow-flies, which will lay eggs in exposed meat and hatch maggots. If you didn't bring netting, keep a smudge burning under the hanging deer during the daytime.

Just Sit a Spell

Patience, like red hair or inherited wealth, is something you've either got or you haven't got, and I don't think there's much you can

do about it. If you haven't got it, you might just as well resign your-self, as I have, to catching fewer fish and shooting less game than people who do have it.

Take, for example, deer hunting. Most hunters will agree, I think, that the surest way to put venison in the freezer is to pick a crossing and sit there quietly till a deer comes along. This may happen in a few hours or, in extreme cases, in a few days, but sooner or later some fiddle-footed hunter like me will push a deer out, giving the patient soul such an easy shot he'll be ashamed to pace it off.

People who are naturally patient probably don't mind sitting still for long periods of time. I find it extremely irksome, myself. After five minutes I get small itches that demand to be scratched. My nervous system cries for nicotine. I begin thinking I picked a poor place to while away the dragging hours.

So I get up and go somewhere else. A short while later a placid-type hunter from New Jersey shoots a fat spikehorn from the very spot I left.

When I offer these three rules for sitting still successfully, please remember that I don't claim to follow them myself:

1. Get comfortable. Find something smooth or soft for your fanny, arrange a back rest, and stretch out your legs. If you can relax, you won't wriggle and itch so much.

2. Smoke if you must. Deer will smell your body odor first anyway, and pulling on a pipe or cigarette helps to relieve the tedium.

3. Stay put. There may be a better stand somewhere else, but there's probably another hunter in it, wishing he'd picked the place you did.

TAP'S TIPS

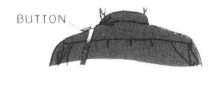

BUTTON

(Anything you hang over your shoulder has an annoying habit of slipping off. You can keep your gun sling, camera or binocular strap in place by sewing a large button on the shoulder of your shirt or hunting coat.

(If, heaven forbid, a hunter takes a shot at you when you are deer hunting, don't run, because that might excite him still more. Instead, throw yourself flat on the ground and start yelling as loud as you can. What you yell doesn't matter, although in these circumstances a little profanity would be forgivable.

(Save those plastic bags that practically everything is sold in these days, and take a few when you go deer hunting. You will find them useful for packing the luncheon sandwiches, for keeping your seat dry while watching a runway and, on the lucky day, for carrying the deer liver back to camp.

Make Noise Quietly

The purpose of a deer drive, obviously, is to push deer out to where the posted hunters can get a shot at them. Given favorable terrain (desirable) and some deer (absolutely necessary), a well-organized drive can produce some pretty exciting results.

The drivers, of course, must start the deer moving by making some sort of a noise. On this phase of the subject, opinion divides sharply. In remote northern areas where I've hunted, the oldtimers favor a hound-like baying, and I can testify that deer react promptly when they hear it. Whether they fear the sound instinctively, or because "dogging deer" is still practiced covertly back in the big woods on frosty November nights, I would rather not guess. But if you can bawl like a hound on a smoking track, deer will not linger long in your path.

Many "city" hunters, I've noticed, seem to operate on the theory that the kind of noise doesn't matter, as long as it's loud. They beat on dishpans, whoop, holler, and blow police whistles, yet deer still leak out the sides or circle around behind them.

Perhaps you have been fortunate enough to observe the way deer react to different sounds. I have seen more than one merely lift his head curiously at the sound of a shot, and then calmly resume feeding. I have observed the same response to such sounds as woodchopping, the whine of a power saw, even to shouts between two hunters.

But let a twig snap and see what happens!

The sounds that cry "Danger!" to deer are pretty much the sounds a hunter makes walking through the woods. Therefore, if you drive quietly you increase your own chance of getting a shot, or push deer toward one of the posted hunters. By traveling a zigzag course you will flush any deer that might try to sneak back between drivers, or lay tight while they pass.

Actually, wind direction is probably more important than whatever noise you make, anyway. Whether you sound like a hound or a dishpan, you always smell like a man. So before you plan your drive, hold up a wet finger and make the wind work with you.

TAP'S TIPS

(Here's a way to rig a hunting coat so it can be worn when needed and carried conveniently during

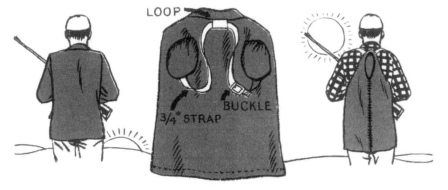

LOOP

3/4" STRAP   BUCKLE

midday when it isn't. First, sew a tunnel loop beneath the collar on the inside. Through this loop, thread a web strap about ¾-inch wide and 3½-feet long, with a buckle near one end for adjusting the length. Sew the ends of the strap to the inside of the coat at the lower edges of the armholes. When the coat becomes too warm to wear, button or zip it inside out, slip your arms through the straps and wear it on your back.

¶ The tracks of a small buck and a large doe look very much the same. But it is possible to identify each of them. The buck's tracks will be deeper, larger, more widely spaced, and will point out. The doe leaves smaller, sharper tracks that point almost straight ahead, and her hind feet sometimes partly cover the forefoot tracks.

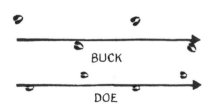

BUCK

DOE

Through the Looking Glass

"So help me, I'll never hunt deer again without a scope!" Every year thousands of hapless hunters with unfilled deer tags take this mournful vow. Since you rarely hear of a scope manufacturer moving into the poorhouse, a great many of them apparently mean it.

Whether or not it's fair to blame the open sight for missing a standing deer at 50 yards, a distressingly common complaint, the truth of the matter is that the modern scope sight with its fine optics actually can help the average shooter to hit what he aims at.

But as the drunk said to his wife when he rolled in at 2 A.M. with lipstick on his face, let's not form any hasty opinions. After all, the scope doesn't point the rifle. It merely helps the hunter to aim more accurately under certain conditions.

So if you have considered mounting a peeking tube on Old Heartseeker, here are a few things to think about.

On the negative side, the scope costs money. Not more than most of us can afford, but it's an item that can run anywhere from $20 to $80 or more, plus mounting cost if you give the job to a gunsmith. The scope is not practical on rifles that kick their empties from the top of the receiver, as it cannot be mounted low enough. The lens must be kept clean of dust and fog. Most experienced hunters—although not all, by any means—agree that the scope is slower than open sights for shooting running game at close range. And, of course, the scope exaggerates those faint tremors that afflict all of us when we aim a rifle.

Now look at the advantages.

The big one, obviously, is magnification. A 200-yard deer offers a duck-soup target when viewed through a 2½- or 4-power glass, and can

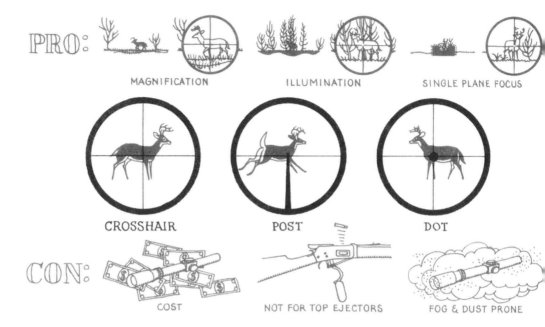

PRO:

MAGNIFICATION   ILLUMINATION   SINGLE PLANE FOCUS

CROSSHAIR   POST   DOT

CON:

COST   NOT FOR TOP EJECTORS   FOG & DUST PRONE

be clearly identified as a buck, doe, spikehorn, Jersey milk cow, or one of the guys you played poker with the evening before.

Due to its light-gathering ability, the scope actually illuminates the target in morning or evening dusk. As these are by far the best times of day to hunt, this factor alone can make the scope a good investment.

As he enters the mellow, or bifocal, years the open-sight shooter notices that the rear aperture and front post on his rifle have acquired quite a bit of fuzz, which makes it difficult to align them accurately with a distant object. That's because he tries to see things that are in three different planes. The scope puts everything on a single plane, a blessing indeed for old geezers like me.

The reticule of the scope, whatever its type, provides a more efficient aiming device than any metal sight with the possible exception of the rear peep. For all-around hunting, most scope shooters prefer the medium cross hair, as it permits pinpoint aiming without obscuring the target. The post reticule is perhaps a bit faster on running game—this statement is admittedly debatable—and ideal for target range shooting. The dot offers the advantage of enabling the mathematically-minded hunter to estimate the range of his target, if he knows how much area the dot covers at various distances, and the approximate measurement of the animal on which he wishes to inflict rigor mortis.

What power? Depends on where and how you hunt, and for what. The 2½-power scope is plenty strong enough for most deer hunting and

Saturday afternoon varminting. The dedicated varminter or the sheep and goat man who considers 500 yards pointblank range will want something a bit stronger. The thing to remember is that the high-power lens has a smaller field of view and seems to shake more on a hand-held rifle.

TAP'S TIPS

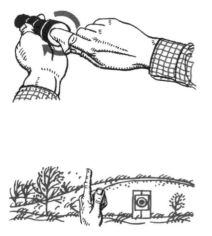

⟨[When cleaning the lens of a scope, be careful not to scratch the glass. Clean only when necessary. Blow off loose dust first, as it is slightly abrasive, then moisten the glass with your breath and wipe it gently with a circular motion. Use special cloth or paper, available at any camera store or optometrist's.

⟨[Deer grow antlers, not horns. Antlers are solid and, except in the case of caribou, are worn only by males. Horns are hollow, and both sexes have them. The pronghorn antelope is the only animal that develops branched horns and sheds them every year.

⟨[If your deer rifle suddenly starts hitting to the left or right after it has been sighted-in, wet a finger and check the breeze. It is surprising how far off course a little wind can "blow" a bullet over a hundred-yard range.

Aim for the Chest

Anyone who has ever dressed out an animal, whether it be a moose or a mouse, must have noticed that the body is divided in two parts, separated at about the line of the last rib by the diaphragm, a wall of thin, tough tissue.

To a deer hunter, this simple study of anatomy is of great importance. Knowing which part of the body to aim for can mean the difference between the triumph of hanging a buck on the game pole and the tragedy of knowing that a wounded animal is dying in silent agony somewhere out in the thickets.

A hit almost anywhere in the rib cage, from the diaphragm forward, is nearly certain to bring the animal down within a few hundred yards, perhaps almost instantly. The lungs fill the lower two-thirds of the cavity, and a bullet smashing through that area is sure to destroy a great amount of tissue and perhaps cut the heart as well. A high shot that misses the lungs can hardly miss the backbone. And a shot in the forward section of the chest will probably break a shoulder, possibly both.

So any hit, high or low, left or right, in the area forward of the last rib should put the deer down. And any shot in this area, except for a shoulder hit, will destroy very little meat.

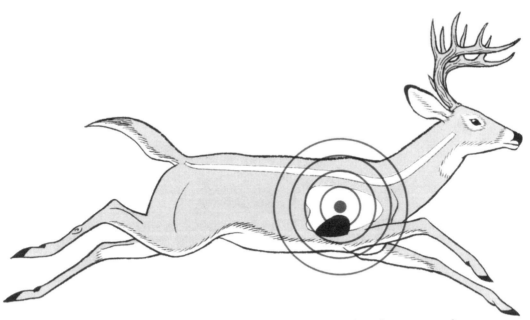

Rearward of the last rib, the body cavity contains the organs of digestion and reproduction. Any hit behind the diaphragm wall and below the backbone, itself a small and difficult target, is nearly always fatal. However, it is slow to take effect, and a gut-shot deer may run for miles before pain and weakness force it to the ground.

The blood trail often tells the experienced hunter where his deer was hit. Dark blood usually indicates a shot in the paunch; pink-colored blood a hit in the chest area. Whatever color it is, the hunter would do well to smoke a pipeful of tobacco before following the deer. Then he should stay with it till he finds it, no matter how far it goes or how long it takes. A man owes the deer that much.

TAP'S TIPS

⦗ A deer bounding across an opening offers a very difficult shot. However, if the deer has not been too badly frightened it will often stop to look back as soon as it reaches the cover on the other side. Unless the cover is very thick, this may give you a much easier shot at a standing target.

⦗ Smart hunters, like experienced sailing skippers, are always conscious of the wind and take advantage of it as much as they can. Its direction and strength are both important, whether you are hunting deer or ducks. So develop the habit of checking the wind frequently, and then try to make it work in your favor.

Buckshot, Oh-Oh

Last fall a friend of mine bought a deer rifle, his first. He came out of the sporting goods store cradling a beautiful piece of artillery, along with an excellent hunting scope and enough ammunition to carry him through several hunting seasons. Then he took the rifle to a range nearby and sighted it in until he could dot i's with it. By that time things were looking pretty bleak for the deer population, and my friend had already picked out a spot in his house where he thought the rack of antlers would look best.

But alas, no deer died by his hand that fall, although he spent two weeks trying. He saw several deer ghosting through the brush, and a couple of them were wearing the kind of antlers he had in mind, but he never got any of them in his scope soon enough. He took a few shots and missed all but one. That deer ran off with a foreleg dangling and doubtless provided a meal for the foxes and bobcats a few days later.

None of this was any fault of the rifle's. The clerk had sold him a good one, mounted with one of the best scopes made. But the rifle was intended for long-range shooting in open country, and my friend went hunting in a heavily-wooded area. He would have done better to carry his duck gun loaded with 00 buckshot.

If this sounds like heresy, let me tell you quickly that one of the top hunting guides I know, in one of the best deer-hunting states in the country—Maine, of course—always carries his shotgun when he hunts

240

deer for his own larder. Over the years George has shot about every kind of deer rifle made. But for hunting in thick, brushy country, he much prefers the shotgun.

You hear a lot about spectacular shots at ranges of 100 and 200 yards and even more, but little is said about the thousands of deer that are killed each year within 40 yards of the gun. Such shots do not give the hunter much excuse to brag, but they account for an amazing lot of venison.

With a rifle you must hit your deer or miss him with a single slug, and often without a chance to get in a second shot. But when you touch off a 12-gauge shotgun loaded with double-ought buck you are sending nine hard-hitting pellets out there, and can expect more than half of them to group within a 30-inch circle at 40 yards. And many a deer has died with only a single 00 shot in his neck or heart.

To most of us who hunt rabbits, ducks, and upland birds, a shotgun is a much more familiar weapon than a rifle. It comes up to the shoulder easier, seems almost to point and shoot itself without conscious effort on our part. Therefore, it is not surprising that it may connect with its deadly spread of heavy shot when a rifle might miss with its single slug, especially when you have just a fleeting glimpse at a buck crashing through the brush 30 or 40 yards away. And in heavily-wooded country you won't see many deer much farther away than that.

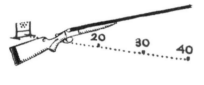

([If you decide to try your shotgun for deer hunting, take time first to pattern it with buckshot. When you see the patterns it throws at ranges from 20 to 40 yards, you will have more confidence in its ability to knock down deer.

([Take along two sets of antlers (if you can find or borrow them) when you plan to hunt from a stand. By rattling the antlers together occasionally you may be able to fool a buck into thinking two deer are fighting, and "call" him up to you.

([Rifled shotgun slugs deliver surprising accuracy, often grouping less than 12 inches at 100 yards. This accuracy, plus the tremendous shocking power of the big slug, make it an excellent deer load for medium ranges. Many hunters load their shotguns with two buckshot shells and then a slug, on the theory that the third shot at a deer will probably be a fairly long one.

The Prevention and Cure of Buck Fever

Most deer hunters have a favorite buck-fever story. Mine concerns the novice hunter who took a stand at dawn on the opening day of the season, and less than five minutes later saw an enormous buck deer walk out of the brush and stop broadside, not 30 yards away.

Now, this hunter had never before shot a deer, or even shot at one. But to hear him tell it, his pulse never so much as stuttered. As he later reported the incident, he mentally drew an X behind the buck's right ear and carefully covered its intersection with the front bead of his rifle. Then, reflecting that he might wish to have the magnificent head mounted, and not wanting to risk damage to the antlers, he drew another imaginary X just under the animal's right shoulder, and shot the deer dead through the heart.

"No buck fever at all?" I asked him.

"None whatever. However," he added, "when I knelt down to dress him out I began vomiting rather violently."

Buck fever strikes in many different ways. The hunter may simply freeze and remain incapable of motion while the deer saunters from his sight, or he may empty his rifle in the air or into the ground. Frequently the fever does not overwhelm the hunter until after he has shot the deer, as in the case described above. A similar delayed reaction struck another acquaintance of mine who, upon shooting his first deer, a large buck, recalled that one friend had advised cutting off the geni-

tals immediately to preserve the flavor of the meat, and another had asked for the flag, for tying bucktails. So the lucky hunter quickly de-sexed the deer and then whacked off its tail. As it happened, the shot had only stunned the animal, for a moment later it scrambled to its feet and bounded off into the woods, leaving the hunter standing there waving a bloody trophy in each hand and shouting "Come back! Come back, you damned fool!"

Some hunters never get buck fever, while some keep on getting it year after year, as if it were recurrent malaria. It is brought on, of course, by excitement. If excitement can be eliminated from the act of shooting a deer, no one need ever suffer from buck fever. And obvi-ously, if the hunter really doesn't *want* to shoot a deer the prospect of doing so will not excite him. Therefore, buck fever can be either pre-vented or cured simply by convincing yourself that shooting a deer is not an especially desirable thing to do.

Before you start hunting, stop to consider what you are letting your-self in for. You are going to walk miles before you see a deer, more miles before you get a shot at one, and still more miles before you finally hit one. This will probably occur at the most distant point you have traveled from camp, and you will be alone. After dressing out the crea-ture and discovering that one of your bullets has mashed up most of the best hindquarter meat, you will carry, drag and roll the carcass over hill and through freshet until you reach camp exhausted and drained of triumph.

The next day the weather will turn warm and you will have to keep a smoky fire smouldering under the deer to protect it from blowflies till time to start home. Having already spent more than you could afford for license, guide's fees, camp board and transportation (and possibly having also lost heavily at poker), you will then spend still more for a freeze locker and for mounting the head, which your wife will soon consign to the attic.

You will have promised the neighbors venison, of course, and naturally they will expect only choice cuts. So you will pass out the tender loin chops and the forequarters, leaving yourself nothing but the neck and some leathery flank meat, suitable only for stewing. By this time you will hate your deer, and wish you had never shot it.

If you consider all this carefully before you plan a deer hunting trip you will never become excited over the prospect of shooting a deer. Once you conquer excitement you will be completely immune to buck fever.

There's just one little catch, though. You won't have any fun hunting, either.

TAP'S TIPS

⟨ After shooting a deer, approach it carefully and watch its eyes. If they are open and glassy, the animal is probably dead. However, watch out if the eyes are closed, because the deer may be only wounded or stunned.

⟨ If you plan to hunt deer with bow and arrow, remember that most states require that you use a bow with a certain minimum pull, usually from 40 to 50 pounds. Also, don't forget to put your name on your arrows.

⟨ Venison makes sorry table fare when it is cooked to a crisp. Overcooking toughens meat and destroys much of its natural flavor. So cook venison as you would beef, brown on the outside, pink or even red in the middle. To make up for its lack of fat, add a hunk of beef suet or a few strips of bacon.

How to Field-Dress a Deer

To anyone who has never done it before, dressing out a deer looks like a difficult and messy job. But it needn't be. If you go at it right you should be wiping the blood off your knife fifteen minutes after you take it from the sheath.

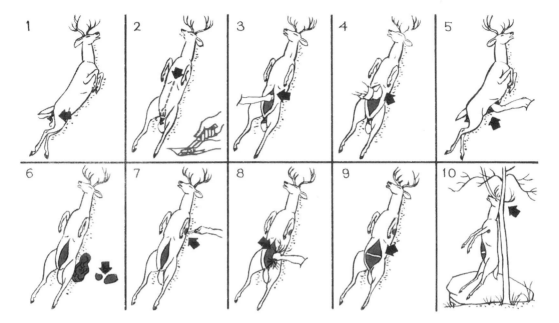

Let's say you have just knocked over your first deer and you are alone, with no one to help. Here's what you do—and if you jot this simple step-by-step procedure down on paper and tuck it in your hunt-ing-coat pocket, you won't have to cudgel your buck-fevered brain try-ing to remember.

First, make sure the deer is dead. You can tell by its eyes. If they are open and glassy, he is thoroughly deceased. If they are closed, poke one of them with a long stick or bounce a rock off his ribs. Finish off the deer with another shot if he so much as twitches. It is not necessary to stick a deer to bleed it, as blood flow stops when the heart does.

Now roll or drag the carcass to sloping ground and place it on its back with the head uphill, so it will drain from the rear end. Then follow these steps in order.

1. Cut completely around the anal vent and pull it out a ways. If you want to be neat about it, tie it off with your bootlace to prevent droppings from coming in contact with the meat.

2. Start the abdominal incision at the V formed by the rib cage. To avoid puncturing the intestines—this is very important—cut with the edge of the knife blade up and guide it between two fingers of the left hand, to hold the skin away from the gut pouch. Slit the skin down the belly and around both sides of the genitals to the crotch.

3. Pull the abdominal contents out far enough so you can cut away the diaphragm, a wall of thin tissue that separates the chest area and belly.

245

4. Reach into the chest with your left hand, grasp the windpipe and throat cords as high as you can, and cut them free.

5. Roll the deer on its side and gently pull the viscera out of the carcass. Be careful not to puncture the bladder, for obvious reasons. Draw the rectal tube and its contents in through the anal opening.

6. Pick the heart and liver out of the mess and lay them aside to cool. These are the only parts of the deer that should be eaten fresh, and you will want to cook one of them for your victory supper.

7. Look for bloodshot muscle or shattered bone and cut away these areas, as they spoil quickly and will taint the surrounding meat.

8. Wipe the inside of the carcass with a cloth, grass, fern, anything dry. Never use water, as moisture hastens spoilage. Don't try to remove every last bit of red blood. Instead, spread it evenly over the meat and bone. As it dries it forms a hard glaze that will discourage blowflies.

9. Prop open the belly cavity with sticks so the meat can cool and dry quickly.

10. If you can't get the deer into camp immediately, drape it head-high over a large rock or wedge the neck or antlers in a tree crotch. But get the deer on the game pole as soon as possible, because predators and scavenging birds will soon find it in the woods. Then let it hang as long as the weather stays cold, preferably a week or two, whether from the head or heels doesn't matter, now that draining is complete. In warm weather the aging period can be prolonged by sprinkling black pepper over the exposed meat or by covering the carcass with cheese-cloth to keep the blowflies away.

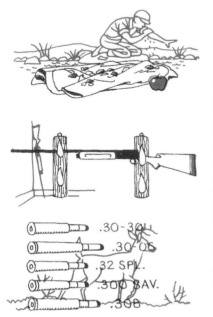

TAP'S TIPS

(After a few days in camp, deer hunters begin to smell very unlike a rose. This can be a factor in hunting success, as deer have keen noses, and human BO travels far on a light breeze. For that reason, smart hunters defy camp custom and wash often. Some even scent their clothing with crushed apples.

(When putting away a rifle or shotgun at the close of the hunting season, it is best to place it on a horizontal rack or stand it on its muzzle, rather than in the usual butt-down position. This prevents excess oil from seeping out of the metal parts and soaking into the stock.

(In Maine, where hunting deer is almost a way of life, the most popular deer rifle is still the .30-30, according to a recent survey. Second in popularity and gaining fast is the .30-'06, then the .32 Special, .300 Savage and .308 Winchester in that order.

DUCK SHOOTING

Puddlers in the Potholes

IT SEEMS very strange, when you stop to think of it, that duck hunters should tend to congregate so heavily in certain places when there are so many other places where they could enjoy their sport in peace and privacy. Maybe wildfowlers are naturally more gregarious than normal people, or perhaps they get more fun out of trying to shoot the same ducks other hunters are trying to shoot. In either case, they would probably have better luck if they would just go and find themselves a little pothole somewhere.

A pothole, in the sense that duck hunters use the word, is any small body of water patronized frequently by ducks but seldom by duck hunters. It may be a beaver pond, a widening in a stream or irrigation ditch, a swamp hole, or just a patch of casual water no bigger than a tennis court. If part of it remains open in cold weather, stirred by an inlet or spring, and if you find breast feathers drifting on its surface, it is a place well worth visiting. Blacks, mallards and other puddle ducks like to use such places to rest and drink and to keep themselves from being continually shot at.

There are two basic ways to shoot a pothole. One is to creep up to

247

it in the early morning, try to knock down a bird or two when they flush, and then hunker down for a while to see if they will come back and give you another crack at them. The other way is to set out some decoys and make a day of it.

You don't need much of a set to shoot a pothole over decoys. A half-dozen will be plenty, and just two or three will do quite nicely. The purpose of the decoys is not to attract birds, because they are coming to the pothole anyway, but to make them think it is safe to light.

The trick is to scatter the decoys here and there so they look like ducks contentedly feeding or resting. Bunching them in front of your hiding place makes them appear frightened and ready to take off. At least, that's the theory.

Most potholes are heavily fringed with brush and trees, so it is sel-dom necessary to build a blind. In fact, it's better not to. Puddlers, being by nature a suspicious breed of fowl, are quick to spot changes in a familiar shoreline. So if the cover is sparse, kneel in it, sit in it, or lie face down in it if you have to, but don't rearrange it any more than absolutely necessary.

Yes, a call will help. You can't get away with false notes and you shouldn't be too talkative. But a little happy gabble will convince the birds that the coast is clear and it's safe for them to come down and sit a spell.

TAP'S TIPS

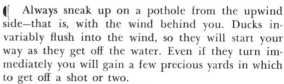

(｜ Always sneak up on a pothole from the upwind side—that is, with the wind behind you. Ducks in-variably flush into the wind, so they will start your way as they get off the water. Even if they turn im-mediately you will gain a few precious yards in which to get off a shot or two.

(｜ To fight off duckblind shivers and goosebumps, wear a light rainshirt under your shooting coat or parka. It will cut the wind and provide extra insula-tion on a cold day.

(｜ When you cripple a duck, watch his head. If he can hold it up he still has enough life to get away unless you finish him off quickly. But if his head is down or noticeably drooping, you can be sure he is too far gone to travel very far.

Blinds Are for Fidgeting

Here is an interesting experiment worth trying some day when ducks keep flaring away from your setup for no apparent reason: Get

out of the blind, lie down in front of it, and see what happens the next time birds take aim on the decoys.

What may happen is that they will drop into the stool as trustingly as chickens running to cracked corn. If they do, it shouldn't take long to figure why they came in this time and refused to decoy before. Sitting inside the blind, you felt that you were so well hidden you could safely peer over the top to see if the birds were still coming. You may have waggled your gun barrel a little as you shifted into a better shooting position, or snapped away a cigarette, or pulled the glove off your trigger hand, and the ducks saw you do it. But when you lay completely exposed outside the blind you knew you couldn't move so much as an eyelid. The ducks undoubtedly saw you, but they had no reason to take alarm. For all they could tell, you might have been only a log or a windrow of marsh grass.

Many years ago I hunted with an old Cape Codder who in his early days had earned a major part of his livelihood shooting ducks for market. In his time he must have killed a sinful quantity of ducks and geese. Yet he never bothered to build a blind when he hunted alone. He told me he simply hunkered under the bank of a tidal creek or squatted in any natural cover available, anything that would break the outline of his body. However, when he guided for pay he always provided a blind for his clients, because he believed that city people are physically incapable of sitting still. Honesty compels me to confess that he made no exception to the rule in my case.

None of us likes to admit that we tend to fidget inside a duck blind when birds are moving, but most of us do. The temptation to lift up and see if the ducks are still coming is almost beyond human power to resist. Cramped muscles cry for relief. Itches demand to be scratched. Yet it takes only a tiny patch of white face, the glint of sunlight on glasses, the merest movement of any kind, to make approaching ducks do a back-flip, for it is the nature of wild ducks to be suspicious, and they have amazing long-range vision.

I do not mean to imply that some sort of a blind is not desirable. Building a snug hidy-hole in the morning dusk is part of the ritual of wildfowling. However, the blind does not have to be large or solid. It should, in fact, be as small as practical and as sparse as the gunner dares to make it, and designed primarily for the purpose of disguising the occupant and not of completely hiding him. If the hunter wears clothing that blends into the background of the marsh or swamp, the blind will serve its purpose if it only fuzzes the outline of his body. In that case, it doesn't matter whether the hunter sits in the blind or in front of it. What does matter is that he sits still, at least while ducks are moving.

TAP'S TIPS

⁅ Motionless decoys on glassy water rarely attract passing ducks. To make them look more like live, feeding birds, run lines from a couple of them to the blind, and twitch the lines when birds approach. String the line under water through a ring anchored between the decoys and shore.

⁅ Many hunters wake up with a "morning headache" after a day of duck shooting. Eyestrain often results from long hours spent looking into the dazzle of sky and water. Blackening the cheekbones will reduce some of the glare. Sunglasses help even more, but they must be slipped off when ducks approach so they can't flash a warning to the birds.

⁅ For a quick hand-warmer in a cold duck blind, cut vertical slices in the paper case of an empty shotgun shell and touch a match to it. The case will burn with intense, smokeless heat for a couple of minutes—long enough to limber up frozen fingers.

Bags for Blacks

No question about it: the more lifelike your decoys, the more eagerly ducks will come to them. You can't improve on solid blocks,

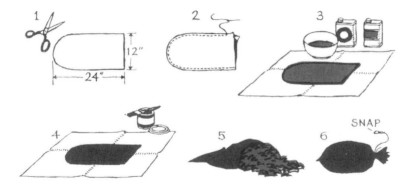

carefully painted in the natural colors of the fowl they imitate, true to life in size, shape and silhouette. When conditions are right ducks light into them in the trusting manner of a chick running to its mother.

But other types of decoys fool the ducks, too. One November day at Barnstable Marsh on Cape Cod, Massachusetts, I saw a gunner banging ducks over a set of tin cans—big, square, 5-gallon-size oil cans painted flat black. He killed a limit of birds over the tinware, too.

Throughout the range of the black duck, and in mallard country as well, stuffed bag decoys turn the trick as well as the fanciest of hand-painted blocks when birds are moving, and almost as well when they're not. The bags offer certain advantages over other kinds of decoys, also, being light in weight, easy to carry, and both simple and inexpensive to make.

Get some lightweight canvas, light cotton duck, or unbleached muslin, and cut matched pieces about 22 to 24 inches long by 12 inches wide, square at one end and round at the other. Pair up the pieces and double stitch them together on a sewing machine to form bags, with the opening at the square end. Turn the bags inside out to hide the seams.

Place each empty bag flat on some newspapers and slather both sides liberally with linseed oil and turpentine mixed half-and-half. When the cloth is thoroughly saturated, let it dry and then paint both sides with the flattest, dullest black paint you can buy. If the bags dry with even a suggestion of gloss, apply a second coat of flat black and while it is still wet dust the surface evenly with lampblack powder. Enough of it will adhere to kill the shine.

The bags can be filled with anything that is light and buoyant. I used the stuffing from a discarded mattress. Kapok is ideal, and if you're lucky you might lay hands on some old boat cushions and get all you need. Shredded excelsior is quite suitable, too. Cram as much of the stuffing into the bags as you can, using heavy pressure, and then tie off the neck with tarred line, leaving a pucker to suggest a duck's head and neck. Tie snaps to the ends of the cord so the bags can be clipped easily to rings in the main line, which will be anchored.

Two or three strings of bag decoys, with four or five bags on a string, are enough to toll in blacks and mallards. The bags can also be turned into whistler and sheldrake decoys by tying a white cloth around them. When the shooting's over, it is a simple matter to haul in the strings, snap the bags together by their neck cords, and carry them home like a bunch of overgrown grapes.

TAP'S TIPS

◖ If high-base duck loads give you "shooter's head-ache," a sore shoulder, and a pain in the pocketbook, don't hestitate to switch to the lighter field loads. They are just as effective within sensible range, particularly when hunting over decoys. When I stopped shooting heavy loads I found that my ratio of shells-fired-to-ducks-killed improved greatly.

◖ If ducks flare away from your blind for no apparent reason, look around for empty shells lying in the open where your pump or autoloader shucked them out. Glitter from the brass cases may be scaring the birds away.

◖ Cardboard shell boxes have a disconcerting habit of collapsing after they have been wet, and spilling shells all over the car or duck blind. It can't happen if you dump them into a metal box or can, or a strong plastic bag. I carry mine in the outer shell of a canvas minnow bucket.

"Confidence" Decoys

The first confidence-type decoy I ever used was a defunct sea gull I found on the marsh at Barnstable, Cape Cod. It was bitterly cold that day, and the ducks were paying scant attention to my decoys. So I took a walk to thaw my legs and came upon the gull, doubtless done in by a bored and lawless marshwalker the day before. Mostly, I guess, because it seemed a shame to let the creature go to waste, I picked it up and propped it at the water's edge near my blind.

Perhaps birds would have started to decoy anyway. I'll never know. But it is a fact that the next bunch made one swing and barreled into the stool as if the place were baited. And so did the next. By the time we ran out of legal shooting time my partner and I had collected quite

SEA GULL TERN BLACK DUCK SLEEPER

a respectable bag of black ducks, and we figured the gull had something to do with it.

Anyone who has read the literature of oldtime wildfowling knows that confidence decoys are old stuff. The Shelburne Museum in Shelburne, Vermont, has gathered a remarkable collection of old decoys, numbering more than a thousand, and a couple of the more interesting specimens from this collection are illustrated here so you can see what confidence decoys look like. Perhaps you might wish to invest a few evenings to making a couple for use next fall. If duck populations continue to dwindle, you may desperately need their help.

When live decoys were outlawed in 1935, many duck hunters resorted to confidence decoys to compensate for the loss of their flyers. Cranes, gulls and swans were most commonly used, and sometimes a few merganser blocks were placed among a raft of broadbills, or a goose decoy in a stool of blacks or mallards. It would be a pretty silly duck that would shy away from a place where a Canada felt safe.

"Sleepers" and "feeders" are also confidence decoys. Their purpose is mainly to allay suspicion, rather than to attract ducks to the area. No doubt decoys with raised heads look more like ducks from a distance, but the alert posture also indicates suspicion or alarm, and approaching birds may shy away unless they also see a bird sleeping, feeding or casually preening itself. I imagine confidence decoys must give ducks the same promise of good food and hospitable treatment that the presence of trucks outside a roadside diner gives to a passing motorist.

The most common type of confidence decoy is the sleeper with its head snugged down tight to the body or turned so it rests on the back. In the turned position it could also be called a preening decoy. Small matter. To a duck a couple hundred yards up in the sky, it wouldn't make much difference whether it looked like a sleeping duck or a duck fussing with its feathers. It would certainly look like a duck that had very little to worry about.

Some gunners would never think of investing a day in a duck blind without having a couple of feeding decoys in their spread. Strangely, I've seen very few feeders used where I have done most of my duck hunting, along the northeastern seaboard. But it stands to reason that a decoy dipping his bill into the water or standing on his head in feeding position must give passing birds the idea that there's a square meal to be had if they'll come down and join the party.

If you do plan to make or buy a set of decoys for the coming season, it would do no harm to stop when you have an uneven number. There is an interesting theory that an odd number of decoys will attract birds better than an even number because the extra one appears to be unpaired and hence available for companionship. If this sounds fanciful, stop to think how you would feel if you arrived at a party alone and late and, upon counting the couples, discovered there was a luscious blonde left over. Wouldn't *you* decoy to her?

TAP'S TIPS

⟦ Reloading in cold weather can be speeded up by carrying two or three extra shells in loops sewn to the back of the left-hand mitten. It's much quicker than fumbling around in a pocket with frosty fingers.

⟦ A long-billed cap such as salt-water fishermen wear is ideal for duck hunting, as it helps to hide your face while you peer skyward at approaching birds. However, if the visor has a shiny surface it should be dulled so it won't reflect sunlight. Covering it with mud will do the trick.

⟦ When touching up battered decoys with fresh paint, avoid a shiny finish. Flat paint thinned with turpentine dries dull. If it isn't dull enough, buff the decoy with fine steel wool.

Why Ducks Don't Fall

If statistics have ever been compiled to show the number of shells it takes on the average to bag a duck, I've never seen them.

What's your guess? Five shells per duck? Much too low, I think. Nearer ten, probably. A lot of ammunition, anyway, and most of it shot away foolishly.

It costs close to 15 cents to fire a shotgun nowadays. Yet I have talked with pass shooters and marshwalkers who didn't appear greatly distressed at bagging only one duck with a box of shells, and who seemed to count "feathered" birds and cripples as a tribute to their wing-shooting skill.

Obviously, long-range shooting burns up a large part of the wasted ammunition. Yet anyone can learn to estimate 40 yards merely by pacing it off, or by hanging a dead duck against the sky and observing its size from the distance. A duck hunter who passes up shots beyond that range will almost surely bag more ducks with fewer shells, and reduce his crippling loss by 50 per cent or more.

Oddly enough, a lot of ammunition is wasted by shooting at birds on the water. A sitting duck just doesn't kill as easily as one would think. Part of the body is protected by water, and the heavy wings form a shield around most of the rest. The head looks inviting, but at 30 or 40 yards a spreading pattern may never touch it. Many experienced duck hunters carry a few $7\frac{1}{2}$'s or 8's for finishing off cripples, as the thicker pattern is more likely to put a couple of pellets in the head or neck.

A flying duck, on the other hand, offers his entire body for a target. When shooting over decoys I prefer to take my ducks as they come in, rather than letting them light and then jumping them. The incomer shows his underparts, he's got his brakes on, and he's moving into closer range, whereas a duck rocketing off the water gives you less time for a somewhat more difficult shot.

Another suggestion: You may find that you stop more birds with smaller shot in regular field loads. No. 6's, even 7½'s, increase your chance of hitting with an extra pellet or two. The lighter loads may also help you to resist the temptation to take crippling long shots, and if the high-base stuff brings on flinching or "shooter's headache," your accuracy may improve dramatically.

TAP'S TIPS

◖ For many duck hunters the incomer passing over at top speed is the toughest shot of all. The trick is to blot out the bird with the gun muzzle as you shoot. If you can see the target when you press the trigger you are probably not leading the bird enough.
◖ When jump-shooting ducks from a canoe, tie a length of light cord to the paddle and attach the other end to a thwart. When ducks get up you can drop the paddle and let it trail in the water while you grab for your gun. The split second you save may mean the difference between a hit and a miss.
◖ Anyone with average eyesight can distinguish a duck's colors when it is within 40 yards. So if you wait until the colors show distinctly you can feel confident that the bird is within killing range.

Duck Blinds I Have Shot From

Over the years, man and boy, I have shot at ducks from almost every kind of hideaway known to wildfowling. Strangely enough, I have done my best shooting in the worst blinds, and vice versa.

A case in point is the wooden barrel I sank in the marsh at Orleans on Cape Cod, Massachusetts, the first year of the four-bird limit. The operation was conducted with painstaking care. If I had used an engineer's transit I couldn't have determined more exactly the precise spot to place the barrel, after due consideration for tide, prevailing wind, and the known habits of the ducks that used the area. The Orleans Barrel was perfect in every way but one.

It didn't fit.

256

You'd think a person launching such a project as this would have the foresight to try on the barrel for size first, but not me. At high noon of opening day I tossed out my decoys and inserted myself in the barrel. Part of myself, that is. The lower part. The bigness of me, head, shoulders and chest, wouldn't go in. I folded my legs every way they would fold. I squatted and scrooched. I still looked like a sprung jack-in-the-box.

As I writhed within my tomb vainly trying to compress myself to its dimensions, I heard the whicker of wings, and screwing my head upward espied a pair of black ducks rocking over the decoys on cupped wings. Straightening my tortured legs under me, I shot the pair of them.

Ordinarily a double with the cold barrels of opening day would fill a nondoubling duck hunter like myself with elation. Instead, I felt only grimness. "Two more," I prayed, "oh, God, give me just two more so I can get out of this thing and go home!"

I waded out to pick up my birds and stuffed myself back into the barrel. During my brief absence it had shrunk considerably, for now I couldn't worm myself deeper into it than the fourth button down on my shooting coat. But while I hunkered there trying to ease the torture in my cramped and aching legs, a single black duck buzzed the decoys, and with tears in my eyes I killed him.

I gathered him in and staggered back to the barrel, now half filled with muddy water. I looked up at the skyful of scudding clouds with skeins of waterfowl drawing crazy patterns across it. And I squeezed myself in again.

A man with a watch on his wrist might say I waited perhaps a quarter of an hour for my fourth bird. I'd say it was several weeks later when three black ducks peeled off a ragged formation and headed for my decoys. I know I loomed up like a massive wart on the marsh—but the birds came in just the same. I picked the nearest one and lowered him to the water. Then I gathered my decoys and tottered back to the car.

Never before and never since have I killed a legal limit of ducks at the outlay of one shell per bird. On opening day the next fall I sank another barrel in the same spot, a barrel spacious enough to accommodate an expectant cow moose, and killed two birds, one of them a sheldrake, with 27 shells.

The most luxurious and by far the most commodious blind I have occupied is the rambling structure which Ransom Kelley operated on the shores of Merrymeeting Bay in Maine. This blind offered many creature comforts, including a spacious bedroom with beds, a kitchen with stove, cooking utensils and a large table; a cupola on top for observing the comings and goings of waterfowl, and a downstairs shooting battery that could have been used to excellent advantage at Bastogne.

The way it worked was this. Out on the water, a couple hundred yards in front of the blind, were three or four sets of goose decoys, attached to the end of a long outhaul. When geese lit among the decoys, someone in the blind began turning a wheel, which slowly drew them nearer to the blind. The geese followed, and when they had been tolled within shotgun range the hunters pushed the baffle board down and put the lead to 'em.

We were sipping coffee in the kitchen when the lookout in the cupola pressed the buzzer three times—oh, sure, the blind was wired for electricity—to warn us that geese were a-wing. We finished our coffee, lit cigarettes, and sauntered downstairs to the shooting battery. Upon peering out we saw that a flock of six geese had settled among the decoys. After waiting a few minutes to let them relax their vigilance, one of the guides began turning the outhaul wheel, very slowly. The decoys inched closer to the blind, followed by the geese. Before long they were nearly within range, so the hunters deployed to battle stations.

I took the right flank and picked out the bird I wanted. He was somewhat apart from the others, on my side, and a large, majestic honker he was, sailing like a gondola out there on the ripple. This, I thought, is duck soup. Actually, such shooting should be outlawed, else we soon would have no geese left.

A goose at 30 yards looks like a goose into whose eye you could spit. Mine looked like that as the baffle boards crashed down and the enormous creature took wing. I rammed three loads at him and watched him flap out to midbay, the lone survivor of his flock.

All the others got theirs, and one hunter got two. I still maintain, though, that a gunner can't do his best work standing comfortably on his two feet, with ample headroom and elbowroom, and birds as close as that.

Midway between the original Orleans Barrel and the Merrymeeting blind is the Barnstable duckboat. This craft is indigenous to Cape Cod's Barnstable Marsh, where it is employed with deadly results by the native gunners and the shooters from the city who go out with them. The Barnstable boat is flatbottomed, with a covered foredeck and a cockpit amidships girdled with a coaming to keep out the slop in rough weather. It slides over mud like a toboggan, floats on a moderate dew, and is amazingly seaworthy for such a low-slung craft.

To transform the Barnstable duckboat into a blind, you insert forked sticks into holes drilled into the coaming. Next, you gather several armfuls of marsh grass and drape it over the sticks. Then you simply throw out your decoys, anchor the boat, and crouch in it like a robin in a nest. If you sit still enough, ducks will swim up to you and climb out on the foredeck for a sun bath.

258

My first introduction to the Barnstable duckboat gave me a memorable experience. Howard Marks, grizzled Cape Codder who recalls with nostalgia the good old days of market gunning and spring shooting, took me out in his two-seater back in the era of the ten-bird limit. We left Calf Pasture Point well before daylight, and as Howard unerringly oared his way through the labyrinth of creeks in the inky darkness, he regaled me with an account of his adventures on the previous evening.

"We wuz sittin' around drinkin' a little," he said, "an' I guess I drank a drop more than I intended. Anyway, when I got up to go home, 'round midnight, I felt a mite dizzylike. I made it out the door all right, an' started up the lane. But I got tangled up in a stun wall somewhere along the way, an' 'fore I knew it I wuz a-layin' on the grass with my foot wedged between a couple of stuns.

"Well, sir, I laid there a while tryin' to figger out where that stun wall could have come from, an' then I began to feel so comfortable I decided I might's well spend the night there as anywhere. So I put my arm under my head an' went to sleep. Had a lot of frost on me when I woke up, but I got my foot out of the wall all right, an' come right along to keep my date with you.

"It's goin' to be a nice mornin' for ducks," he added cheerfully. "Wind's beginnin' to whisper out of the nor'east, an' I bet she'll be blowin' some, come sunup."

We set out our decoys at a creek mouth in gray dawn, thatched the boat with marsh grass, and pulled it up under the steep bank. Howard reached inside his shirt and pulled out a wooden duck call which hung from his neck by a piece of tarred cod line. "Soon's the birds start movin' we'll have a little music," he grinned. "I c'n hardly wait till we've got the first bird in the boat."

"Where's your gun?" I asked, noticing for the first time that it was missing.

"Oh, I don't never shoot when I take somebody out. I'll get my birds this afternoon after I've set you ashore with your ten."

"Supposing I don't get ten?"

His eye kindled. "You'll get ten," he said. I got the uneasy feeling that I had damned well *better* get ten, and no foolishness about it, either.

"Mark left!"

I dropped my head and peered through an interstice in the thatch. Upcreek, to our left, three black ducks were barreling along, straight for the blind. I put my finger on the safety button. "Say when," I whispered.

The birds cut a short circle, cupped their wings and dipped over the decoys. "When!" Howard grunted.

I came to my knees and let 'em have it, one, two, three. And one, two, three they clawed up and poured off over the marsh.

Keeping my head averted, I jammed three fresh loads into the pump.

Howard said nothing for a moment. Then he asked, "You done much shootin'?"

I started to say "Quite a lot," but caught myself. "Some."

"Nex' time lead 'em a little," Howard said. "Lead 'em a helluva lot, in fact."

The next bird was a single that cut straight across the water and hung over the decoys as if suspended from a string.

"For gawd's sake, don't lead this'n," Howard said under his breath. "Take 'im!"

I hit the bird squarely amidships and it came down with a splash among the decoys.

Almost before it landed Howard had the oars out and was rowing wildly after the bird. He grabbed it by the neck and tossed it into my lap. "There," he said with relish. "First bird's in the boat. Now to wet him down. Hand me the bottle."

"What bottle?"

He rested on his oars and looked me straight in the eye. "*Your* bottle."

"I haven't got a bottle."

"You mean you didn't bring anything to drink?" His voice trembled with disbelief.

"I never drink when I'm shooting," I told him severely.

"Well, great balls of fire, man, *I'm* not shootin'! I allus wet down the first bird my gunner kills. You mean I can't have a drink till we come off the marsh? Nine more birds? Oh, my God!"

The implication was clear enough. A blind man might reasonably be expected to kill nine ducks, given sufficient time and opportunity. A three-year-old child might do it, or even Howard's spinster aunt. But not me. Mumbling something unintelligible under his breath, Howard rowed back to our mudbank and anchored the boat. I couldn't think of anything to say, so I kept my counsel. But I remembered Howard's experience of the night before, and the fact that he hadn't even fortified his spirit with a cup of coffee this morning, and determined to shoot as I had never shot before.

Four black ducks whistled over our heads from back up the marsh, cut a wide circle and swung over the decoys. I watched them through the thatch until they came within gunshot of our boat, and whispered "Now?"

"Wait," Howard whispered back. "Let 'em light."

The ducks dropped into the water and paddled about among the decoys.

260

"Now?"

"Wait," Howard told me again, with an edge in his voice. "Let a couple of 'em line up an' give it to 'em."

"I'm damned if I will," I said. "I'm not going to shoot them on the water."

"You need nine birds," he reminded me hoarsely, "an' I need a drink. Line 'em up!"

I cleared my throat loudly. The four ducks leaped off the water on wildly beating wings. I blotted out the right-hand bird with my barrel and dumped him. Swinging over to the next one, I pumped the other two loads well under him as he gained altitude and flew off with the others.

Relations were somewhat strained in the duckboat after that. Howard sat licking his dry lips. I scanned the sky with elaborate care, but confined my attention to the upcreek side, which kept my head averted from Howard's end of the boat. Birds were flying, but as other gunners began getting in their licks they moved higher. From the corner of my eye I saw Howard fondle his duck call.

A flock of ten or a dozen birds winged by, high and well out, heading for the open waters of the harbor. As I watched them, wishing they'd turn, Howard's call sounded in my ear.

"*Quack!* QUACK-*quack-quack-quack!*"

The flock wavered, but didn't quite turn.

"*Quaaaaaack! Quack-quack-quack!*"

The effect was astounding. As if he had a string tied to them, Howard pulled the ducks out of the sky and drew them straight toward our decoys.

"Wait, now," said Howard. "For Pete's sake, wait'll they're right in your face and eyes!"

I waited. The birds swung wide over the decoys once, set their wings and scaled right into my face and eyes. Without waiting for instructions, I rose to my knees and drove the sixes at them. When the barrage lifted, one duck thrashed on the water, wing-tipped and able. I stuffed the magazine full and dispatched him with three shells.

As Howard rowed out to pick him up he eyed my shell box, now nearly half empty. "You'll be runnin' out of shells pretty soon," he observed. I thought I detected a note of cheer in his voice.

I hated to say it, but I had to: "I brought an extra box."

Howard swallowed once, hard. He opened his mouth as if to say something, and then clamped it shut. I had the feeling that it was just as well he did.

Before very long I had torn the cover off the second box and was scrabbling in it to feed my gun. Like a trumpeter in a jam session, Howard poured his soul into his duck call. Birds that winged by high and far out turned and hurtled through my spirited anti-aircraft fire like kamikaze pilots. The race became one between the slowly mounting pile of dead birds and the fast-dwindling store of shells in the box. As my fingers scraped bottom and came up with the fiftieth shell I turned to Howard.

"How many we got?"

"Nine," he said, as if he had the number memorized. "How's the ammunition holdin' out?"

"Last shell," I told him.

I pumped it into the chamber and waited. From out of the sky Howard pulled two black ducks. Like maple leaves falling on a windless day in October, they drifted down on the decoys. I laid the muzzle on the bill of the nearest and, with a short prayer, pulled the trigger. Glory be, the bird fell.

So far as I know, records have never been kept on the quickest pickup ever made by a ducking guide, but if there have, Howard broke the record that day. The mudbanks of the marsh raced by as our flat-bottomed boat, never designed for speedy travel, planed homeward. When we hit the beach Howard jumped out and accosted a perfect stranger in gunning clothes.

And *that* duck hunter had a bottle. . . .

Probably the most remarkable of the blinds I have shot from was not a blind at all, but a Sears Roebuck nightshirt. Late in the season, when snow blankets the marsh, or the tidal waters have frozen, a long nightshirt draped over the person effectively disguises one as a lump of snow or ice, especially if the individual has become so numbed with cold that he cannot move.

Late in the same fall that I gunned with Howard, Ollie Rodman and I landed on Sand Island, where Barnstable Marsh opens up and becomes the head of Barnstable Harbor. That morning when we arose at Mother Mortimer's, where we laid over after driving down from Boston the night before, the thermometer outside the kitchen window registered a frigid five above. The wind, keening out of the polar regions, made it even colder on the bare and frozen expanse of Sand Island. But off the south shore we found a patch of open water, perhaps 50 yards across. Into it we flung our decoys, and by the edge of it we crouched miserably, clad in our white nightshirts, scanning the skies for ducks.

Although wildfowl are said to be nearly impervious to cold, I believe that day was too much for them, for we saw only an occasional sea gull until nearly midmorning, when a flock of three black ducks materialized out of the gray heavens. Too cold to move, and probably too cold to shoulder our weapons, we watched them draw closer, until they were heading straight across the ice for our decoys. Closer they came, and still closer. Then, just as they should have set their wings and dropped in, they flared and scampered off.

I turned to Ollie accusingly. "Did you move?"

Through purple lips he said, "I couldn't m-move if I w-wanted to. It's the decoys. They're all iced up."

I hadn't noticed the decoys but they were, indeed, iced up. Ice sheathed their backs like silver armor. It hung from their bills, reminding me of pictures I'd seen of stalactites hanging from the roof of a cavern.

"You better go out and knock the ice off them," I said.

"I'm thinking of a number," Ollie said. "Odd or even?"

"Even."

"Nope, odd."

I got to my feet somehow and waded out into the icy water and kicked the decoys until they were free of ice. By the time I rejoined Ollie they had started to ice up again.

"Your turn next time," I said.

"Let's match for it again."

"You go to hell," I told him. "We'll take turns."

Some time later a flock of five geese winged over our heads, a hundred yards high. We watched them longingly.

"Heading out for the harbor," Ollie said. "If it gets rough out there, they'll be back."

"The decoys need kicking," I said.

As Ollie got up, groaning, a rattle of gunfire sounded to the east of us. I picked up the flock of geese, and saw them flaring over Thatcher's Island beyond us. One bird dropped out and sagged over the ice. A small figure darted after it.

The remainder of the flock never re-formed. Two of the geese disappeared harborward while the other two—the other two headed straight for us!

"Mark!' I bellowed at Ollie, who was by now wading among the decoys. "For the luvva Mike, geddown!"

He looked up and spotted the geese. Like a heron about to spear a minnow, he bent over quickly with his nose inches from the water. "Maybe," thought frantically, "he looks like a piece of floating ice."

The geese bore down on me, one slightly ahead of the other, flying straight and true at the height of about 40 yards. I let my eye flicker down to Ollie's double, which he had laid carefully over a lump of ice to keep the muzzles out of the snow. Two shells in that, three in mine. Five shells. Even with 6's, that ought to do it.

"Take 'em!" Ollie yelled.

I came to my knees and poured three loads from my pump into the nearest broad white breast. In one motion I laid my gun on the ice and grabbed Ollie's. As I brought it up I saw the first bird falling, so I rammed the two loads into the other. As the last charge thumped into him, his wings folded and the two birds crashed down almost together.

Ollie waded ashore with a broad grin on his face. "On that note," he said, "leave us pick up our decoys and go someplace where it's warm so you can brag about it!"

We gathered in the blocks and made shore by alternately rowing over the open water and dragging over the ice. Howard Marks was waiting for us at the landing, a binocular slung around his neck.

"Been watching you two from Calf Pasture Point," he grinned. "You looked cute, layin' out there in your nighties. Who was it killed the geese?"

"He did," Ollie said, jerking a thumb at me.

Howard looked at me speculatively. "You don't say. That guy has owed me a drink since last October." He grabbed me by the arm. "And now, by God, I'm gonna collect it."

264

GUNS AND SHOOTING

Popping for Practice

WHATEVER YOU HUNT, or however good a shot you are, you're going to miss a few easy ones in the course of a hunting season. So if you've got a certain number of misses in your system, the best time to use them up is before the season opens.

If you haven't handled your shotgun since last gunning season, pick it up now and snap it to your shoulder a few times. You'll probably find that your swing is creaky, your eye dim, and the gun doesn't come up quite as effortlessly as it did the last time you shot it.

Smooth, accurate gun-mounting results from muscular coordination. You get it, or regain it, through practice. And the simplest way to regain mastery over your gun is to handle it. First, make absolutely triple-sure the gun is empty. Then stand in one spot, fix your eye on any object—a picture or clock, for example—and quickly point your gun at it. Now close your left eye and sight along the barrel with the right. You'll probably find you are pointing a bit over, under, or to one side or the other. Correct the hold and try again—and again and again. Before long you'll be on target every time. And if you feel a little foolish taking imaginary shots at Cousin Mike's picture on the piano, remember that many of the country's top skeet and trap shots spend hours "dry pointing" to keep on familiar terms with their guns.

A few rounds of skeet or a couple of afternoons at the trap range will work wonders in helping you to get some of the misses out of your system. Your gun will begin to feel comfortable once more, and the comb will start snuggling up to that familiar spot under your cheek bone, where it belongs.

If you can't get to a skeet or trap field, then beg, borrow or buy a hand trap and take turns throwing clay pigeons with your gunning partner. Sure, shells cost money these days, but missing a clay target isn't nearly as painful as missing a cock pheasant, and both wasted shells cost exactly the same.

Or, if the high cost of ammo scares you, go out back of the house and dry-point song birds. Slip a dead shell into the chamber to protect your firing pin, and snap away at flying swallows or robins. You'll know if each "shot" would have been a hit or miss, whether you shot over or under or behind, and you may even correct a tendency we all develop at times of stopping the gun in midswing.

You'll find it much easier to correct your shooting faults now, when misses don't count. Before long you'll get back into the sweet-shooting groove you enjoyed so much at the end of last hunting season when you were hitting just about everything that flew.

TAP'S TIPS

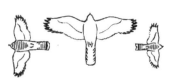

([Of all the species of hawks native to this country, only three are considered undesirable—the Cooper's, sharpshin, and goshawk, all notorious killers of song and game birds. All the others are beneficial, and feed mainly on insects and rodents. The three villains have long, banded tails and short wings. Learn to recognize these three, and spare the others. If you can't make a positive identification, don't shoot, because the desirable hawks greatly outnumber the harmful species.

([Always remove ammunition from your car at the end of each hunting trip. First reason, safety. Second reason, excessive heat may affect the loads if the car should be left in the sun with the windows closed.

([Hunting in the winter poses a constant hazard—snow in the barrels. Sometimes shooting will clear a snow-clogged tube, but sometimes it won't. When it doesn't, the barrel may burst. So play it safe and check your barrels every once in a while to make sure they are clear.

Tapply's Secret of Successful Scattergunning

If you know someone who has trouble hitting game birds or clay saucers in flight, I think you could tell him in one short, four-word sentence how he can become a better wingshot almost instantly. Not overnight; instantly.

Maybe I should hire a smart advertising man to handle this thing for me. There might be a fortune in it. See how this sounds: "You, too, can become a crack wingshot! Bag twice as many birds with half as many shells! Send only one dollar TODAY for Tapply's Secret of Successful Scattergunning! Endorsed by world's top shooters! Satisfaction guaranteed or money b—" On second thought, perhaps it would be just as well not to say anything about refunds.

Besides, anyone could discover the Secret himself, if he watched a good wingshooter for a while.

It was the late William Harnden Foster, one of the originators of skeet, who revealed the Secret to me, many years ago. I had just broken 10 out of 25 clay targets, which was my miserable skeet average at the time. Bill took me aside and said:

"Straighten your left arm."

And that is the Secret. Just slide the left hand farther out on the fore-end.

Analyze, if you will, what each of a shooter's hands must do when he mounts his gun to shoot at a moving target. The right hand (port-siders will have to reverse these directions, naturally) merely guides the butt to the shoulder and performs the relatively unskilled jobs of pressing safety button and trigger.

The left hand does the important work. It supports the weight of the barrels, swings them smoothly through the flight-path of the target, making adjustments for changes in its speed and direction, and guides the shot charge on a collision course toward the swift-moving bird or Blue Rock.

Look up right now and point at something with your left forefinger. Did you extend your arm, or did you bend it so the finger was only a foot from your face? You extended it, because it is instinctive to point that way.

Now point again, and turn your palm up. If you dropped the fore-end of a shotgun in it you would be in good shooting position, with your left hand pointing at your target.

If you've got a minute, get out your shotgun, check it for empty chambers, and aim it for a few seconds with your left hand extended and elbow tucked directly under the gun. Then slide your hand back close to the trigger guard, the position so many beginning shooters use. You'll notice the barrels feel much heavier now, the whole gun suddenly out of balance.

Swing the muzzles along a horizontal line, such as the molding at the top of a wall or a telephone wire, and notice how the muzzle tends to wobble off line when you bend the left arm, and how much easier it is to stay on the line when you extend it.

Same thing happens when you swing on a bird. So anyone should shoot better if he straightens his left arm—as long as he also remembers to keep his head down, pivot from the hips, and swing through as he shoots. These all help, too.

TAP'S TIPS

((Those who own two or more shotguns of different gauges always face the risk of mixing their ammunition—like a friend of mine who arose at 2 o'clock one winter morning, drove a hundred miles to go duck shooting, rowed a mile to reach his favorite gunning spot, built a blind, and then discovered that he had brought 12 gauge shells for his 16 gauge gun. So unless you have a strong preference for a certain brand of ammunition, you can avoid such a monumental mixup by color-coding shells to shotgun—red cases for the 12, green for the 16, purple for the 20.

268

⟮ Here's something everyone who is just starting to use a pump-action shotgun should remember: Never hold the trigger down when working the action between shots. We have seen some close calls due to accidental firing, so the cornsheller should be reloaded carefully until the shooter becomes familiar with his new gun.

Deadly "Little" 20

It has always seemed to me a little ridiculous that anyone should consider a 2-ounce fly rod more "sportsmanlike" than a 5-ounce rod, or think that a shotgunner deliberately handicaps himself in the interest of good sportsmanship by shooting a 20 bore instead of a 12. I think it's just the other way around, or at least that the advantages of using light and heavy gear cancel out.

During the past thirty-odd years I have used a 20 bore Model 21 Winchester double for everything from ducks and even geese down to crows and woodcock. During that time I've had one or two pretty good days, but my gunning partners have always appeared less impressed with my wingshooting skill than with the fact that I performed these miracles with such a piddling little gun. If I tell them I shoot better—to put it bluntly, kill more game—with a 20 than I do with a 12, they charge it off to modesty. Modesty, hell. On the rare occasions when I shoot well, I'm the first to mention it. Whenever I can brag without lying, I brag.

True, the 20 bore load has fewer pellets and less velocity than the 12. For comparison, in regular field loads the 12 gauge shell holds about 460 No. 8 pellets, the 20 gauge only 360. Velocity of the 12 is about 855 feet per second, of the 20, around 835. So the bigger gun gives you a denser pattern and just a bit more sting.

However, the 12 gauge gun will weigh from 1 to 1½ pounds more than the 20, roughly speaking. Along toward the end of a long day in the uplands the 12 seems to come up slower, drags when you swing it ahead of a fast-flying bird. If you'd like to compare the difference sometime, borrow a 20 from someone in the party and see how much lighter and faster it feels. When the sun slants out of the west and you're beginning to become conscious of your age, you'll hit birds with the 20 you'd miss with a 12, the extra pellets and load speed of the bigger gun notwithstanding. And the 20 costs less to feed.

Gun weight isn't such an important factor when you're squatting in a blind or pit, of course, and ducks kill harder than quail, so the 20 has less to offer the wildfowler. Even so, the full choke tube of a 20 will do a nice job on decoying ducks within 40 yards.

20 GAUGE GUN

FASTER HANDLING

LIGHTER WEIGHT

12 GAUGE LOAD

GREATER VELOCITY

MORE SHOT PELLETS

During the last few years there has been a definite trend toward lighter sporting gear—in guns, rods, hunting bows, clothing, camping equipment. If this gear is more efficient and more pleasant to use than the heavier stuff, obviously using it doesn't make a man more "sportsmanlike." So let's have no more of this nonsense about gunners who "give the game a break" by shooting a 20. Because the simple truth is, the 20's as deadly as the 12. In some ways, deadlier.

TAP'S TIPS

⟨ The next time you see a gunner about to close the action of his double-barreled shotgun, notice how he does it. If he slams it together as if he were banging a gate shut, he either doesn't know how to handle firearms, or doesn't have much respect for fine mechanism. But if he holds the piece by the fore-end and lifts the stock up to it, mark him down as a man who knows what he's doing—and why he's doing it.

⟨ There are still a great many Damascus, or twist-barrel, shotguns around, and one way to live dangerously is to shoot them with modern loads. The tubes in these guns were not constructed to take the pressures generated by the beefed-up stuff we shoot today. They may stand up under a dozen shots or a hundred, or they may burst the next time the trigger is pulled, and blow off a finger or two. The chief value of these old guns is as souvenirs of the black-powder era.

Sight Unseen

Quick, now: What is the color of the front bead on your shotgun?

If you can't remember, your memory is no worse than mine. I've peered down the rib of my pet feather-duster literally thousands of times since I acquired her 30 years ago, yet I couldn't recall what her front bead looked like. I guessed it was probably white. But when I took the old girl from her case a moment ago, I found that her nose was red.

A friend of mine, about to put away his shotgun after a highly profitable day in New England woodcock covers, happened to notice that the front sight was missing. After a long search he found it in the bottom of his gun case, so he had hunted all day without once seeing his muzzle clearly enough to note the absence of the bead. He has never bothered to replace it.

If sighting devices could help us hit birds we'd all be deadeyes, for an infinite and wondrous variety of them has been offered for public sale. Only a few have survived. Perhaps the most popular sighting aid is still just a strip of adhesive tape wrapped around the muzzle. The white blob helps some acutely farsighted shooters to keep their barrels in the dim foreground of their vision as they concentrate on the distant target.

I have asked many hunters, some of them top wingshots whose names you would recognize, what picture they see when they shoot at

271

a flying bird. "Nothing but the bird itself," is the typical answer. All admitted that they made no conscious effort to relate the barrels to the flight of the bird.

Last fall I asked Burton L. Spiller, author of several authoritative books on upland shooting and still a remarkable wingshot at 70-odd, how he learned to hit grouse. "By missing so many of them," he told me. "I just kept burning powder till they started to come down."

This supports the common theory that the ability to hit moving targets with some degree of consistency—say, one grouse out of four, two pheasants out of five—is basically a conditioned reflex, established after a great deal of practice with a gun that fits well or, just as important, one to which the shooter has fitted himself. Beads, rings, bars and other sighting aids seldom help, except occasionally in the case of a shooter with an eye problem. I've been told that a low-power scope has helped many shooters, but even that is no substitute for shooting and missing and shooting some more.

TAP'S TIPS

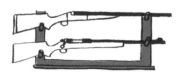

⟨ Before putting a shotgun away after a hunt, always release the spring by snapping the trigger. To avoid damage to the firing pin, let it hit a block of wood or a dummy shell. If the spring remains under tension for a long period of time it may become weakened.

⟨ When a covey of birds explodes in front of you the temptation to shoot into the thickest part of it is almost too much to resist. But no matter how closely bunched it is, the covey pattern contains more air space than birds, so the chance of not hitting a bird is much greater than the chance of hitting one. The experienced gunner picks one bird and stays on it until it comes down, then picks another if he still has time for a double.

⟨ Moisture that goes into a gun case with the gun stays there and forms rust on unprotected metal. Or moisture may collect from condensation with temperature changes—and if the gun remains in its case rusting may not be discovered until it has done considerable damage. That's why many hunters prefer to store their guns on an open rack. Ventilation of air keeps the exposed guns dry and the owner can check their condition at frequent intervals.

What Load Does Your Gun Like Best?

Patterning a shotgun is something like Mark Twain's weather: everybody talks about it, but no one ever seems to do anything about it. Probably not one shotgunner in ten has ever bothered to find out if his pet fowling piece has any preference for certain loads or shot sizes. Yet it's a very simple thing to do, and the results may prove surprising.

The inside of a shotgun bore is (theoretically, at least) perfectly smooth and round, with a tapered constriction, or choke, at the muzzle. You would think that every 12-gauge, 28-inch, full-choke barrel would be exactly the same as every other barrel of similar dimensions, and throw exactly the same shot patterns with every load. Yet it is a proven fact that one such barrel may deliver perfect patterns with No. 6's and another may pattern badly with 6's but beautifully with 7½'s.

Anyone who has never patterned his shotgun can easily find out what kind of food it likes by tacking up some large sheets of paper and sprinkling them with shot. Standard procedure is to fire four or five test patterns of each load at 40 yards and count the pellet holes inside a 30-inch circle drawn around the thickest area of the pattern.

A full-choke barrel should put about 70 per cent of its shot charge inside the circle; modified, or half-choke, 60 per cent; improved cylinder,

273

or quarter-choke, 45-50 per cent; cylinder, 30-40 per cent. You have to know the number of shot in the load, of course, to get the percentage figure. As a guide, No. 9 chilled shot run about 585 to the ounce, or 660 to a 1⅛-ounce skeet load; 8's, 410 to the ounce; 7½'s, 345; 7's, 300; and 6's, 225.

While counting pellets, it is a good idea to compare the distribution of shot in the various test patterns. In a perfect pattern the pellets inside the 30-inch circle will be spaced uniformly, without patches or holes. However, if the pattern is otherwise satisfactory, don't fret about the thin spots. A hummingbird or a wren might "fly through" a spotty pattern without getting nicked, but it is very unlikely that any bird on the game list could make it.

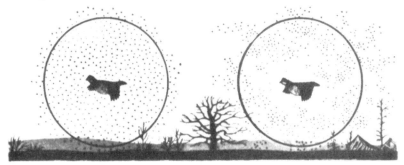

TAP'S TIPS

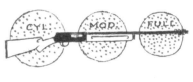

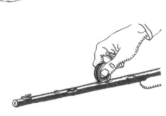

(It's hard to understand why every owner of an autoloader or pump-action shotgun doesn't have a variable choke fitted to its muzzle. The investment will pay big dividends, for the gun can be used for any species of game, from quail to geese, just by making a simple adjustment. Many shotgunners also claim that the device helps them to "see" the barrel better when they swing on a flying target.

(A typewriter eraser can be used to remove small blotches of rust from a gun barrel. The fine abrasive rubs away the rust and, unlike sandpaper or steel wool, does not damage the finish. If spots prove stubborn, soak them first with solvent.

(Dents can be removed from gunstocks by covering the dented area with a damp cloth and pressing it with a hot iron. The steam lifts the dent up to the level of the wood. If the dent is deep, several steamings may be needed.

The Bossy Master Eye

Every one of us has a "master eye," which takes charge of such matters as peering through a microscope or aiming a gun. If you are righthanded, chances are you are right-eyed, too. But you may find, as I did several years ago, that the opposite eye butts in when you shoot a rifle or shotgun. The simplest way to determine which eye is the master is to point your forefinger quickly at an object, keeping both eyes open. By closing one eye, you can easily see which one took charge of aiming.

The wrong-eyed rifle shooter has no particular problem because he can close the troublesome eye and get a reasonably clear sight picture with the other. But the shotgun shooter needs all the vision he can get, and shooting with one eye closed seriously handicaps his view of the target and his judgment of its speed and distance.

Some left-eyed shooters learn to shoot lefthanded and, after a lot of practice, often become as deadly off the left shoulder as they ever were off the right. And I know of at least one topnotch skeet and trap shooter who fitted his gun with an offset stock that brought his left eye in line with the barrel. Once he became accustomed to it, he shot better than ever before.

But there's a simpler way than that. If you find you are cursed with a master eye on the wrong side of your face, practice squinting it as you shoot. Close the bossy eye enough to kill most of its vision at first, gradually opening it to regain as much binocular vision as possible without letting the eye take complete charge again. Spend as much time dry-pointing as you can spare, always squinting that troublesome master eye. After a while the squint becomes automatic, and soon you will not even be conscious you're doing it. When the eye-squint becomes a reflex, like pressing the trigger, you'll find that the birds are falling before your gun as they never did before.

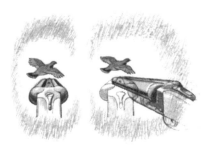

TAP'S TIPS

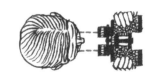

([Seeing double through binoculars results when the eyepieces are not properly aligned with the eyes. If vision overlaps, vary the adjustment until the interlocking circles disappear and you get the same single picture you see with the naked eye.

([If glasses interfere with the use of binoculars, try looking through them with the eye-shields removed. This lets the eyes come closer to the lenses and gives a much wider field of view.

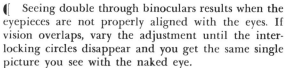
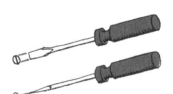

([When removing screws to dismantle a shotgun or rifle, make sure the screwdriver blade fits snugly in the slots. If the blade is too large or too small it can damage the screw heads or, worse yet, slip out and gouge the metal or wood. If necessary, file the blade to the proper size before using it on small, tight-fitting screws.

Caliber and Gauge

Whenever a shotgun figures in the crime news, the reporter who writes the story almost invariably describes the weapon as a ".12 gauge shotgun" or, even worse, as "12 caliber." The difference between gauge and caliber is as great as the difference between an ounce and an inch. For the benefit of all hands, including cub reporters, let's get this matter straightened out now.

We inherited the term "gauge" from the olden days of the smooth-bore musket, which fired round bullets cast of lead. A modern 12 gauge shotgun barrel will accommodate a perfectly round lead ball weighing

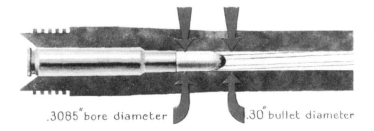

.3085" bore diameter   .30" bullet diameter

$\frac{1}{12}$ pound; balls weighing $\frac{1}{16}$ pound are 16 gauge, and so on. The only exception is the .410, which is not a gauge but a caliber, because a lead ball measuring .41 inch in diameter would fit snugly into the bore of a .410 barrel.

So caliber, as you can see, is a measurement in inches of diameter, either bullet or bore. Theoretically, a .30 caliber bullet measures exactly .30 inch; actually, it doesn't. A rifle barrel is not smoothbore. Spiralled grooves are cut into it to make the bullet spin as it leaves the barrel. The bullet must bulge into the grooves to prevent powder gas from leaking around it as it twirls down the bore. For that reason, the diameter of bullet and bore cannot be the same. The .30 caliber Government bullet, for example, is cast oversize to .3085 inch, thus ensuring a tight fit. The popular long rifle rimfire .22 goes into a bore measuring from .217 to .219 inch, depending upon who made the rifle; the .303 Savage goes in a bore of .300; the .32 Winchester Special in a .315-inch bore, and so forth.

But in general, just remember that caliber means diameter in inches and gauge means fractions of a pound. We'll let the manufacturers worry about oversize bullets and undersize bores.

TAP'S TIPS

❲ Your shoulder absorbs up to 30 foot-pounds of recoil energy every time you touch off a heavy load in a 12 gauge shotgun. To soften the blow, and perhaps avoid the possibility of developing a "flinch," it may be necessary to have the stock altered for a better fit in drop at the comb, length, and pitch. Sometimes merely adding a recoil pad to lengthen the stock will greatly reduce the recoil effect and improve the ratio between hits and misses.

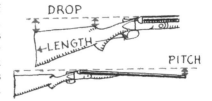

❲ The rimfire .22 is essentially a short-range rifle, although its little slug can be "dangerous up to a mile," as the ammunition companies claim. So if you set your sights for 50 yards, you need to hold only a little high or low for every shot within its effective range.

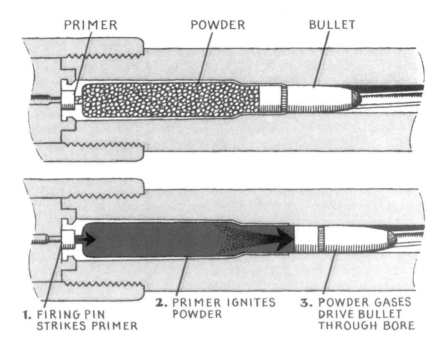

PRIMER   POWDER   BULLET

1. FIRING PIN
STRIKES PRIMER

2. PRIMER IGNITES
POWDER

3. POWDER GASES
DRIVE BULLET
THROUGH BORE

How Ammo Goes Off

Can you remember the last time a shotshell or rifle cartridge failed to fire when you pressed the trigger? I can't, and I've been burning powder for more than 30 years. When you think of it, the reliability of modern ammunition is a wonderful thing.

Picture all that happens in the tiny fragment of a split second after you release the firing pin on a chambered center-fire rifle cartridge. First, the pin plunges against the primer and shoves the entire cartridge forward, forcing it snugly against the front end of the chamber. Then as the pin continues forward it dents the primer cup and creates friction in the priming mixture, causing it to ignite. The burning mixture generates gas pressure inside the primer, forcing flame through the flash hole and touching off the powder charge.

The burning powder builds up tremendous gas pressure inside the cartridge case, as much as 50,000 pounds per square inch. This pressure expands the brass case to the limit of the chamber wall, which prevents gas from leaking into the breech of the rifle. As the case is thinnest at the throat, that part expands first and loosens its grip on the bullet, allowing the pressure to force it into the rifling. Here the lands engage the slug and give it spin as the ever-increasing pressure pushes it down the barrel.

278

As the bullet emerges at the muzzle, traveling as fast as 4,000 feet per second, the gas pressure behind it celebrates its freedom with a loud bang. If the powder is still burning, you may also see a flash at the muzzle, especially in shade or dim light.

Meanwhile, things are still happening back in the chamber. The hot case, remember, has expanded to fit the chamber tightly, and you couldn't possibly extract it in one piece. But after the powder has all burned, the case starts to cool off, and shrinks away from the chamber walls enough to let go when the extractor grabs it.

From that instant on, that case will fit that particular chamber exactly, because it has expanded to compensate for the minute tolerances allowed in the manufacture of both the cartridge and chamber. If you handload, that can be important, for the case will not be weakened by further stretching in strange chambers, and will therefore last longer and give you maximum accuracy.

TAP'S TIPS

(A clinch-on lead sinker and length of cord make a handy substitute for a cleaning rod. Pinch the sinker to one end of the cord and tie a cleaning patch to the other. To clean the bore, drop the sinker through the barrel and pull the patch through. It's much more convenient to carry on hunting trips than a rod.

(When you use a gun during the winter, let it warm to room temperature before cleaning it and putting it away. If you store it cold, moisture may condense on the metal and cause rusting.

(Will your deer rifle give you the same dime-sized groups in November that you got when you sighted it in during the late summer? Perhaps not, if the barrel was warm that day, because expansion and contraction of the metal can affect accuracy. Better sight it in again when the barrel is cold, as it will be when you are hunting deer.

It Was an Accident!

But was it? The newspapers will call it that when they break out the big black type to headline their stories of shooting mishaps during the hunting season. "Accident" strikes me as an inaccurate word for describing what happens when someone does something stupid while crossing a fence or cleaning a rifle.

Tragic and inexcusable as such "accidents" are, even more tragic

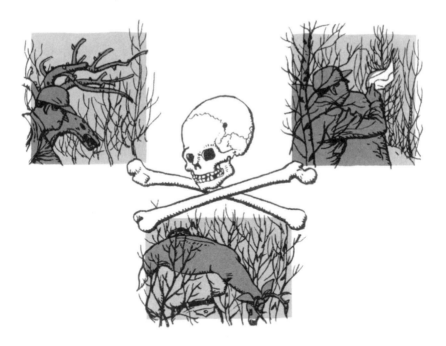

and unforgivable is the case of one hunter mistaking another hunter for a deer.

Think of it! A man aims his rifle at another man and deliberately pulls the trigger!

Calling it "carelessness" doesn't come even close to the reason for it. No one could possibly mistake a man for a deer because of indifference or lack of "care." To commit such an enormous blunder, a man must become so emotionally charged with the overpowering need for killing a deer that his mind plays tricks on him, as if in the grip of a raging fever—as indeed it may be at the moment.

And the headlines scream out the shame of it while a dozen automobile "accidents" resulting from too much speed or alcohol get only a few inches of space on a back page.

What can you and I do about it? Well, I can write about it and you can talk about it, and maybe we'll get through to a few people who will remember what we've said.

We can stay home and give the woods to the goons, just as a cop could stay off the streets when hoodlums are loose, but that wouldn't solve the problem either.

One thing we can do, and must do, is to make it as difficult as possible for anyone to mistake *us* for a deer. We can wear plenty of yellow or red. We can be careful not to stop in a clump of brush and shake out a white handkerchief before blowing our nose with it. We can drag

280

out our deer instead of carrying it over our shoulders. In camp, we can demonstrate our experience with firearms by handling them with the respect they deserve.

Above all, we can remember that shooting a deer really isn't terribly important, and certainly not worth the risk of becoming involved in an "accident" ourselves.

TAP'S TIPS

❨ A wooden box makes a sturdy rest for sighting-in a deer rifle. Saw V-shaped notches in each end of the top, making them deep enough to hold the rifle firmly. Place a couple of stones inside the box to anchor it. If necessary, wedge a board under the front or back to obtain the correct shooting angle.

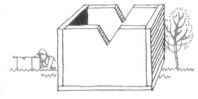

❨ A bit of cellophane tape stuck over the muzzle of a rifle or shotgun will keep the barrel free of dust in storage or of mud or snow when hunting. The tape breaks easily when the gun is fired, so if you forget to remove it there is no danger of bursting the barrel.

CELLOPHANE

❨ If you have trouble finding the front bead on your rifle when shooting against a background of dazzling snow or dark woods, paint it fire orange and, if necessary, also paint a triangle on the face of the rear sight. The paint can be removed later with turpentine. Or use bright-red fingernail polish.

❨ A short length of rope will come in handy many times on a deer hunting trip. You can use it to hang your deer while the blood drains, as a drag rope for a one-man haul, or to bind the carcass to a pole or litter for a two-man carry. To save pocket room, some hunters carry the rope wound around their middle.

❨ If you are one of those who can't enjoy drinking from a spring while lying flat on the ground with your nose buried in ice water, get a length of plastic surgical tubing and use it as a drinking straw. A coil of it fits in any small pocket.

DOGS

Pick of the Litter

SOME DAY, if you lead a virtuous life, make friends with a great number of dog breeders and wave enough money under their noses, you may be offered your pick of a litter of hunting dogs.

When you go to select your pup, don't bring your wife. I can tell you just the pup she'll pick. It will be the wistful little fellow sitting all alone in a corner—that cute one over there, Henry, look, the one with the floppy ears and big sad eyes. Can't you see, Henry, he's practically *pleading* with us to take him.

Leave her home, Henry. Leave the kids home, too; they're no help, either. This is a man's work, requiring a frosted heart and the calculating eye of a pawnbroker.

Maybe the flop-eared pup will turn out to be the best of the lot, but the law of averages says he won't. The pup to put your money on is the biggest, toughest, roughest, noisiest one of the bunch, the one who swaggers when he walks and bullies his way to the head of the line at the feed pan or nipple.

Chances are he'll be a male. If you're shopping for a bitch, pick the gal who snaps at the roughneck, and cocks her head when she's whistled at, as any high-spirited female should.

282

It's a tough choice, and you'll never know for sure you've made the right one. But as long as you're going to gamble, you might as well bet on the favorite. That will be the tough little guy who learns fast and doesn't scare easy. Trouble is, that's generally the one the breeder has already decided to keep for himself.

TAP'S TIPS

❨ Many hunters believe that early spring is the best time to shop for a new bird dog pup. By the time summer comes the youngster is ready for simple yard training and can be worked on young birds in September. Some exceptionally precocious pups develop early enough to shoot over by the time the hunting season opens.

❨ If you accept a pup at weaning time, remember that he requires frequent feedings. Five meals a day are none too many at first. Cut feedings gradually until, at six or seven months of age, you are feeding him twice a day. I put my dogs on a single evening meal when they are a year old and full grown.

❨ A new puppy's first night in a strange home can be a fearsome experience, and he usually expresses his unhappiness by wailing from dusk till dawn. To keep him quiet, put an old-fashioned alarm clock beside his bed. The loud ticking seems to provide the companionship he longs for.

❨ Most trainers insist that a dog should be taught to heel at his master's left, opposite the shooting side. In practice, it doesn't seem to matter much; the important thing is to teach the dog to come to heel instantly on command and to stay there. Fortunately, most dogs learn this quickly.

Who Trains the Pup?

Because the life expectancy of a dog is roughly one-seventh that of a man, hunting dogs wear out faster than hunters. Therefore, in the natural course of events it becomes necessary for most of us to find a new gun dog on the average of once every 10 years—perhaps oftener, if we live near heavy traffic—nurse him through the perils of puppyhood, and somehow or other make him worthy of sleeping in Old Dog's kennel.

This poses no great problem for the hound dog man. He can pick a lively pup, turn him loose with an older dog, and wait. Sooner or later the pup will train himself.

But the man who likes to have a well-mannered bird dog quartering the covers ahead of him faces the prospect of breaking in a new feather-finder with misgivings. Should he unbelt a month's salary for a ready-trained dog, make a modest investment in a well-bred pup and turn him over to a professional trainer, or should he try to train the youngster himself?

Don't look at me. I'm strictly the do-it-yourself type, and have always trained (I use the word in its loosest sense) my own bird dogs.

The answer may be found in any standard dog-training book. An hour's reading will help the owner decide whether he has the time, patience, and facilities for teaching the multitude of things a well-trained dog ought to know.

If it looks like a bigger job than he cares to tackle, the owner can save himself a lot of time and trouble, if not money, by handing the job over to a professional trainer. But if reading the book encourages him to try it, all the better. Working with a young dog, watching it develop, is an enormously gratifying experience, and many amateurs have produced topflight performers, even field trial winners.

TAP'S TIPS

❡ When it becomes necessary to teach a young dog the error of his ways, give him a whack with a loosely folded newspaper. It doesn't hurt him a bit, but the loud noise makes him think it does.

¶ The quickest way to win a dog's affection is to feed him. Dogs associate the pleasure of eating with the person who supplies the food. Such a relationship will prove valuable during the training program and in actual hunting.

¶ Never risk confusing a pup with commands that sound alike. "Whoa" and "No," "Here" and "Heel" sound similar even to human ears. You can make it easier for your pup to understand what you want him to do by substituting "Stop" for "Whoa" and "Come" for "Here." Also, remember that the dog may respond to your tone of voice more readily than to the words you use.

The Carsick Pup

Anyone who has ever owned a young puppy knows that upchucking is likely to start any time after Mile One of any given automobile ride. It's a miserable experience for the pup, but it isn't a perfumed chariot ride for Old Folks, either.

In most cases a dramamine tablet given about an hour before the ride will prevent carsickness. Also, it helps if the owner makes sure the pup has nothing to eat or drink for a couple of hours before leaving. The pup may feel just as sick on an empty stomach, but there isn't as much he can do about it.

Personally, I've found that short, frequent rides cure a pup of carsickness as quickly, and much more permanently, than is possible with pills or withholding food, especially if the ride is turned into a play period.

Put the pup on the front seat with you and play with him a while. Drive slowly to the next corner and back, still talking to him and

285

roughhousing him a little with your free hand. Next day take him a little farther. Keep the rides short so he doesn't have time to become sick. If you drive to the store on an errand, take the pup along. Give him a ball or a stick to play with while he rides, to divert his attention.

You can tell if he starts to feel squeamish, because he'll begin to drool. Stop the car, take the pup out and let him walk or run around a while. Then stuff him back in the car and drive home the shortest way.

Most pups—and older dogs too—betray their tendency toward car-sickness by the way they approach a ride. If yours doesn't want to get in the car, it is probably because he has learned to fear the consequences—in other words, he has developed a conditioned reflex by associating the car with sickening nausea and so, up come the biscuits. You may be able to overcome this by feeding the pup in the car for a few days. In a week's time the ever-hungry pup should jump into the car eagerly when his feed pan is put on the floor or seat. After that, short rides on an empty belly, with dramamine if necessary, should cure him.

TAP'S TIPS

(Save the water drained from cooked vegetables and use it to moisten your dog's kibbles or meal. The pot liquor flavors the food and contains vitamins and minerals that would otherwise be wasted.

(Most pups can begin to "learn English" as early as their tenth week. Start with a simple command, such as "Come," and introduce new words one at a time according to the pup's ability to grasp their meaning. End each lesson when the pup's tail stops wagging.

(Here's an easy way to prevent a dog from climbing all over a car on long trips. Cut a sheet of ¼-inch plywood to fit into the rear floorboard well. Attach a short rope or chain to a ring bolt in the center of the board. Then tether the dog to it. He can't possibly move the board or get off it.

When Dog Meets Gun

The worst time to let a young dog hear the sound of gunfire for the first time is when hunting. With your mind on flushed or fleeing game, you can let off an indiscreet shot that might ruin your pup for life. So it's safer and wiser to make gun-conditioning a definite part of his early training. Then you will have nothing to worry about when the hunting season comes along.

286

Start the program by making a lot of noise when you feed the pup. Rattle his pan loudly, slam the door. If he's jumping all over you for his chow, he probably won't mind the noise a bit. Next, fire a cap pistol while the pup is playing or eating or doing anything interesting. If he jumps or flinches—and he may at first—don't make the mistake of reassuring him with words or petting. Ignore him, and your indifference will show him that nothing has happened that he should worry about.

When the pup has become thoroughly accustomed to the cap pistol, move up to the .22. At first, wait until he is tremendously interested in something before you shoot off a blank, and then only when he has moved a reasonable distance away. If he shows no fright, close up the distance gradually.

By then you're ready to introduce him to the boom of a shotgun. Repeat the same procedure, starting some distance away and shooting only when he is chasing a songbird or sniffing eagerly on ground scent. When he begins to show interest, rather than alarm, at closeup shooting, you can be sure he'll never be a gun-shy dog.

And if you think this ounce of prevention isn't worth the time and effort, just ask anyone who has ever tried to *cure* a case of gun shyness.

TAP'S TIPS

[Most owners of male dogs, and people who live near people who own male dogs, have the same problem—damage to shrubbery. Try sprinkling some mothballs around the bushes. Dogs seem to dislike the odor as much as moths do. The same treatment also repels skunks, mice, raccoons, and even ground-nesting hornets.

[A rolled-up newspaper provides the best means I know of to discourage a dog from barking. Keep the

weapon handy, and when the dog barks follow this simple, three-step procedure immediately: 1. Grab newspaper. 2. Grab dog. 3. Apply newspaper to dog's backsides. The paper won't hurt the dog, but the noise will make him think it does. If *every* outburst of barking is followed immediately with a loud and vigorous whacking and shouts of "No! No!," most sensible dogs soon catch on to the idea.

(After a dog stops hunting his toenails grow faster than he can wear them down. Long nails may split and become painful. If you don't like to cut or file them, sink a flat stone or cement slab in front of his kennel gate or wherever he spends a lot of time. The rough surface will help to keep them worn down.

Porky-Proofing the Pup

A young dog's first dose of porcupine quills will either cure him or make him seek revenge by tackling every porcupine he sees from that day on. At best he ruins one hunt; at worst, several.

Fed up with pulling quills and having my hunts spoiled, I worked out a way to break my last two young bird dogs instead of waiting to let nature take its unpleasant course. And I am happy to report that both treatments were successful.

Since porcupines are plentiful in the New England country I hunt, it has been easy to locate one of them for training purposes. In each case I spotted one while driving along country roads. Snapping a long check cord to the pup's collar, I let him discover the porcupine. When he made a joyful dive for the creature I was ready for him, and upended him with a hard yank on the cord.

Loudly shouting "No!" in an angry voice, I then grabbed the pup by his collar and began dusting him with my cap. When I felt I had convinced the poor dog that he had just committed the most terrible sin of his life, I let him pass near the tree where the porcupine had taken refuge. When the pup looked up at the cause of all his troubles I shouted "No!" again, whacked him with the cap, and dragged him away.

The single lesson stuck. The next time the pup saw a porcupine he looked at me apprehensively, backed away gingerly, and went about his business. During all the years I hunted him he never tangled with a porcupine.

The next pup proved a bit more stubborn, and showed enough interest in his second porcupine that I had to repeat the treatment. But after the second lesson he reached the reluctant conclusion that porcupines were associated with unpleasant interludes with the boss, and he hasn't touched one yet.

TAP'S TIPS

❴ If you hunt in areas where porcupines are common, it is a good idea to carry small needle-nose pliers in your hunting coat at all times. Then if the dog tangles with a quill pig, you can go to work on him immediately. You will probably find most of the quills in the dog's mouth and tongue. Grip each one firmly and tweak it out with a yank—it hurts less than drawing it out slowly. Lacking pliers, clamp the quills between two coins. Never cut the quills off.

❴ Many hunters shoot every porcupine they see, just on general principles. I don't, but the act can be easily justified by remembering that the damage done to our forests by a single porcupine during its lifetime has been estimated at up to $6,000.

❴ Here's an easy way to remove dog hairs from clothing and furniture: Wrap cellophane tape around your hand with the sticky side out and rub it lightly over the surface. Even the tiniest hairs adhere to it.

Lessons with a Check Cord

Training a bird dog pup for field work is largely a matter of keeping him under control until he learns what you expect of him. And the only way I know to control a rambunctious, hell-for-leather pup (the only kind worth training) is to hang a 50-foot check cord to his collar and keep a firm grip on the other end.

"Whoa!" (or "Stop!") is one of the first commands he should learn. Let the pup go, and when the check cord starts to straighten out, yell

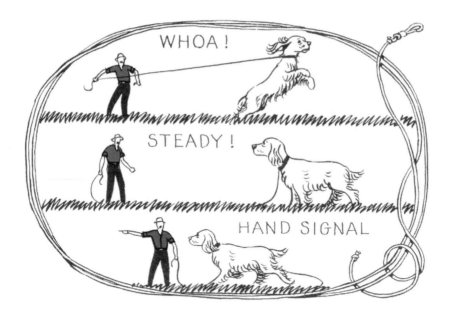

"Whoa!" and lean back on it, hard. A couple of doses of this usually convinces a pup that if he doesn't stop on your command, something's going to make him do it anyway.

"Steady!" comes next. When you've got the pup whoaing pretty well, hold him in position with the check cord and give him the "Steeeeaaaaady" order. When he settles down, walk around him and then walk away from him; if he moves, return him to position and hold him there. He'll soon catch on.

Next you'll want the pup to obey hand signals. Let him get out to the end of the cord and catch his attention by whistling. Wave your hand toward a new direction and start walking that way at an angle, holding the cord. He'll have no choice but to turn that way, too. After a while you'll have him quartering by himself, and turning at your hand signals from as far as he can see you.

All this pays off when he first comes in contact with game. With the check cord you can guide him to a spot where you've marked down a flushed bird, you can slow him down as he starts making game, whoa him when he gets close to his bird, and hold him steady on point while you walk up and flush it.

Later, you can teach him to hold steady at wing and shot, if that's what you want him to do.

A smart pup soon learns to respect his check cord, and hesitates to take liberties as long as it's snapped to his collar. In fact, you may want to keep the check cord on your dog for the first hour or two of each day's hunting, so you can hold him under control while he runs off his head of steam. And if he shows signs of forgetting his manners, don't hesitate to hang it back on him for a while.

TAP'S TIPS

¶ Plastic-covered clothesline makes a much more serviceable check cord than either cotton clothesline or sashcord. It doesn't fray, resists kinking and knotting, and rarely tangles in brush or stone walls. It slides over the ground like a greased snake and a 50-footer will last for a couple of seasons.

¶ When picking ticks off a dog be careful not to leave the head buried in the animal's skin, as it may cause severe irritation. Before trying to pick off the ticks, cover them with a gob of grease or petroleum jelly. Deprived of air, they let go so you can remove them whole by lifting them out with tweezers.

Dogs on Trial

It usually takes just the first touch of autumn color to start the average sportsman thinking about getting a gun dog. With the very first frost, in fact, he probably rushes in his order for the hound or bird dog he should have sent for months ago.

Naturally, he wants a dog that's fully trained and ready to find game as soon as he steps out of the crate. That accounts for the large numbers of gun dogs bought on trial on the very eve of every gunning season. It also accounts for one of the dog breeder's biggest headaches. He knows that no matter how careful he may be to sell nothing but finished gun dogs, exactly as advertised, a certain number of his deals will go sour.

Of course, there are always a few crusty customers who will be satisfied with nothing short of a field trial champion. Most hunters, however, will gladly settle for a broken dog of average ability. Yet misunderstandings still crop up between breeder and buyer. Most of them are due to the fact that dogs are not machine-made items of sporting equipment, but living creatures of flesh and blood.

A hunting rifle made in Connecticut will shoot accurately in Arizona, but a hound raised and trained in Arkansas might not be worth an empty shotgun shell in Michigan until he stops hankering for the swamps and woodlands of his home country. If he's not actively homesick, he's pretty sure to be confused and travel-worn for a few days after his arrival at his new home.

291

But the dog's on trial, and there's only a limited time in which to find out if he's any good. How can you tell, quickly enough to back out of the deal if you think you've got a dud?

All too often, you can't. But remember, reputable dog breeders are honest men. When you pay a fair price for a trained dog chances are you'll get one. If you've got the bargain bee in your bonnet, you'll probably get stung.

It's only fair to give your new dog plenty of time to get used to you and his new surroundings before you take him afield. Many good dogs won't hunt for strangers. The dog you thought was useless might have turned into a worldbeater after he got to know you.

Finally, add about 50 percent to whatever the dog shows in his first performances. If he does a fair job during his trial, you can usually count on him to improve as you become better acquainted with each other.

So don't be too hasty or critical when you buy a dog on trial. You may succeed only in building up business for the express company.

TAP'S TIPS

 If fleas make life miserable for your dog during the hot summer weather, sprinkle salt over his kennel bedding and into the hole he has probably dug for himself in a piece of shaded ground. The salt discourages fleas from collecting in such places, where

they can re-infest the dog. Dusting the dog with powder before turning him loose will repel fleas that might jump aboard him from other dogs, too.

¶ You can get a rough idea of a dog's age by examining his front teeth. If they are worn, the dog is probably on the downhill side of middle age. Not that there's anything wrong with middle age—but if you think you are buying a young dog, the condition of the teeth will tell you whether you are getting what you are paying for.

YOUNG   OLD

No Soap!

Some people claim they enjoy bathing their dogs, and it is even possible, I suppose, that some dogs enjoy being bathed. But I never got any fun out of wrestling with a wet dog, myself, and if any of my animals derived pleasure from it, they didn't show it.

The large and powerful English setter who presently occupies my kennel had a couple of baths shortly after he signed up with us nine years ago. These were such traumatic experiences for us both that I decided I'd rather have a happy, dirty dog than a clean dog burning with master-hatred, and I've never bathed him since.

Nine years is a long time to go without a bath. Yet people comment on Duke's glossy coat, and the only noticeable odor about him comes from the aromatic cedar shavings on which he sleeps.

Every dog authority I've ever read agrees that the best way to care

293

for a dog's coat is to brush it thoroughly and often. Most dogs that howl in anguish at being lathered and rinsed will express pure ecstasy all the while you brush them. So it's a much happier arrangement for both parties.

I start with a steel comb to weed out the solid matter and tease out the tangles in Duke's feathers and tail. Then I go over him from nose to tail tip with a stiff brush, the kind with the bristles set at an angle. There's no need to be gentle about it, either; the harder I brush, the more Duke seems to enjoy it. Then, when the brush no longer picks up loose hairs, I finish by slipping on a soft leather glove and "gloving" him all over while he wriggles with delight.

Fleas? Cedar bedding discourages them in the winter, and a weekly dusting with powder keeps them under control during the summer months. But soap and water—never again!

TAP'S TIPS

⟨ You may have read that the best way to clean a dog's eyes is to wipe them with the tip of his ear. Your vet will suggest a much better way: Flush out the weed seeds and dirt with a mild solution of boric acid, or any commercial eyewash, applied with a dropper. If the eyes have become inflamed, follow the washing with a small dab of ophthalmic ointment under each lid.

《 Summer is a tough time for hunting dogs, and many of them suffer more than their owners realize, both from the heat and the inactivity. Yours will be both healthier and happier if you make sure he has constant access to shade and fresh, cool water. Exercise him for at least a few minutes in the cool of the evening and keep him slightly underfed until it is time to start hunting again.

《 To teach a dog to walk at heel, hold him on a tight leash with his head beside your knee. When he tries to move ahead, twitch him back and say "Heel!" sharply. If he is slow to catch on, tap his nose with a folded newspaper or twirl the end of the leash in front of him so it strikes him whenever he tries to go forward.

The Pointing Frenchman

The most precocious bird dog I ever owned pointed a ruffed grouse staunchly on opening day of his first hunting season, only eight months after he was whelped. George, my hunting partner that day, seemed to regard it as a flagrantly unnatural act.

"Dang it," he said, "I thought you told me he was some kind of a furrin' span'l."

To anyone who had never seen a Brittany at work, the sight of a stub-tailed spaniel behaving like a pointer or setter would indeed seem strange. But the Brittany came by his pointing instinct honestly, as a result of crossbreeding between some of his early ancestors and French and Italian pointers and possibly Irish and English setters as well. However he got it, the Brittany of today points as naturally as any of the better known pointing breeds.

Even so, the spunky little Frenchman has not proved to be quite the perfect, all-round gun dog some of us once hoped he'd be. For one thing, he simply doesn't have the wheels to get out and find quail or Huns in big country. He handles pheasants well enough, but no better, in my experience, than any of the other pointing breeds.

It is in grouse and woodcock cover that the Brit displays his brightest talents. The typical Brittany hunts companionably close to the gun and is not prone to crowd his birds or overrun them, as is the unhappy habit of many pointers and setters I've known. In addition, the Brit is a natural-born retriever, and can dig grounded birds out of the thickest jungle of alder or grape.

It is said that the Brittany is a timid dog and for that reason difficult to train. It would be fairer to say that he is by nature a gentle dog. He does not respond well to harsh training methods, but he learns fast and requires very little retraining between seasons.

The most common complaint about the Brittany is his lack of a tail. An erect plume unquestionably adds stature to a dog on point. But dogs point with their noses, and the Brittany must have been sitting in Row A, Seat 1 when noses were issued to the dog family. So anyone looking for a dog that can find birds, point them, and bring in the dead and wounded should not let a little thing like an abbreviated tail prevent him from enjoying the services of a Brittany.

TAP'S TIPS

([Before taking a long-haired dog afield, trim the hair around the ear openings. Burrs and weed seeds will not stick to the clipped areas, and thus cannot work into the ear canal and cause irritation. When it becomes necessary to clean out a dog's ears, twirl cotton batting on the end of a toothpick or crochet needle, dip in baby oil, and swab out the easily-reached sections gently.

([Some bird hunters are worse shot-breakers than their dogs. After shooting, they run ahead to mark down the bird or retrieve it, and of course the dog feels free to take off too. If the hunter stands still after shooting and reloads before ordering the dog to fetch, the dog is more likely to hold steady to both wing and shot.

Belling a bird dog helps the hunter to keep track of him in heavy cover. Some say birds won't lie well to a ding-dong dog, but I am not one of them. In fact, I sometimes think birds lie better to an approaching dog when they can keep him located by the sound of his bell.

Beagles for Ringnecks

The best pheasant dog I've ever known, bar none, was old Molly, who used to live with my wife's brother. Molly was a beagle, country bred and self-trained, but I have never seen her equal for running down ringnecks and putting them up close to the gun. If I wanted a dog just for pheasant hunting I would try to find a beagle that looked like Molly, name her Molly the Second, and hope that she turned out to be just half the pheasant dog the first Molly was.

Pheasants are difficult birds for a pointing dog to handle. The cock, especially, is restless and fiddle-footed, prone to run instead of squat, sneaky in his habits, and fond of dense cover. But none of these things bothers a beagle. He just lowers his head, turns on the steam, and crowds the bird until there is no place left for it to go but up.

Hunting pheasants with a beagle can be fast sport at times, but it is the hunter who must be fast. Strictly a trail hound, the beagle doesn't "handle" on game, so the way to get a shot is to keep up with him while he trails and flushes the bird.

The beagle usually opens on a cold trail and you have little trouble keeping up with him as he slowly untangles it. As it warms up, the beagle yells louder, and you've got to step along a little livelier. When he lets go with a high-pitched squeal that tells of tail feathers practically between his jaws, you shed all remaining dignity and run like a halfback. When the bird rockets up, you're there, puffing and blowing, but close enough for a good shot.

It sounds rugged, but the beagle saves you footwork, too. You don't have to founder through heavy cover as you do when following a setter or pointer. You just turn your beagle loose and loaf along the swamp edges till he gets a bird going or reports no one home. When he does open up, you have little trouble getting to him, for thick cover cuts his speed down, and he must follow a twisting trail while you can go to him in a fairly straight line.

The beagle will flush plenty of birds for you, but you'll appreciate him most of all when you scratch down a wing-tipped cock that lands running. Here again, you'll get no fancy bird work, and few beagles

take kindly to retrieving. But the beagle will take out after the cripple, yelling like a banshee. When he stops yelling, you know he's made a "catch," and you can tuck the bird in your game pocket. That's what counts.

Nope, there's nothing about houn'-dogging pheasants that would appeal to an artist painting a sporting magazine cover. But I can't think of a more efficient way to get a ringneck into the air, back on the ground, and into the game bag.

TAP'S TIPS

❡ Never judge a new hound only on his performance with other dogs. You can evaluate his ability better if you let him run alone; then after you have satisfied yourself on that score, you can turn him loose with other hounds to see how he stacks up in competition. If you feel dubious about a new dog, give him every possible chance to show what he can do before shipping him back. With a little more time, he might prove to be the worldbeater you have always hoped you'd find.

❡ When a hound is trying to work out a check or a loss, refrain from encouraging him (although it seems the natural thing to do). His job is difficult enough without complicating it with commands and "atta-boys." If he succeeds in solving his problem he will do

it with his nose, and without any help from a cold-nosed human.

❮ Let your hound's collar out an extra notch or two when you turn him loose to hunt. Then if he should run a tree stub under it or get himself tangled in a wire fence, he has a good chance to wiggle out of it. This may cost you a collar or two, but it could save you a valuable dog. Some hunters even make a special "stretch collar" out of inner tube rubber or elastic garter material, just to hold the dog's identification tag while he's out hunting.

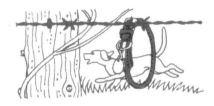

"Garaging" Your Dog

Does your dog live outdoors? Then are you positively sure, not just pretty sure, that he's warm and comfortable during cold winter nights? Sure, he's grown a thick overcoat and he's tough, and probably he hasn't complained about his present accommodations. But many a valuable hunting dog has grown old before his time, creaky and rheumatic in the joints, only because his winter quarters failed to protect him from drafts and dampness.

Perhaps the answer lies in your garage. If you can spare a couple of feet of space in one corner and still find room for your car (I managed; I traded for a compact), you can easily build a snug box kennel where your dog will sleep through the coldest winter nights without so much as a shiver.

Cut the entrance first, locating it between the corner stud and the next one to it. Draw a pencil outline on the inside of the garage wall. Bore 1-inch holes at the corners of the door-to-be and cut out the entrance with a keyhole saw, starting at the holes, of course.

Building the kennel box itself is easy. Frame it with 2 x 4's, nailed to the garage studs, and cover the frame with tongue-and-groove siding or economize with plain pine boards. The top of the kennel box should be hinged so you can lift it to get inside and change the bedding occasionally. You can insulate the kennel inexpensively by filling the spaces between floors and walls with sawdust, wood shavings, or sheets of newspaper.

Inside the kennel nail a wide board across the bottom just within the entrance. This partition protects the sleeping dog from drafts and prevents the bedding material from spilling out. The sleeping area itself should be as small as you dare make it, allowing the dog just room enough to curl up comfortably while keeping his body heat confined to his bedroom.

Cover the kennel entrance with a flap of canvas or burlap, cut to the exact size of the doorway and weighted at the bottom so that it falls back in place after the dog pushes through it. Outside the entrance build a simple platform comprising a couple of wide boards supported by posts. Your dog will use it as a sunning bench in winter, and when summer comes he'll burrow under it to escape the hot sun.

Now that you've gone this far, how about adding a wire-enclosed dog yard outside the garage? All you need is a half-dozen cedar posts, a roll of 4-foot chicken wire, and a little ingenuity. Space the posts to make the yard as large as possible, and sink them at least a couple of feet into the ground. Run wooden stringers between posts at top and

300

bottom, four feet apart, for added rigidity as well as something to staple the wire to. If your dog is a digger-outer, sink a second strip of narrow chicken wire into the ground, as deep as you think necessary. At a convenient point set in a gate where you can let the dog in and out and where you can enter yourself to do the needful with a shovel.

It makes a happier, healthier home for your dog. It certainly did for mine.

TAP'S TIPS

◖ If your dog lives in an outdoor kennel, you can winterize it by lining the inside with Homasote. This inexpensive building material cuts easily, provides excellent insulation, and resists dampness. The panels can be removed in the summer if you wish, but the insulation will probably keep the interior cooler, if the kennel is exposed to the hot sun.

◖ When carrying a dog in the trunk of the car, don't prop the lid open a crack thinking you are giving him fresh air. More likely he will get fumes sucked in from the exhaust. Close the lid and stop to let the dog out for a breather every half-hour or so. Better yet, train him to ride quietly inside the car with the rest of the hunting party, where he belongs.

◖ Some of us tend to neglect our hunting dogs during the fishing season. You can tell if your dog is packing on surplus fat by running your hand over his rib cage. If you can't feel his ribs, better cut down on his grub or give him more exercise, or preferably both.

301

Fetch!

Met up with a grouse hunter one day last fall, a real serious type feller. He told me he always takes his annual vacation in the fall, guns two solid weeks for grouse and woodcock, plus weekends and odd days he can steal from the office.

Dog? He had one. Said he was worried, too, for the old boy was getting along in years, and he didn't know where he could get another half as good. Breed? Mostly fox terrier!

He had tried the pointing breeds and spaniels, he told me, and they only loused up his particular style of hunting. He kept his terrier at heel and walked up the birds himself. The dog's one and only job was to bring in the dead and wounded, and he was a whiz at it.

Disagree with him if you like, but this grouse hunter firmly believed he owned the perfect grouse dog. Personally, I've owned pointers, setters, and Brittanies, and I never could say that about any of them, although I did come close—just once.

It's a thrill to see a high-headed pointing dog lock up on a grouse, but the cold truth of the matter is that it happens pretty darned seldom. I'm speaking of grouse now, mind you, although I might stretch that to include pheasants without too much of an argument. Woodcock and quail are birds of a different feather.

302

Maybe the terrier man had something. It's a rare dog that can learn to handle grouse perfectly, but almost any dog can learn to retrieve, and a nonslip retriever will surely put birds in your game pocket.

Start out with a well-bred bird dog, by all means. If he finds birds for you and points them, wonderful. If he doesn't, or can't, or simply won't, teach him two things: to walk at heel and to retrieve. When he brings in the first bird you thought you'd missed, you'll take a more charitable view of his other shortcomings, believe me.

TAP'S TIPS

⟨ Wear pant legs outside boots when hunting in the rain, so water can drain off them. Tucking pant bottoms inside the boots allows water to run in, soaking feet and keeping them soaked.

⟨ Although commercial worm remedies are perfectly safe for dogs when administered according to directions, it is always wise to have a vet check a fresh fecal sample first. He can identify the type of worm and prescribe the proper treatment for it—or perhaps tell you that a worming isn't needed, and thus spare the dog a violent purging.

⟨ Next time you get stuck in the mud on a remote woods road, try this trick. Jack up the wheel on the muddy side, block it up with flat stones, and remove the jack. Then jack up the dry wheel. Push the car off the blocks and jacks toward the driest side of the roadway. Repeat, if necessary, till the wheels are on firm ground.

MIXED BAG

The Noonday Break

THE OLDER I GET, the more I enjoy putting aside my rod or gun at noon to build a little Indian fire and fix something hot for my belly. Cold sandwiches eaten standing up don't seem to satisfy the way they used to ten—no, twenty—well, actually more than thirty years ago.

Coming to a complete stop for a noontime cook-out makes a pleasant break in any day's fishing or hunting. While the kettle's boiling you have a chance to sift through the highlights of the morning and savor the goodness of the day. You can even take time to notice that the sky is blue and the birds are singing. With a mug of steaming coffee under your nose, and perhaps a fresh-fried trout in your fingers, you can relish the thought that you still have a long half-day ahead of you. Then, with a full, warm belly, you can lie back and digest for a while. You'll feel ever so much better when you pick up your gun or your rod and start out again.

For the benefit of those who would like to try it, here's what I take stowed more or less neatly into a wicker market basket: coffee pot, small frying pan, wire grill from an old gas stove oven, heavy coffee

304

mugs, a couple of tin plates, knives, forks, and spoons. I also pack instant coffee, powdered cream, tea bags, sugar, salt and pepper, all in small screw-top jars. Then, last thing before leaving, I put in the perishables—bread, butter, cheese, frankfurters for toasting; whatever sounds good at the time. In case of rain, I carry a one-burner propane gas stove. The whole works stays in the car, so I plan to hunt or fish toward it as the sun warns me that lunch time is near.

But the deal won't work if you're in too much of a fever to stop fishing or hunting long enough to give it a try. The idea is to pick a spot where you can hunker down comfortably, forget the fish or the game for an hour, and just relax. You'll find that you enjoy the rest of the day all the more when you do.

TAP'S TIPS

⟨ You have probably heard that water will purify itself by running over seven stones. Don't believe it. Bacteria can travel the entire length of a stream and give anyone who drinks the water a serious case of dysentery or worse. Play it safe and drink only from bubbling springs, or boil the water. After boiling, pour the water from one container to another several times to restore aeration.

⟨ A vacuum bottle can provide a great variety of lunchtime beverages if you fill it with boiling water and take along some packets of instant coffee, cocoa, tea, bouillon, powdered soup, etc. Thus, every member of the party can enjoy the drink of his choice—all from the same bottle.

⟨ An empty plastic household bleach jug provides an ideal way to chill a luncheon cooler. Clean the jug, fill it with water (leaving some room for expansion), and keep it in the freezing compartment overnight. It will refrigerate the cooler and provide ice-cold drinking water as it melts.

Kindlin', Cracklin', and Coals

The fire you build is no better than the wood you put into it. You can't get chummy with a blaze that snaps hot coals at you, or cook over one that burns out the instant you turn your back on it and contributes nothing to the cook-out except a layer of black soot on the utensils. On the other hand, you can't prepare a quick lunch over a hardwood fire that requires an hour or more to burn down to a bed of red coals.

Every camper knows that birch bark offers the best kindling mate-

rial, because of the highly flammable oils it contains. Wet or dry, in fair weather or downpour, birch bark burns. However, the woods-wise camper doesn't depend entirely on birch bark. He takes his ax in hand and looks for a dry standing cedar. Split fine, dry cedar catches fire quickly. Next best common kindling is dry pine.

Most resinous woods snap and crackle as they burn, often throwing hot sparks on clothing, tent, and the dry duff of the forest floor. The worst offenders are hemlock, spruce, red cedar, balsam, tamarack (larch), chestnut. Use these in your campfire only if you must to get it going, then switch to one of the nonsnapping woods.

For a quick, hot fire, virtually smokeless and ideal for boiling the noontime kettle, look for dry poplar. This wood burns out quickly, leaving a fine white ash, so keep feeding it to the fire.

For long-lasting fires that burn down slowly to a bed of glowing coals, turn to the hardwoods. Hickory is the best of all, but hard to find in many areas. Other slow-burners are oak, apple, hard maple, white birch, beech, and ash. Yellow birch burns as well green as when dry; hickory and beech nearly as well. All hardwoods burn better in the fall, after the sap has left them. Wood growing on high ground is drier than wood cut near a swamp, stream, or lake. Pass up white elm, cherry, and willow. They are almost fireproof.

You can always recognize the experienced camper and woods-cook by the fuel he chooses for his fires—and also by the care with which he douses every last spark and coal after he has finished cooking over them.

306

TAP'S TIPS

《 Pots and pans used for open-fire cooking soon become black with soot. To prevent this, carry a few discarded aluminum foil dishes that heat-and-serve frozen foods come in, and put the cooking utensils on them. The foil transmits heat and collects most of the soot.

《 There are several ways to waterproof matches for rainy-day use. Dip them in fingernail polish, melted paraffin, or spar varnish. If you forgot to dip them, rubbing the wet match through your hair will dry it if it isn't hopelessly watersoaked.

《 When you have trouble lighting a match in the wind, try lighting two. Hold them parallel, about an eighth of an inch apart. When one flares the other will also ignite, and each will help to keep the other burning despite the wind.

Pull up a Chair

Wild meat being what it is, a game dinner should rightfully be considered a special treat, reserved only for those who appreciate the finer things in life. It should be preceded by much careful planning, accompanied by many choice fixin's, and followed by a general letting out of belts. Just "cooking" a couple of pheasants doesn't do justice either to the birds or your guests.

307

The way to start, I've found, is to hoard game in the freezer till you've saved enough to make a real banquet of it, and then to invite some close friends who enjoy adventurous eating.

Some wives can cook game, and some never really get the hang of it. If your life partner wrinkles her nose at the "gamy smell," chase her out of the kitchen and take over the job yourself.

Make sure you can dress the table with plenty of extras, such as wild grape jelly, pickles and olives, all clustered around a big wooden bowl of tossed salad, made with water cress if you can get it.

And here's a tip. Wild rice is just scarce enough to be a novelty to most people, and goes perfectly with every kind of game. So do fiddle-head ferns and wild mushrooms. And a flagon of red wine. When in doubt, make it Burgundy, not too sweet.

If you've shot well and hoarded your game, maybe you can start off with woodcock or quail, lightly broiled and dressed with a garland of crisp bacon. Next, bring on the barbecued breast of grouse or pheasant, to be sliced thin and splashed with just a smidgin of the basting sauce. That sets the stage for the main event, the roasted ducks or goose, or the venison haunch, whether deer, elk, or antelope.

If at this point you observe one of the ladies fidgeting with her girdle, you can consider your dinner a success.

Anyway, that's the basic formula. By stockpiling game in the freezer till you've got the proper amount and variety, you can put on a feed that will making dining room history.

TAP'S TIPS

⟨ Fish or game will not spoil in the home freezer if it has been properly quick-frozen, but in time it will lose some of its flavor. To enjoy it at its best, plan on serving it up within six or eight months of the time you tucked it away.

⟨ Any old frying pan won't do for the experienced camp cook. Thin-bottomed pans heat up fast, but are notorious food scorchers. Thick pans make their weight felt in the pack basket, but they spread the heat and cook evenly. The new plastic-coated (Teflon) pans are a blessing, as they require no cooking grease and are easy to wash.

⟨ To keep fish from falling apart in the skillet, scale them but leave the skin on, then split or fillet them. Drop each piece flesh side down into the hot fat. When golden brown, turn gently with a spatula and cook till the skin peels off easily, leaving a solid chunk of succulent meat.

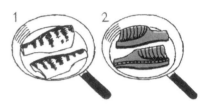

Tricks with Aluminum Foil

Getting ready to go fishing is no longer a simple matter of picking up my rod, reel, and box of lures and kissing my wife goodby. I wouldn't think of starting off on a day's fishing now without my collection of accessories—plastic bag, in case I want to bring home a brace of trout for my daughter's breakfast; a tube of patching cement, a roll of mending tape, sunglasses, headache pills, a bottle of stuff to make flies float, a bottle of stuff to make leaders sink, line dressing, flashlight, pocket bird book and, of course, a complete arsenal of fishing gear.

And now I have been told that I really ought to add just one more item to my packet of essentials, some aluminum foil.

This came up during a discussion recently with Joe Bates, Jr. who, for business reasons, has made a rather profound study of the multitude of uses to which fishermen, hunters, and campers can put this common kitchen commodity. I told Joe that I can hardly straighten my knees under the load of stuff I take fishing now, but promised him I would try to find room for some aluminum foil if he could convince me I needed it. Shortly thereafter Joe sent me a list of things I could do with foil, and this is it:

Use a crumpled wad of foil to burnish corroded fishing lures, automobile chrome, boat brightwork.

When cooking over an open fire, lay a doubled sheet of foil over the grill for frying hamburgs, steaks, fish. In camp, cover stove burners with foil and fry food on it, after turning up the edges to prevent the

grease from running off. Saves carrying cooking utensils, also washing them.

Attach strips of foil to tree branches to "spot" a trail through woods, or to mark a narrow passage between lakes or among islands. The foil is easy to spot with a flashlight when returning after dark.

To make a clean, smooth breadboard, spread foil over a plank. Roll out biscuit dough with a bottle.

Cover the bait bucket with foil. It will reflect the sun's heat and keep the minnows cool and lively. Be sure to punch holes in the foil for ventilation.

To make a beacon that will guide you back to a boat landing after dark, line a box with foil and put a low-lit lantern in it. Even simpler, wrap a band of foil around a tree near shore; it will reflect a flashlight beam, even catch light from the moon.

When baking biscuits over an open fire, form an arch of aluminum foil over the pan. The reflected heat will brown the top of the biscuits evenly.

If a sudden shower catches you without rain gear, spread a sheet of foil over your shoulders, under your shirt or jacket. Much of the rain will run off instead of soaking in.

To start a fire quickly on rain-soaked ground, build it on a sheet of foil. Then make a foil reflector to dry wet clothes in front of the fire.

If you need a cup or dipper, simply mold aluminum foil around your fist—or better still, around a tin can. To make a still larger pan, form it over a small, smooth-cut tree stump.

310

When rain threatens, or when wading in treacherous currents, foil-wrap items you want to keep dry—your watch or billfold, for example. Fold and re-fold the edges of the foil to make the wrapping watertight.

Joe said he could suggest a great many other uses for aluminum foil if I would like to hear them, but I told him it wouldn't be necessary. However, I did point out that a roll of foil was a bit too bulky to fit in a fishing jacket pocket. He said I could pack quite a lot of it into a flat package no bigger, hardly, than a folded handkerchief. I agreed that sounded like a sensible idea and promised to take some with me the next time I went fishing.

TAP'S TIPS

⟨ To make sure of having a quick fire when you need it most, such as to get yourself dried out while hunting or fishing in the rain, tuck the stub of a candle in your tackle box or jacket pocket. With the help of the candle you can always coax a blaze from the soggy kindling.

⟨ "There's nothing like steak broiled over an open fire," they say, smacking their lips. They're wrong. Meat broiled *against* a fire is much better; fish too. The blood and juices dribble down over the browning surface, adding moisture and flavor to the fillet or steak. But wait until the fire has burned down to a bed of glowing hardwood coals before leaning the meat or fish against it.

⟨ Even a watched pot boils over occasionally. To prevent kettles from bubbling into the cooking fire, cut a couple of green hardwood sticks and lay them across the top of the pots or pans. The boiling water quiets down when it hits them.

How to Waterproof a Tent

Every camper knows the joy of drifting off to sleep while rain beats a soothing tattoo against taut canvas overhead. But neither the joy nor the sleep lasts long if the rain comes through as fine spray or if cold droplets bounce off the camper's forehead.

Tents can be waterproofed by two methods. One fills the fabric, the other renders the material water repellent without plugging the weave.

There are many commercial preparations which are completely satisfactory for either job, but for the benefit of those who enjoy doing such things themselves, here are two oldtime methods that give excellent results.

To fill the fabric, shave paraffin into turpentine in the proportion of 1 pound of paraffin to 1 gallon of turpentine. Place the container in a tub of hot water and stir until the paraffin melts. Set up the tent with canvas taut and paint the hot solution into it, using a fairly stiff brush. Allow the tent to dry thoroughly.

To make the fabric water repellent, stir ½ pound of powdered alum in 2 quarts of soft boiling water—rain water preferably. When the alum is completely dissolved, add 2 gallons of cold rain water to the solution. In a separate container dissolve ½ pound sugar of lead in 3 quarts of soft boiling water, then add 3 gallons of cold rain water. Soak the fabric in the alum solution for at least six hours. Wring or shake out the surplus fluid, then soak in the sugar of lead solution another six hours. Wring out and hang smoothly to dry. This waterproofs the fabric without clogging the weave, leaving the tent flexible, light, and reasonably fire resistant. Fine-weave cotton clothing can also be made water repellent by the same process.

TAP'S TIPS

⟨ For comfortable camping, pitch your tent facing the prevailing wind, normally the dry quarter, so rain won't beat in on you at night; away from overhanging

trees so the sun can dry it quickly after a shower; and on a breezy knoll, for drainage and freedom from biting insects.

(To keep tent ropes tight but not too tight, tie heavy rubber bands cut from a discarded inner tube to each rope. Set the stakes out far enough so you have to stretch the bands. The rubber keeps even tension on the ropes in any weather.

(Small rips and burn-holes in a tent can be repaired permanently with a fabric-wader patching kit. For a temporary repair, use waterproof adhesive tape.

Fishermen *vs.* Water Skiers

There is a rocky bar in Winnisquam Lake, New Hampshire, where smallmouth bass come to feed on quiet summer evenings. My son and I have paddled our canoe out to this bar many times after the breeze has died, and sometimes we have lifted some bass off the rocks with fly rod and bug. As often, perhaps more often than not, we have sat clutching the gunwales of our rocking canoe while large speedboats dragged water skiers around us in roaring circles.

Of course, we could have waited till darkness drove the skiers ashore before venturing onto the bar, and as a matter of fact, that is what we

finally did. Perhaps that will be the only recourse left to fishermen if speedboating and water skiing continue to flourish. However, it seems to me that if fishermen must become strictly nocturnal, like raccoons or bats, the choice should be made freely, and not forced upon them.

Water skiers need about thirty times as much lake surface as fishermen do, according to figures I've read, yet are outnumbered by fishermen at a ratio of approximately nine to one. That makes it a lopsided deal, if nine-tenths of the people are free to use only one-thirtieth of the available water.

It has been suggested that skiers and fishermen could fly flags to show what they are doing, and thus keep out of each other's way. The idea may have some merit, but it seems to me that a fisherman looks pretty much like a person fishing whether or not he waves a flag with a sunfish painted on it, and certainly the fisherman could identify someone careening over his pet fishing grounds on a pair of slats as a water skier, flag or no.

Another solution might be to divide the water so that fishermen could have it on odd days of the month, or afternoons. This suggestion also has a little merit. But to be perfectly fair about it, the division should be made on the nine-to-one ratio, giving fishermen rights to the water nine-tenths of the time. I doubt that many skiers would go for a deal like that.

In California some of the larger lakes have been zoned, with cer-

314

tain areas closed to fast outboarding, over 5 mph, so fishermen, duck hunters, and swimmers can pursue their simple pleasures in peace. This is perhaps the most practical solution to the problem. However, there is an even simpler one. If fast boats would just steer clear of fishermen —keep, say, at least one hundred yards away—there wouldn't be any problem at all. But perhaps that is *too* simple.

TAP'S TIPS

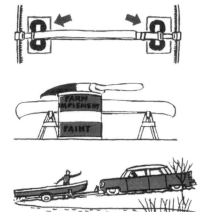

(To prevent boat-rack suction cups from leaving marks on the roof of the car, cover contact spots with Saran Wrap. This thin wrapping material clings to the surface, protects the paint, and peels off easily when the rack is removed.

(Farm-implement enamel is excellent for repainting canvas canoes and car-top boats. It comes in many popular colors, wears well, and costs much less than canoe enamel. A quart will cover an 18-foot canoe.

(Putting trailer hitches on both the front and rear bumpers of the car makes it much easier to maneuver a boat into and out of the water. The front hitch lets you see what you are doing in cramped quarters and keeps your rear wheels on dry land where they can get solid traction.

Trim Ship

George was a State of Maine guide who knew his business thoroughly, but I used to get terribly impatient with him when he loaded the big canoe for a fishing trip down-lake. Being at the time young and bushy-tailed, I wanted to hop in and start digging with the bow paddle. George, however, insisted on shifting the heavier duffel around till the old Sprague double-ender lay just so on the water.

Later, when I graduated to the stern paddle and assumed the responsibilities that went with it, which included coping with the quick squalls that often blew up on the big lakes, I began to understand why George was so fussy about how the canoe load balanced. For one thing, George had never learned to swim. For another, he was bone-lazy, and naturally wanted the canoe to slide along with an absolute minimum of effort on his part.

They tell us that there are more than forty million people riding around in boats today. I shudder to think of the tons of gasoline and the barrels of sweat they're wasting on boats that move sluggishly or steer hard due to improper loading.

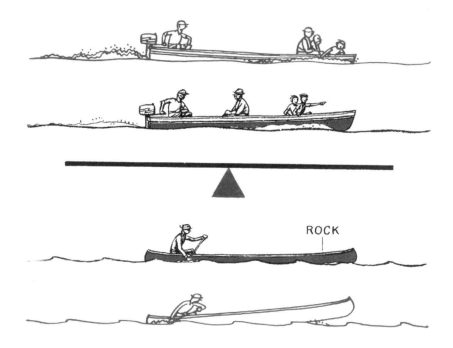

ROCK

You've seen them, I'm sure—outboard boats plowing along with their noses buried and motors roaring; canoes half out of water at the bow, yawing back and forth in the wind; rowboats so side-heavy the oarsman can't reach the water on the high side.

It takes only a few moments for a solo boatman to find a rock to hold the bow down out of the wind, and it's just as easy to distribute passengers and gear evenly as it is to let them ride wherever they happen to land. The prop, paddle, or oars will produce more speed with less energy, and all hands will enjoy a faster, safer trip.

TAP'S TIPS

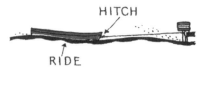

HITCH

RIDE

(A towed boat slides over the water much easier if the towline is attached to the middle of the bow instead of to the top. This prevents the bow from nosing down and plowing. Also, adjust the line so the boat rides on the forward slope of the second wave. It's surprising what a difference it makes.

(A strong, inexpensive boat anchor can be made by filling a 5-quart oil can with cement. Before the cement hardens, sink a large eyebolt into it to receive the anchor rope. It's just as easy to make a couple, so the boat can be anchored from both bow and stern.

(To prevent lake charts and topographical maps

316

from becoming so tattered that you can't read them, rubber-cement them to cotton sheeting or muslin. If the map is to be folded, first cut it into pocket-sized squares and mount each section with a quarter-inch of folding space all around. Then waterproof the surface with thinned clear varnish.

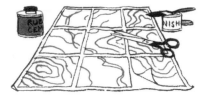

Feel Like an Argument?

After all the uncounted millions of man-hours that have been spent fishing and hunting, plus all the research the wildlife scientists have done, you'd think it would be impossible to ask a question about fish or game that didn't have a simple Yes or No answer, wouldn't you?

For example, fishermen still write to fishing editors to ask if fish are colorblind. The answer is No. Research has proven conclusively that fish can distinguish colors, although perhaps not exactly as we do. End of argument.

But some questions can't be answered as simply or easily as that. If you want to start something, some time, just pick any of the following —and jump back when you ask it.

How does a hound know which way to follow a trail on bare ground?

As far as I know, this one has never been answered satisfactorily, and probably it never will be. The obvious answer is that the hound merely follows the strengthening scent. However, suppose the trail is four hours old, a perfectly reasonable supposition, and that each individual track, or patch of scent, was laid down at leisurely half-second intervals. In that case, the hound must detect the difference in scent strength between a track made 14,400 seconds ago, and one made 14,400½ seconds ago. You think he can do it? Don't forget that the hound may not follow an old trail as fast as the fox or bobcat made it, so the scent may be actually weakening all the while the dog is working on it. You could argue that one all night.

Or try this one: Which lure requires the most skill to fish properly —a wet fly, dry fly, streamer, or nymph?

If you lean on the word *properly*, most experienced trouters would probably vote for the nymph, followed by the wet fly, streamer, and dry fly in about that order. Some dry-fly addicts may howl, but most of them will confess that the floater isn't really so difficult to fish. It's just more interesting . . . to a dry-fly fisherman, anyway.

And if that one doesn't stir up an argument, this should: Which is the best all-round trout—the brook, brown, or rainbow?

The answer, if there is one, depends of course on what criteria you use to rate the fish. Most trout fishermen, although perhaps only a thin

317

WHICH WAY ?

STREAMER

DRY

MOST SKILL TO FISH ?

WET

NYMPH

BROWN   BROOK   RAINBOW

BEST ALL-AROUND TROUT ?

majority, will say the brookie is the handsomest and most flavorsome, the brown the smartest, the rainbow the scrappiest. However, voting along straight party lines would probably go more like this: Dry-fly fishermen, the brown by a landslide; bait and sunken-fly fishermen, the brook trout; spin fishermen, the rainbow.

While the trout fishermen are fighting over that one, let's see if we can stir up the deer hunters. Who gets the deer, the man who wounds it or the man who finishes it off?

This argument is usually settled in favor of the man who actually nails the deer for keeps. But circumstances alter cases. Putting a quick shot into a deer someone has just knocked down certainly should not establish unchallenged ownership thereof. On the other hand, suppose you shoot a crippled deer and the man who crippled it comes along while you're dressing it out, and claims it? Technically, it's your deer, but if he were clearly following a wet blood trail, you would probably abandon your claim. *But,* again, if the deer were very lightly hit—just belly-creased, say—wouldn't you feel justified in leaving your tag on it? Besides, how do you know this is the deer he shot at?

And while we're on the subject of deer, can you *always* tell a buck's track from a doe's?

Some hunters claim they can, but most experienced backwoods guides will admit they can't—not always. If the tracks are broad, blunted and deep, toe out and show drag marks, you can bet it's a

318

buck and perhaps you will collect your money. But if it's a medium-sized track, better keep your wallet buttoned.

It seems presumptuous for the average sportsman to question an authority like the late Dr. James A. Henshall, who wrote the classic *Book of the Black Bass*. It was Dr. Henshall, you will remember, who said of the smallmouth bass: "I consider him, inch for inch and pound for pound, the gamest fish that swims."

Many fishermen will say "Amen" to that. But a few who have tangled with landlocked salmon and grilse may feel inclined to debate the issue. Me, for one. And a 2-pound brook trout hooked with light fly-fishing tackle can make you forget your worldly problems for a while, too. I also wonder if Dr. Henshall had done much bonefishing when he wrote that book.

Do you really believe that a crippled duck will dive, clamp its bill on a root, and hang on till it drowns?

Or that a treed raccoon will cover its eyes with its paws when a hunter tries to shine them with a flashlight?

That pickerel and pike fishing is poor in August because these fish suffer from sore teeth and jaws at that time of year?

That crippled woodcock always lie where they fall without trying to crawl away and hide?

That red squirrels castrate gray squirrels?

That a bullet drops faster over water than over land?

That a wise old buck will deliberately run with its head low to conceal its antlers?

That ruffed grouse become drunk from eating fermented fruit?

True or false? Fact or fancy? It doesn't matter, really, because most of us would rather not know. It's better to have these things to argue about when the hunting boots are off and the fire is snapping in the fireplace.

TAP'S TIPS

⟨ You can't tell a male from a female woodcock by their plumage, but the size of the bird and the length of its bill will provide a reliable clue. Full-grown hens average 6 ounces or more, cocks almost always less than 6. The hen's bill measures 2 11/16 inches or more; the cock's less than that.

⟨ Can porcupines throw their quills? No—but sometimes they do. When threatened by an enemy, they lash their tails angrily and occasionally a loose quill flies off and scores a hit.

❨ Instead of blazing a trail through the woods with an ax, mark the trees with a squirt of yellow or orange paint from a spray can. The spot of paint shows up better in dim light and doesn't damage the trees.

❨ Washing clothes in camp is easy if you use a "plumber's helper." Just dump the dirty duds in a pail of soapy water and agitate them with the rubber suction cup.

Weather Rhymes and Fishing Times

Weather jingles make more sense than most people think. Taking into account such factors as the sun, moon, wind, clouds, fog, and even rainbows, they can forecast changing weather with sometimes uncanny accuracy.

For example, as everyone knows, *Red in the morning, Sailors take warning; Red at night, Sailors delight.* This may be the oldest of all weather rhymes (a version of it appears in the Bible) yet any present-day meteorologist will agree that it is almost 100 per cent infallible.

Another old rhyme, still quoted in Spenserian English, predicts weather by wind direction: *When smoke goes West, gude weather is past; When smoke goes East, gude weather is neist.* However, fishermen are more familiar with this version: *Wind in the West, fishing is best; Wind in the East, fishing is least.*

If the wind doesn't blow at all, there is a rhyme to cover that situation too. *A stormy day will betide Sound traveling far and wide.* As

RED IN THE MORNING...

WHEN SMOKE GOES WEST...

...SOUND TRAVELING FAR & WIDE

RAINBOW AT NIGHT...

MORNING FOG WILL BURN ERE NOON...

RAIN BEFORE SEVEN...

you may have noticed, noises carry with startling clarity on still days when a low-pressure system settles in, and you can plan on a rainy day to follow.

The next time you see a rainbow, note its location and the time of day, then recite this easily-remembered jingle: *Rainbow in morning, Shepherds take warning; Rainbow at night, Shepherds delight. Rainbow to windward, Foul fall the day; Rainbow to leeward, Damp runs away.*

The fall of dew provides still another reliable weather sign. This simple couplet tells you how to interpret it: *When the dew is on the grass, Rain will never come to pass. When grass is dry at morning light, Look for rain before the night.*

But never let a foggy morning keep you from a fishing date. *Morning fog will burn 'fore noon; Evening fog will not burn soon.*

Even a day that starts fair can turn stormy. The clouds may tell you if you remember this bit of seagoing verse: *Mackerel scales and mares' tails Make lofty ships carry low sails.* "Mackerel scales" are cirrocumulus clouds in a mottled pattern, and "mares' tails" are wispy, upswept clouds at high altitude. They promise wind and rain within two days.

On the other hand, some weather rhymes aren't to be trusted. I have fished in many a downpour because I once believed rain before seven meant it would clear by eleven. It is true, though, that a fair day usually follows a brief morning shower.

There are dozens of weather signs that don't rhyme but are worth remembering when planning a day's fishing. You should prepare for rain if an old wound aches or all the cows in a herd are lying down in the morning, if swallows fly low and spiders stay in their webs. Expect the worst when you see a halo around the moon or if noises sound hollow and hardwood leaves turn up their undersides. If you're still not sure, look in your fireplace. As any oldtimer will tell you, soot falling from the chimney means rain is coming and you can bet on it.

TAP'S TIPS

❨ Most fishermen string up a fly rod by pushing the fine leader tip through the guides. Here's a better way to do it: Double the fly line above the line-to-leader connection and push the doubled line through. It's much easier on the eyes, reduces the chance of skipping a guide, and the line won't slither back through the guides if you lose hold of it.

❨ October and June are generally considered the two best months of the year for bass fishing. One reason for this is that bass feed at or near the surface during these months. Another is that they feed in the daytime, so it isn't necessary to get up at the crack of dawn or stay out till midnight to enjoy good fishing.

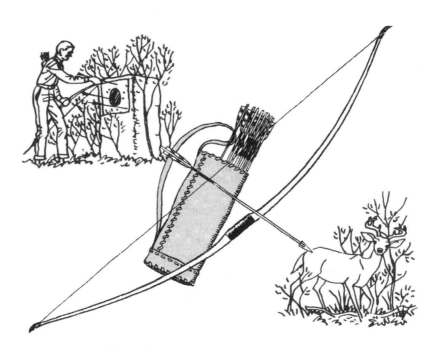

Hunting Robin Hood's Way

Giving the bow-and-arrow boys first crack at the deer herd is a sensible idea that many states have adopted. It has been a wonderful thing for the archery tackle manufacturers, too. Thousands of gun hunters have bought a bow and some arrows, thinking it would be mere child's play to stick a broadhead into a deer before it had been scared silly by the roar of musketry.

According to figures released each fall after the special archery seasons, collecting a deer with bow and arrow isn't quite as easy as it looks. Plenty of archers get shots, many at intimate range (a friend of mine once missed a *standing* buck at 25 feet!), but arrow and deer seldom arrive at the same place at precisely the same time.

The reason for this low ratio of bow-killed deer to bowhunters is not the inaccuracy or inefficiency of the bow. The glass-powered, scientifically designed hunting bow of today is a powerful and deadly weapon capable of amazing accuracy with properly matched arrows. Within its range it can kill a deer as surely and as quickly as a rifle bullet. It inflicts a free-bleeding wound that can be easily followed. And it is a silent weapon, so that one man's shot does not spoil his neighbor's chances.

So the failure of the bow to kill more deer must be blamed on the archer. Most of the deer-hunters-turned-archers simply never bother to learn how to aim and shoot an arrow. Archery looks too much like kid stuff. Shucks, all you've got to do is draw back and let 'er fly.

Like shotgun and rifle shooting, bow shooting requires practice. The best place to get it is at an archery club's field course. There are hundreds of them scattered around the country, one of them probably a couple of miles from where you're sitting now. The man at the archery shop will tell you where it is. You'll find twenty-eight hay-bale targets laid out in a meandering course through the woods, offering shots from as close as ten yards to as far away as eighty. Sporty shooting! And the same kind of shots you'd get at deer.

When gearing up for deer hunting with a bow, most beginners assume that they must have a heavy, and hence powerful, bow, capable of flat trajectory over long range, with enough force to drive a broadhead arrow deep into a deer's interior. The power of a bow is rated by the number of pounds of pull required to draw it back to the point of a 28-inch arrow.

Howard Hill, who won 196 field archery tournaments and seven consecutive national flight championships, once killed an African elephant with a hunting bow that was said to pull over 100 pounds. Elephants being the size they are, the impressive thing about this is not so much Mr. Hill's markmanship as the fact that he could shoot an arrow out of such a tremendously powerful weapon.

While it is true that heavy bows shoot flatter and harder than light bows, most experienced bowhunters and hay-bale archers nevertheless prefer bows that pull between 40 and 60 pounds and averaging somewhat under, rather than over, 50 pounds.

Modern bows of that weight, with their glass-powered, recurved limbs, develop more than enough zing to drive a broadhead completely through a deer, yet are light enough to permit the archer to shoot a field course of 112 arrows without suffering discomfort or muscular fatigue.

As most archery dealers will agree, beginners tend to overestimate their ability to pull a bow. They don't realize that bending a bow of, say, 70 pounds is quite different from lifting a 70-pound weight.

Even Howard Hill, who once pulled to full draw a bow of 175 pounds, said to be the heaviest ever shot, advises the beginner to choose a bow "light enough to be pulled easily." For you, that may be a 50-pound bow. For me, a middle-aged man of sedentary habit, it's nearer 40.

Anyone who intends to use his bow for hunting will find that his state's game laws usually specify the minimum bow weight permitted for deer hunting. In most states the minimum is around 40 pounds, give or take a pound or two. So if you're one of the thousands who will take up the challenging sport of archery this year, and wonder how much bow to start with, that may be the best weight for you. Later you can move up to a more powerful bow when you develop the muscles and skill to handle it.

TAP'S TIPS

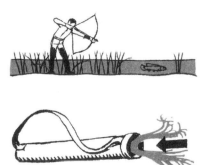

⟨ Spring is the prime season for the bowfisherman. Carp, suckers, and other rough fish come into the shallows and tributaries to spawn or bask in the warm water, making them vulnerable to a barbed arrow. Best times to "fish" are mornings and evenings when the water is calm.

⟨ Here's a simple way to prevent arrows from rattling in the quiver and possibly spooking a deer: Bend a clump of dry straw or grass into a U shape and stuff it loosely into the top of the quiver. It holds the arrows in place, comes out easily if the barb of a broadhead catches in it.

Fun with Frogs

Frogging may not be the most exciting sport in the world, but it isn't dull either if you go at it right. Probably the most challenging way to do it is to paddle slowly along the shore of a pond at night, shining the frogs' eyes with a flashlight and trying for head shots with a .22. The ammunition companies must approve of this method very highly, because you'll miss a lot of frogs. But you'll get some, too. Be sure that there's a steep bank beyond to smother your ricochets; in flat country gather your frogs some other way, for safety's sake.

The easiest and surest way to collect a mess of frogs is to spear or gig them under a light. If you approach slowly and quietly they usually hold still until you get close enough to jab them with a spear. You can make your own frog gig if you like, simply by straightening out three

324

or four long-shank pickerel hooks and screwing them firmly to the end of a pole, flattened at the end so you can spread the prongs about an inch apart.

If you're made of sterner stuff than I am you can catch frogs on hook and line, for they'll grab a bright fly or a bit of red cloth on a hook. But their struggles are not pleasant to watch, and frogs caught that way never tasted quite right to me.

For real sport, try shooting them with bow and arrow—but only if you're more interested in sport than in frogs' legs, because it takes expert archery to nail one out of five at average ranges.

My son, who was then in his teens, introduced me to frog hunting with a bow and blunt-headed arrow. He had been making life a thing of great uncertainty for the frogs in a weedy pond a short distance from our home and, being a tolerant and indulgent parent, I let him stay out frog hunting later than his mother thought reasonable. Then one evening I took my bow and joined him to see what was keeping him out so late—and we didn't come home until midnight. Next, a few members of our local archery club drifted over to find out if frogs were really as hard to hit with an arrow as we claimed, and lingered long enough to discover that indeed they were.

The bow, shot instinctively the way an upland hunter shoots at a flying bird with a shotgun, doesn't allow you much margin of error on a target as small as a frog. Mostly, you have only two bulging eyes and the dim outline of the critter's head to aim at, usually in the beam of

a flashlight. Even our club champion missed more frogs than he hit. We lost arrows, and broke arrows, and got muddied to the ears. But we had fun, stalking along the weedy margin of the pond like a band of prowling Pawnees, and we even managed to collect enough frogs' legs for a couple of meals.

So if you don't enjoy frogging with rifle, gig or hook, try hunting the hard way, with bow and arrow. You'll see what I mean.

TAP'S TIPS

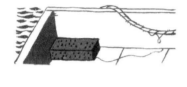

(A bailing can is fine for big leaks, but a sponge is better for little ones, and for soaking up water that dribbles into the boat from anchor rope, oars, and minnow bucket. Gets into the corners and other hard-to-get-at places where a can won't fit, too.

(To bait a turtle trap, punch a few nail holes in a can of sardines. The escaping oil entices turtles to the trap, and the first one there can't eat up the bait.

(Many poisonous snakes, such as copperheads, are nocturnal, and the others don't like to have their sleep disturbed. So it is wise to carry a flashlight when prowling around after dark in snake country.

(Raccoons can be attracted to traps set in shallow water by covering the pans with aluminum foil, shiny side up. Even at night the foil reflects enough light to arouse the coon's curiosity.

Thrills without Kills

You can enjoy all the pleasure fishing can possibly offer by hooking, playing and landing a fish, and then returning him unharmed to the water. But when a pheasant thunders up and you crumple him with a fast, swinging shot, there's no way to put him back so you can shoot him again another day.

Since we can't gun down our game and have it, too, how can we ease the pressure on the supply, which is dwindling so fast in so many areas? The obvious answer is to stop shooting before we fill our legal limit, but bag limits are already pretty realistic these days.

Happily, there are ways to limit the game bag without spoiling the fun. Certainly those who hunt with bow and arrow have found one satisfying way to do it. Even the most avid archer will admit that the bow is less deadly than the gun. You can bowhunt all day with the

determination of a starving Sioux and enjoy every minute of it without seriously depleting the local game supply. "Hunting the hard way" offers such a challenge to a hunter's skill both as a marksman and a woodsman that the weight of the game bag becomes a minor matter.

Hunting with a camera is another way to stretch out the game supply. Once the shutter bug bites, you will brag more about a perfect camera shot than you ever did about your hits with rifle or shotgun. You can shoot pictures all day with never a thought of bag limits, open season or protected species. Better still, a good picture remains a trophy forever, while gun-shot game is all too soon eaten and forgotten.

Still another way to put more emphasis on hunting and less on killing is to hunt with a dog of your own. Well-trained gun dogs save tons of ducks and upland game that would otherwise be lost as cripples and never counted in the annual game bag. Training a promising pup is fun to begin with, hunting with him is still more fun, and when game is scarce or you've shot all you really need, you can keep on hunting just for the pleasure of seeing your bird dog point or hearing your hound bawl on a hot trail.

So if you're looking for thrills rather than kills, lay aside the shotgun or rifle once in a while and bend a bow, click a camera, or fuss with a pup. Each offers a practical way to carry out a personal conservation program—and each will give you just as much sport, if not more.

Choose Your Partner

In the course of a lifetime, fate seems to deal most of us our full share of earthly blessings. We get the One Good Dog, we hook the One Big Fish, and if we're properly deserving, we may even find the One Perfect Partner. That, my friends, is the greatest blessing of them all.

With a good partner, it doesn't seem to matter quite so much if the fish don't bite or if the ducks don't fly. His companionship can contribute more to the pleasure of your day afield than the fish you put in your creel or the game you bag.

The partnership must work both ways, of course. Its bonds must be cemented firmly by both parties, because it will be subject to some severe stresses and strains at times. Your sidekick must be able to laugh off bad weather and tough breaks—and you must do the same. He must have the grace to put up with your faults, and you will have to get used to his. Often it's not easy, but it's worth the effort, for it leads to a relationship much deeper and more enduring than mere friendship.

Also, there's a practical side to this matter of forming a workable fishing and hunting partnership. By sharing costs, two men can own equipment that perhaps neither could afford alone: a fishing boat, outboard motor, hunting camp, a couple of good gun dogs. They can go farther afield, save on lodging and food bills. By traveling together they tie up only one car, leaving the other for their wives. Oh, there are lots of practical advantages.

328

Two men who have fished and hunted together for a while soon develop a pattern of teamwork that often pays extra dividends. By working out the best way to hunt a cover together they can drive game to one another. While fishing, the man with the oars can take as much pride in his boat handling as he does in the fish he helps his partner to catch. By operating as a team they can solve many technical fishing problems that might stump either of them alone.

But best of all is the enjoyment of sharing your good times with someone who can relish them as much as you do, and who understands how you feel about such things.

If you have found your partner, you will know what I mean.

329

INDEX

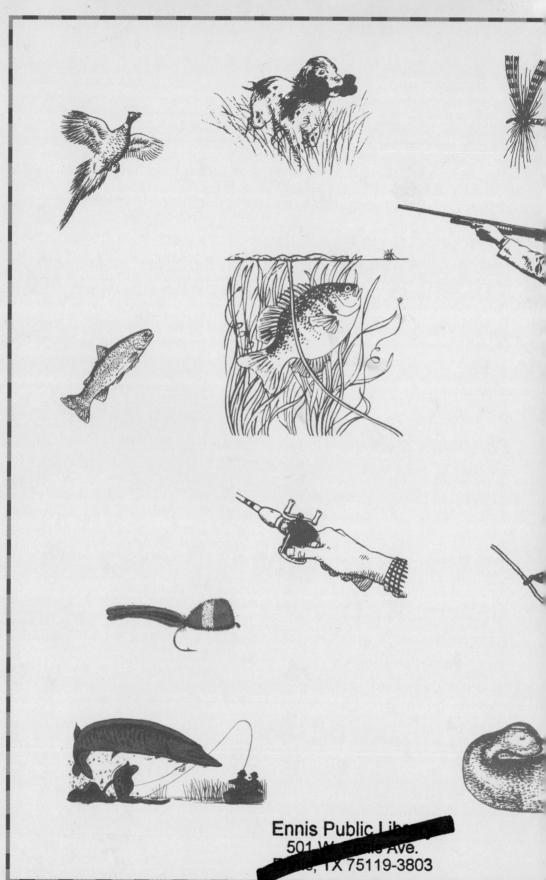